Praise for **FATWA**

"When Pamela Geller talks about Islam, she does it with both barrels. For sparing us the platitudes when confronting this direct and present danger, she is reviled by society's bien pensant. In this book, she recounts her adventures in "hate speech," or as we used to call it, "telling the truth." It is both an enlightening and gripping tale."

—Ann Coulter, Bestselling Author

"This is a riveting tale of a "controversial" woman. She believes in "controversial" principles such as free speech, and holds "controversial" positions such as the right of Muslim girls in the developed world to enjoy the freedoms of all other western women without being honor-killed, beheaded or otherwise murdered. She is so "controversial" that, when Islamic fanatics tried to kill her in the first ISIS attack on American soil, this country's appalling and stupid media blamed her for being so "controversial" as to drive people to open fire on her. In a saner, healthier world, she would not be "controversial" at all, but would be recognized as the brave - indeed, fearless - woman she is. This is her story, and splendidly told."

—Mark Steyn, Bestselling Author

"Over the years, many have made their disagreement with Pamela Geller clear. Islamists fear her; adherents of identity politics loathe her. Threatened with death by ISIS, denounced as a "hater" and "Islamophobic" by others, she is fearless. Even her detractors must concede that Pamela Geller has grit, is passionate and determined. She is a formidable adversary of all those seeking to further the cause of Shariah.

In her book Fatwa, Pamela Geller discusses her upbringing, her family, the ideals that drive her, and chronicles her numerous battles with Shariah law and its defenders. Read this book to see an advocate of freedom in action, defending the right to dissent from orthodoxy, as well as the principles that are at stake in defending the free society."

—Ayaan Hirsi Ali

A courageous book by a courageous woman. This is not just one individual's adventures in defense of freedom - this is a guide for anyone and everyone who is ready to stand for the truth in these days of universal lies. Political correctness is intellectual dishonesty and Pamela Geller isn't afraid to tell it like it is.

—Tomi Lahren, Fox News Contributor and television host

"How did a nice Jewish girl from Long Island become the Joan of Arc of the counterjihad movement? In this remarkably absorbing page-turner of a book, Pamela Geller tells her story – a story of courage in the face not only of the jihadist enemy but of a veritable army of apologists, appeasers, pacifists, whitewashers, self-styled "bridge-builders," and assorted cowards, careerists, and sellouts. Armed only with the truth and a passionate love of American liberty, Geller has survived their smears and kept hope alive. It's an inspiring story that I hope will encourage other freedom-lovers to stand up and be counted before it's too late."

—Bruce Bawer, author of The Victims' Revolution: The Rise of
Identity Studies and the Closing of the Liberal Mind

"Pamela Geller's fascinating book is the vivid chronicle of a courageous woman who fought vigilantly and with fierceness, confronting dangers, threats and vile defamation, to preserve the American soul of freedom and democratic liberties. A most actual record of our perilous time."

—Bat Ye'or, Historian, author of Eurabia: The Euro-Arab Axis, *and
of* Europe, Globalization and the Coming Universal Caliphate

"Pamela Geller is a towering hero of freedom. If free people survive into the next generation, which is by no means assured, Pamela Geller will be celebrated as one of those who stood against the tide of Leftism and Islamic supremacism when it was at its apogee. No proper history of the freedom of the human spirit in our darkening age can be written without including her."

*—Robert Spencer, director of Jihad Watch and author of the New
York Times bestsellers* The Politically Incorrect Guide to Islam
(and the Crusades) *and* The Truth About Muhammad.

"Free-speech advocates who don't make waves are not doing their jobs. Pamela Geller writes a guidebook here for Paladins of the First Amendment."

—Ambassador John Bolton

FATWA

FATWA

HUNTED IN AMERICA

PAMELA GELLER

Dangerous Books

Dangerous Books

2422 South Miami Ave

Miami, FL 33129

Published 2017 by Dangerous Books

Printed in the United States of America

19 18 17 16   1 2 3 4

ISBN: 9781947979000

Library of Congress Control Number: (to come)

This book is dedicated to Floyd Resnick, former NYPD officer and AFDI's longtime chief of security, who dedicated his life to protecting my colleagues and me, no matter how dangerous the situation or circumstance. He was as much a part of the movement as any of us.

RIP

Contents

Foreword
By Geert Wilders

There are just a handful of people on either side of the Atlantic who are on the forefront of the resistance against jihad and Islamization. One of the most vivid personalities in this great fight for freedom, is Pamela Geller. As Mark Steyn has said: "She's a fearless fighter on free speech and other issues, and I wish there were more with her spirit."

In this book, Pamela tells the full story of her many initiatives in defense of the fundamental freedoms that make Western civilization the greatest achievement of human history, such as freedom of speech, freedom of conscience, equality before the law, and individual rights. She has worked with unflagging energy, courage, and perseverance to preserve the fundamental principles of a free society. And as such, she is an example, not just to her American compatriots, but also to Europeans like me.

I first met Pamela in New York in 2008, when she was running *Atlas Shrugs*, a website she started in 2004 to expose the true nature of Islam, a dangerous totalitarian ideology aiming for world domination, and to defend our Western civilization against creeping Islamization. *Atlas Shrugs*, which later became *The Geller Report*, is an invaluable source of information that the fake news media do not want us to hear.

In 2009, Pamela brought me to Washington, D.C. to address the Conservative Political Action Conference (CPAC). A year later, she invited me to address a massive crowd of tens of thousands of lovers of freedom in lower Manhattan who had come out to stand together against the grotesque proposal to build a 16-story mega-mosque at Ground Zero. In 2015, I stood with Pamela for freedom of speech at her Muhammad Art Exhibit and Cartoon Contest in Garland, Texas. That contest, in the wake of the massacre of the

Muhammad cartoonists of *Charlie Hebdo* in Paris, was meant to show that freedom-loving people in the West will never bow to threats and curtail their freedom of speech.

The Garland event became the scene of the first ever attack by the Islamic State on American soil. Two jihadis opened fire on police officers at the entrance to the exhibit. They wounded one officer before being shot themselves. Less than a month after the Garland attack, police in Boston killed an Islamic man who was planning to assassinate Pamela but, becoming impatient, decided to behead a police officer instead. The Islamic response to people expressing their freedom of speech clearly indicates why it was necessary to hold the Garland event in the first place. Either the West is going to stand up for its principles, or it is going to kowtow to bullying and surrender.

Owing to the presence of Islam in our societies, freedom of speech is now no longer a given. What we once considered a natural element of our existence, our birthright, is now something we once again have to battle for. But we do so in an absolutely non-violent way. Like me, Pamela and others fighting Islam in our Western societies abhor violence. Indeed, we oppose Islam exactly because it is inherently violent.

However, for her unwavering non-violent resistance and her efforts to expose Islamic savagery, Pamela Geller has been subjected to abuse and derision from the mainstream media and the political establishment. As I have been in The Netherlands, she has been dismissed as a crank, ridiculed, defamed, and smeared by cowardly political and media elites who have stood by silently when she has been threatened with death.

All this is just one manifestation of how free people are under attack today. They are targeted by the political and cultural elites solely for standing for the dearest of our many freedoms. The "hate speech" charge that has been leveled against virtually all defenders of freedom in the West, and for which I have been prosecuted in my own country, will always be used against people who are defending the West—in order to please and appease Islam.

Its followers can say whatever they want: "Throw gays from apartment buildings," "Kill the Jews," "Slaughter the infidel," "Destroy Israel," "Wage jihad against the West." Whatever their book tells them. But when we call attention to what they are saying, we get charges of "hatred," "bigotry," "Islamophobia" and the like.

This moral inversion, this celebration of the savage and abuse of the civilized man, is a symptom of the cultural relativism that has infected the elites in Europe and North America today. The cultural relativists have opened their minds so wide that their brains are falling out. Most of our politicians and media pundits believe that all cultures are equal. Nothing could be further from the truth. Our Western culture, based on Judaism, Christianity, and humanism, is in every aspect better than the Islamic culture. And as Pamela Geller has said: "In any war between the civilized man and the savage, support the civilized man."

The left once stood for women's rights, gay rights, equality, and democracy. Now they have implemented immigration policies that will end all this, and work tirelessly to destroy anyone who dares mount any opposition to these policies. Many have lost their decency. Elite politicians in Europe have no problem with participating in demonstrations where Muslims openly shout "Death to the Jews." Seventy years after Auschwitz, they have no shame. And then they dare, from their position of abject moral capitulation and compromise, to sneer at those who are fighting for what they should be fighting for.

Back in 2009, I tried to get into Britain, a fellow European Union country. I was invited to give a speech in Parliament. However, upon arrival at London airport, I was refused entry into the country, detained for three hours and sent back on the first plane to The Netherlands. The reason: I would threaten community harmony and therefore public security. It was an absolute disgrace. This ban was eventually lifted, but several years later, Pamela Geller was also banned from Britain. That ban remains in place, and is no less disgraceful. While admitting numerous jihad preachers, Britain is keeping out the voices of sanity that would call that nation back to a path that would secure freedom for her children and her children's children, instead of a path to national suicide.

Meanwhile, Britain has become a war zone, where Islamic maniacs drive cars into people on bridges and children are blown to pieces at pop concerts. And it is not just Britain. All over Europe, all over the West, Islamic terror has become a fact of life. Paris, Stockholm, Brussels, Madrid. But also America: New York, Boston, Orlando, San Bernardino, Garland. Islamic barbarism is just around the corner. And still, the elites refuse to see that Islam is the common denominator behind all these atrocities. And still they refuse to act to preserve our freedoms and security by de-Islamizing our nations. In Europe, they even refuse closing the borders to even more Islam.

The open door policies of many governments in the EU are sheer madness. Suicide policies. Even jihadis who have gone to Syria to fight are allowed to return. We have already seen how dangerous these people are. They have committed terror attacks in Manchester, Brussels, and Paris.

If the resolute and urgent action that is urgently needed, fails to materialize, then in another 50 years from now, Europe's Christians, Jews and atheists will be dwarfed by the followers of Islam. According to Eurostat, the statistical office of the European Union, 2015 was the first time ever in recorded history that the number of babies born in the EU was lower than the number of persons who died. But the total population did not decline. It went up with 2 million, exclusively because of immigration. Europe is in the middle of a process of population replacement.

The consequences will be devastating, because the bulk of the massive flow of immigrants replacing the indigenous Europeans are Islamic. According to the Central Council of Muslims in Germany, at least 80% of the 1.3 million newcomers in Germany in 2015 and 2016 are Islamic. Germany is becoming Germanistan. Holland is becoming Hollandistan. Europe is becoming Eurabia.

If the Europeans do not pull their act together soon, it will be upon us faster than anyone can imagine: America as the last vestige of Western civilization and Europe collapsing, its democratic nation-states finished, its cathedrals in ruins, its works of art gone forever, and persecuted European Jews and Christians fleeing to Israel or your way. Because history shows that wherever Islam becomes dominant, democratic institutions perish, all pre-Islamic remnants are destroyed, and non-Islamic people cease to be safe.

Pamela Geller has made it her mission to warn America against the greatest enemy of freedom in our age: Islam. She urges Americans to avoid following Europe's bad example. And wherever she can, she is helping Europeans like me to turn the tide of Islamization. She is also a staunch defender of Israel, the only democracy in the Middle East, a beacon of light in a sea of Islamic darkness.

In 1982, US President Ronald Reagan gave one of his most important speeches ever. He called the Soviet Union an "evil empire" and urged the West to reject communism and defend freedom. At the time, Reagan's speech was derided and ridiculed by the media and the establishment. Today, however, we know how important it was. It marked the beginning of the end of Soviet totalitarianism. It was a clarion call to preserve liberty and inspired millions all over the globe. Reagan said, "If history teaches anything, it teaches self-delusion in the face of unpleasant facts is folly." What Reagan meant is that you cannot run away from history, you cannot escape the dangers of ideologies that are out to destroy you. Denial is no option.

And as George Orwell once said, "If liberty means anything at all, it means the right to tell people what they do not want to hear."

Pamela Geller's entire career has been one long endeavor to clear away the West's self-delusion in the face of unpleasant facts. She has been telling people what they do not want to hear for nearly two decades. She has given voice to millions who think just like her. She has stood up for the millions who think liberty is precious. And that democracy is better than Sharia.

The question before us in Europe and North America today is this: will free speech be lost to the spurious idea of "hate speech," a term used to stifle legitimate criticism of Islam? And the larger question for the West is: will we leave the children of Europe and North America the values of Rome, Athens and Jerusalem, or the values of Mecca, Tehran and Gaza?

I am convinced that history is on our side. The forces of oppression and subjugation never prevail in the long run. Islam, like other systems that shackle the human spirit, will end up in the dustbin of history. But another thing is equally certain: future historians will marvel at our morally inverted age, in which freedom fighters are derided and harassed, even prosecuted, while globalist internationalists, who are doing all they can to wreck the free world and fit us all in new chains, are celebrated as the enlightened vanguard of a progressive future.

But, fortunately, the historians will also notice that there were people who saved the West by keeping the spirit of liberty alive, by standing tall against Islam, by countering and opposing jihad, by never surrendering to Muhammad's vile ideology of hatred and barbarism. And one of the foremost of these heroes was Pamela Geller.

In this book is the story of how Pamela Geller has stood, and is still standing, for our freedom. She is the Joan of Arc of the counter-jihad movement. Tireless, fearless and brave. And I am immensely honored to stand with her.

Geert Wilders MP
Leader of the Party for Freedom (PVV) in the Netherlands

Pamela Geller

"The most dangerous woman in America" —*The Review, Independent*

"Far-right hate queen" —Max Blumenthal / *AlterNet*

"The anti-Muslim movement's most visible and flamboyant figurehead." —Southern Poverty Law Center

"Noted subway-uglifier" —*New York Daily News*

"One of America's preeminent Islamophobes" —*Village Voice*

"Preaches venomous hatred of Muslims… One of the leading voices promoting the idea of 'creeping Sharia' in the United States" —*Forward*

"Shrieking bigot… lunatic racist" —*The Atlantic*

"A hate-monger to critics, a free speech hero to fans" —*Los Angeles Times*

"Every time I see her on television, I want to take a shower" —Geraldo Rivera

"Not conducive to the public good" —The British government

"A terrible poster child for free speech—and against Islamist extremism" —*Reason.com*

"A lightning rod for anti-Islamic fervor" —*New York Times*

"Incendiary" —*Washington Post*

"America's queen of hate" —*Veterans Today*

– One –
The End of the World as I Knew It

On May 5, 2015, ISIS issued this fatwa calling for me to be killed:

The attack by the Islamic State in America is only the beginning of our efforts to establish a wiliyah [an error for wilayah, administrative district] in the heart of our enemy. Our aim was the khanzeer [pig] Pamela Geller and to show her that we don't care what land she hides in or what sky shields her; we will send all our Lions to achieve her slaughter. This will heal the hearts of our brothers and disperse the ones behind her. To those who protect her: this will be your only warning of housing this woman and her circus show. Everyone who houses her events, gives her a platform to spill her filth are legitimate targets. We have been watching closely who was present at this event and the shooter of our brothers. We knew that the target was protected. Our intention was to show how easy we give our lives for the Sake of Allah.

This was my career in microcosm. I spoke unwelcome truths, and first my character was assassinated, and then the enemies of freedom moved to outright call for my assassination.

It was all because I stood for the freedom of speech. I had no regrets. How could I, for standing for what was right?

I was the unlikeliest of candidates to become a human rights activist, reviled by the enemies of freedom the world over, and designated "the

1

anti-Muslim movement's most visible and flamboyant figurehead" by the uber-left hate group, the Southern Poverty Law Center.

I was the quintessential New York City girl. My career was everything. Every day was new, exciting, different. I loved art, music and fashion. I loved dancing at my favorite uptown club, Bruno Jamais' place on East 81st Street. I loved my life. I loved my freedom. I never thought it could be threatened. I pursued life with a passion—nothing stopped me.

But 9/11 stopped me. 9/11 stopped me dead. Nothing was ever the same.

I was the associate publisher of the New York *Observer,* and before that the Director of Agency Relations at the New York *Daily News.* But I had never been terribly political. When it came to politics, my generation of women was taught to care primarily, and sometimes solely, about abortion rights.

My overarching sense of life was my deep, abiding love of America. America is not the only good thing in the world, but it is the best thing in the world. I was wildly proud of her, and proud to be American, a Jewish American. At no time in history were Jews as free to be outwardly Jewish and proud. No country was better to its Jews.

I didn't grow up like David Horowitz, the famous left-wing activist who later turned conservative. Horowitz's parents were members of the Communist Party until Horowitz was 17, when they left the party upon learning of Stalin's atrocities. They raised Horowitz to be a left-wing activist. By contrast, my home wasn't dedicated to any particular ideology or cause. I had a very normal upbringing. I grew up one of four girls on the South Shore of Long Island. My parents were passive Republicans. My father was always a Republican and voted the straight Republican ticket. My mother was a Democrat before she met my father, but said she soon realized the Democrats were all about government controls and socialism. She was always in favor of individual freedom and capitalism. Right philosophy, wrong party.

It's funny. I remember being very young in the back seat of the car listening to my parents discuss current events and other things I didn't understand, when my father said, "Nothing is forever."

"Not even America?" my mother asked.

"Not even America," he said.

I was dumbfounded. It was inconceivable to me (and my mother) that the greatest nation, the greatest force for good, wouldn't prevail. It was inconceivable. My mother looked at him in shock and bewilderment. I didn't believe him—until September 11, that is.

We were a close-knit family. My parents were tough. They were fearsome but fair.

There was no one sharper or more prescient than my mother. Wicked quick, I almost always hated to ask her opinion on critical things because her answers were never what I wanted to hear. But she was always right. *Always.*

My mother was strikingly beautiful on the order of a Grace Kelly, but my mother's eyes were bigger and wider, and her mouth fuller. Her parents (my grandparents) fled Europe and Russia. My mother was born in New York and grew up during the Great Depression—dirt poor. But hers was not a sad tale. My mother would recount stories of her childhood with wicked humor. She had a real love for life—in spite of difficult circumstances. She was a camera girl at the Latin Quarter, and after work would head uptown to Harlem to listen to Billie Holiday, Dinah Washington and Sarah Vaughan. She loved those 78s. They were the soundtrack of my childhood.

She was tough, scary even—more so because she was right. And we clashed many times, but she was a great teacher, a great mom. Despite hard times, she was always oddly optimistic. You'd give a negative forecast and she'd brush it off, saying, "Whatever it is." She would see a silver lining and keep you focused on good things, worthy goals. Most of all, she had a great sense of humor, and that's what you got from her. When Dad would see everything negatively, she'd call him "Dr. No." And she liked to have fun. Her kids were her life.

And while I had an uneven, and at times contentious, relationship with my mother, I can say, without hesitation, *there was no one like her.* Ever.

The one thing she had was great common sense. My favorite *mommism*? Whenever something really awful happened to me and it wiped me (or my sisters, for that matter) out she would wave her hand and say, "Don't worry, it's nothing." And mean it. And explain it. It may not sound like much, but it saved me more than once. She was a big picture kinda gal. She would always say, "One and one makes two. It doesn't make three, it doesn't make four. Remember that."

It's the best advice she ever gave me.

My father, though rarely home, was my champion. He was always work-ing. In my early teens, I went to work with him on weekends and during split session, and I saw him in action. His pace was unrelenting. He did every-thing—despite the size of the business—from ordering a dozen gross zippers, to pattern cutting, to designing jacquards, sewing samples… I am talking *everything*. So it was a *michaya* to tiptoe around the house Sunday mornings in the wintertime, so that Papa could sleep until all hours. Not spring and summer, though. Oh, no—then he would be out by six a.m. to his 18 holes and spend the afternoon playing gin, nursing a Johnnie Walker on the rocks. And always with a cigarette dangling out of his mouth. Salem after Salem. It's why I love the smell of cigarettes, still.

I loved him. He did everything. I never saw a repairman in my house. He fixed everything: boiler, burner, electric, plumbing, refrigeration, all of it. And he called me to ride shotgun. Always. I would hand him the tools, listen to him cuss like a sailor, and he'd Rube Goldberg whatever he was tackling. And it worked.

Reuben Geller worked his way up from nothing. The oldest of three boys, his father died when he was in junior high school and he took it upon himself to be head of the house. He did every kind of job you could think of, and eventually he built a textile factory in East New York, the tough-est neighborhood in Brooklyn and the murder capital of New York. Geller folklore has it that it was George Gershwin's mother who gave him five thousand dollars to start a garment business. This was a story that was told around the Geller house as long as I can remember, although I have never verified the exact details. No one ever said, "How did you know her? Who was Rose Gershwin to you?" It was understood in my Jewish neighborhood that a wealthy Jew would lend money to hard-working guys. That's how it was, back in the day.

He employed well over 300 folks in that neighborhood. They adored and respected him. They'd invite him to their homes, their family get-togethers. They trusted him and went to him with their problems. And he helped solve them. I speak Spanish fluently because I worked with him, for him, and I wanted to be able to communicate with everyone the way that he did.

And just like in the house, he fixed everything in that shop, from knitting machines to candy machines, elevators to carburetors. He *learned*. He had the first computer, an IBM mainframe, and what a pain in the ass that was. He didn't care. He thought it was the greatest thing since sliced bread. We were going IBM and that was it. I had to learn to do the billing on that damn thing, and it was always breaking down and losing data, and wouldn't it all be easier, Dad, if we could just do it by hand? "No!" He spent hours fixing that baby, too.

I learned everything I know from him. He was benevolent and philanthropic. He was unambiguous, and his life lessons still resonate with me *every day*. He walks with me *every day*. He didn't suffer fools or, in his words, "full of shitniks," a term I love and use to this day. He was unafraid. And so am I.

From the time I was fourteen, I went to work for and with him. Every day I would jump on the 12:15 Brooklyn train to East New York. My high school, Lynbrook High, was on split session, and I would get out of school at 12:30. Since I already spoke Spanish fluently, my Spanish teacher would let me leave early to make that train. Even though I was just fourteen, I would drive my father home every night.

I loved Brooklyn. I would sneak out, take the car, and go to jazz clubs and discos in Brooklyn late at night. It was thrilling and wild. My partner in crime was my best friend, Bonnie Goldsmith, with whom I forged a lifelong friendship at the tender age of eleven at sleep-away camp. Bonnie was the smartest, truest, funniest, loveliest person I have ever known. It was Bonnie who turned me on to *Atlas Shrugged*. We were attached at the hip for close to 30 years. When she passed away at the age of thirty-seven from ovarian cancer, part of me went with her. She didn't live to see September 11, but I know she would have been a fierce supporter of the work I do. Losing Bonnie sharpened everything for me. Life became more precious.

We did everything together. Young, wild, and free. The world was our oyster.

I continued to work in the factory all through high school and my first two years of college. The business world fascinated me. College was a waste of my time, and I left to make my way in the world.

I didn't want to spend my days in a factory. My father was enormously disappointed that I left the business, but I wanted to be in New York City and pursue my career there. I got my first apartment in a one-hundred-year-old brownstone in Park Slope in Brooklyn, a real fixer-upper, like Park Slope itself at that time. Days, I pursued my career with a blinding single-mindedness, and at night I worked without rest on that beloved apartment, stripping the wood mouldings on those towering doorways and that magnificent one-hundred-year-old fireplace, restoring everything to its original beauty. I was utterly happy.

I lived in a post-historical mindset. The good guys had defeated the forces of evil in World War II, and since then, the good cop had been on the beat. What could possibly go wrong?

I assumed my freedom. I never, for one moment, thought it could be taken from me. I had always assumed my freedom. Never questioned its permanence or invulnerability. How wrong I was.

I grew up as one of four girls. Two of my sisters are doctors. Nothing stopped us. Ever. We could do anything and be anything we wanted. One only had to have the will and the drive. And I did. I pursued life with a vengeance. It was a wonderful time to be alive, an even more wonderful time to grow up.

It never occurred to me that growing up in late 20th century America was like hitting the mega millions lottery in the historical game of life. It was a golden era—fun, free, phenomenal. The long coup by the left was still bubbling, not altogether impotent, but certainly not overwhelming, let alone crushing.

America had her morality of individual rights very much intact. The country not nearly as divided and polarized as it is today. For women in my generation, the Equal Rights Amendment that feminists were shrieking about seemed absurd and redundant. Why pass legislation for something we already had?

Politics was not a priority for my generation. Growing up in the seventies, politics wasn't top of mind. No one cared. We were out of Vietnam. And once Nixon was forced out, everyone left the stadium. The big show was over. America was America, land of the free, home of the brave, and whatever it was, we would work out the problem. We were "going to teach the world to sing in perfect harmony" with a Coke and a smile. It wasn't until 1979, when Iran attacked our embassy and took our people hostage, that we began to awaken. That was a defining moment for many of us. That terrible, awful news. Then President Carter's stumbling ineptitude and indecisiveness. In the lead-up to the hostage crisis, Carter backed the Ayatollahs. He helped oust our great friend the Shah. This was the poison fruit of his policy. And the story wouldn't end. Every night at the dinner table, every night on the evening news, there was Frank Reynolds and Walter Cronkite's daily dirge: day 100, day 200, on and on.

Americans were gobsmacked, ashamed and riveted. The *ABC News Hour*, *Nightline*, had its beginnings in 1979 just four days after the start of the Iran Hostage Crisis. At that time, the show was called *The Iran Crisis–America*

Held Hostage: Day "xxx" where *xxx* represented each day that Iranians held our people hostage. The horror of all this and the impotent President made politics wildly relevant for an uninvolved, cynical generation. The bankrupt and bloody policies of the Democrats heralded the age of Reagan.

Through it all, I assumed the permanence of my freedom.

But all that changed on one day, in one moment.

On a beautiful, bright blue sunny morning, a perfect day in mid-September, I went about my usual routine of getting my gym stuff together to head out for my usual killer three-hour workout with my trainer, an ex-Special Forces Marine.

My phone rang. My husband told me to turn on the television. I clicked on my remote—and nothing was ever the same.

The World Trade Center was burning.

The World Trade Center was a city all its own. It had its own zip code, 10048. It was populated by 50,000 people at the height of the day, and 200,000 more people visited it every day. It was iconic for New Yorkers, Americans, and on a personal level, for me. I had my first important breakfast meeting there with the then president and publisher of the New York *Daily News*, Jim Hoge. I was a babe in arms in the newspaper world. What a thrill.

The building was an architectural marvel. It replaced the Empire State Building as the tallest building in the world, and did so with a design that was not just innovative, but revolutionary: it was designed so that columns and walls were not needed for structural purposes, giving tenants open spaces to work with. This had never been done before on this scale. The Twin Towers were the centerpiece of a complex that included four other buildings. Construction began in 1968 and was complete enough for the first tenants to move in in 1970; construction was fully completed in 1973. More innovative techniques were used to protect the structure from fire and even from a passenger plane flying into it, which everyone envisaged as an accident, not a terror attack. (When the planes hit on September 11, however, they caused far more devastation than the architects had ever imagined possible.)

Even its elevator system was designed to maximize efficiency and keep the space used to a minimum. The Twin Towers were full of architectural innovations in keeping with the very idea of a World Trade Center, a concept conceived when the United States was at the apex of its economic power and cultural influence.

The World Trade Center heralded a new age, a gleaming, shining future, especially in the midst of the economically depressed, gloomy 1970s, just as did the Empire State Building when it went up in 1931, during the Depression. The World Trade Center became so much a part and heart of the New York skyline. Movies showcased it. It is the backdrop in hundreds of movies; in one of my personal favorites, *Working Girl*, it's as close to a character as a building can get. It was for the protagonist, played by Melanie Griffith, the dream, the aspiration of bettering herself and "making it." And it was that for us, too. To paraphrase Ayn Rand, it was the will of man made visible.

In *New York Stories*, Woody Allen's mother talks to her son against the backdrop of the Twin Towers. The opening of the Tom Wolfe movie, *Bonfire of the Vanities*, follows Bruce Willis for almost ten minutes marauding in the basement of the World Trade Center. In *Independence Day*, the Towers are the tallest remnants of a ruined New York. In *Ghostbusters II*, the Towers are prominently featured during the citywide blackout scene. I could go on and on, but you get the picture. There are countless, iconic film shots where the Twin Towers play center stage, they were so cinema. Watching those movies today, it's always a ghostly, haunting experience to see the towers—at least for me. These scenes represented life in a New York, and an America, that was gone forever after September 11.

Looking out the passenger window of a 747, they were more than buildings. They were home. Flying into La Guardia Airport was a particular thrill. You could look out of the window and see those impeccable, utilitarian but elegant, towers proudly and loudly standing tall—like the city that loved them.

When they were attacked, I stood in front of my TV, paralyzed. And when the Towers came down in a blinding cloud of flesh, bone, paper, steel—the shreds of life—I wept for the people in the building. I wept for their families. I wept for my city. I wept for my country. I wept because we were at war, and unlike, say, Pearl Harbor, I didn't know who we were at war with. I mourned for an old life, my life, which was over, dead. It had become history, a memory, on that morning. I knew my old life was over when those towers came down. War came to America.

The horror and death was on a scale that was unimaginable in America. People, who just hours earlier, had their morning joe, kissed their wives or husbands, took their children to school, maybe grabbed a McMuffin and hurried into the city to get to their desks, were faced with the most shocking, horrific, imminent death. Men and women waving shirts or jackets stood on the gashed edge of a gaping wound at the top floors of the towers. No one could get to them. No one could help them. The heat from the flames of the airplane turned into a fireball that left people with no choice. Burn to death or jump. Hundreds jumped to their deaths.

Eyewitnesses talked of a couple who held hands as they fell.

> One woman, in a final act of modesty, appeared to be holding down her skirt. Others tried to make parachutes out of curtains or table-cloths, only to have them wrenched from their grip by the force of their descent.
>
> The fall was said to take about ten seconds. If someone fell head down with their body straight, as if in a dive, it could be 200mph. When they hit the pavement, their bodies were not so much broken as obliterated.[1]

The sound of the bodies hitting the pavement was deafening. I did not hear them at the time—but in the beginning, in the news reports, before all the news regarding the jumpers were censored and scrubbed, I heard the sound then. Years later, when I was editing my Ground Zero Mosque movie, I included that footage in the film, and that sound is horrifying.

I thought about John Florio, that big brave firefighter who worked out at my gym. He would come in every morning with a tiny infant and leave her in the windowed childcare center. I wondered if he had rushed to Manhattan when he heard about the attack, to help out.

John Florio had, and he had died there.

As had so many. The images shook me to the core of my being: the unimaginable destruction, the office workers jumping out of the building, preferring a quick death to a slow and agonizing one; the interviews with survivors describing the sound of the bodies of the jumpers as they hit the ground. I thought of the World Trade Center working girls, having ridden the subway to work that morning like so many others, and just arriving at the office a few minutes before the first plane struck and the world was changed forever.

Who had done this? The people who died that day weren't our soldiers. They were regular folks—parents and brothers and sisters and children. And then I realized in this war, they were our soldiers, they were our fighters. And so was I. And so are you.

Who had attacked my country? I felt guilty that I didn't know the answer to the question: who had done this? Then when I found out, I felt guilty that I didn't know who this enemy really was, what they stood for, and why they wanted to destroy my country.

My journey began.

– Two –
The Workshop

The Search for Answers

The indescribable stench of blood and ash, burnt paper and singed hair, remained in New York for months. Before long, a name emerged that shook me: Osama bin Laden. I had heard that name nearly ten years before, at the World Trade Center bombing trial of the Blind Sheikh.

Omar Abdel Rahman, who was known as the Blind Sheikh because he was completely sightless but had nevertheless become a respected Islamic scholar, was the mastermind of the 1993 World Trade Center bombing that had been intended to bring down both towers but failed; the jihadis did manage to murder six people.

Although Osama bin Laden was not indicted in connection with the 1993 bombing, I remember reading about the verdict in the Blind Sheikh's trial in the *New York Daily News*, and one salient fact screamed at me: whether or not he was involved in the Blind Sheikh's jihad attack on the World Trade Center, Osama bin Laden was an international jihadi mastermind, and he was still at large. I thought, *Well, then, it is hardly over—this is just the beginning of a new terrible era of terror.* I understood immediately what Israel had been suffering under for decades. But then I thought, *Well, the authorities must have this problem in hand. They must be on bin Laden's tail, and if they aren't worried, then I shouldn't trouble myself with it.*

How wrong I was. I never made that mistake again.

When the attacks on September 11 were unfolding, I turned to *Fox News* and never turned the channel for 15 years, until Fox began its slow move to the left—or the center, as they euphemistically call it. It's not fair and balanced when your pundits are trimmers, apologists and blank-faced millennials, as they have increasingly become since Murdoch's sons have been in charge.

I saw President Bush displaying true leadership qualities—or so I thought. On September 17, 2001, one week after the attacks, he went to the Islamic Center of Washington, D.C. and stood shoulder-to-shoulder next to the most dangerous Muslim Brotherhood and CAIR operatives in America. He said: "The face of terror is not the true faith of Islam. That's not what Islam is all about. Islam is peace. These terrorists don't represent peace. They represent evil and war."[1]

The fact is that the face of evil and war is the only face of Islam the world knows or sees.

Bush also said: "When we think of Islam, we think of a faith that brings comfort to a billion people around the world. Billions of people find comfort and solace and peace."

It was an extraordinary statement, especially since the last martyrdom letters of the 19 9/11 Muslim terrorists mentioned Allah over 90 times (I know because I counted) and made it clear that they were motivated by Islam and its doctrines of jihad. But I would not learn that for some years to come.

As the hijacked American Airlines Flight 11 sped toward imminent mass death in lower Manhattan, I later learned that Mohamed Atta, the leader of the 9/11 Islamic cell, calmed the passengers by telling them, "Just stay quiet and you'll be okay. Nobody move. Everything will be okay. If you try to make any moves, you'll endanger yourself and the airplane. Just stay quiet."

And President Bush, along with everyone else in a position of power, did just that. They stayed quiet about why 9/11 had happened, and about the ideology behind the global jihad in general. And sixteen years after that act of mass murder, cultural and political elites still obey Mohamed Atta and stay quiet about Islam.

But again, I did not know any of that yet. I believed President Bush, but noticed that he did not explain why, if Islam was a religion of peace, 9/11 had happened at all. Why would these misunderstanders of Islam do such a thing? The media certainly weren't asking this question. Instead, the post-9/11 press conferences were pissing contests: the lapdogs in the enemedia trying to one up Rumsfeld or Cheney or Bush. One only had to watch the daily press conferences with Rumsfeld. It was a nasty business. The Bush Derangement Syndrome as a strategy clearly worked: Bush's name became synonymous with mud. The insane hatred of Trump is merely BDS 2.0. It worked then, so why not ratchet it up? They have.

I watched every Rumsfeld press conference. I adored him, especially when he referred to the press as "thumbsuckers." He said: "People can run around and find somebody who will tell them almost anything they want. But it's interesting how little facts ever get attached to any of these thumbsuckers that get printed in the press."[2]

My saving grace was that I was online... a lot. I had a small fashion business at that time—buying and selling vintage couture—so naturally, instead of searching for, say, Jean Louis gowns, I began to search for information about jihad. This took me to various counter-jihad websites and it was, in a word, revelatory. What I learned shook me.

Counter-jihad websites such as *JihadWatch.org* and *TheReligionofPeace.com* were the only places where honest discussions about jihad, sharia, Islam, and the Koran were taking place. I read the Koran. I examined and then, after about a year, discarded the ideas of historian and Middle East Forum president Daniel Pipes that moderate Islam is the solution. They were nonsensical and fantastical. Moderate Islam is a Western fantasy. As Turkey's then-Prime Minister and current President Recep Tayyip Erdogan said in 2007: "These descriptions are very ugly, it is offensive and an insult to our religion. There is no moderate or immoderate Islam. Islam is Islam and that's it."[3]

And while there are moderate and more secular Muslims, I am hardly concerned with them. Nor am I compelled to applaud them. I do not have to pat on the back every Muslim who does not want to kill me. I expect that. That is my bar. The idea that one should praise them speaks to the soft bigotry of low expectations when it comes to Western dealings with Muslims. It's just absurd.

The Website was My Salvation

One thing was very clear from the outset: the global jihad was not going away anytime soon. The clock was ticking at some warped speed: nothing happened for decades then decades happened in a day. This was a different kind of war. It was a holy war. And it was a different kind of enemy. Devout and savage. The more I sought information on the enemy, the more I faced a brick wall. The media was talking about terrorists, but it wasn't talking about what they believed, or why they wanted to destroy us. Neither was anyone in the cultural arena.

I began to learn what had happened. Islam taught that Muslims must wage war against unbelievers and work to impose Islamic law (sharia) upon them, denying them basic rights. 9/11 was one strike in this war, which had gone on for 1,400 years. It was an attempt to strike a devastating blow to our fierce self-confidence. The attack on the World Trade Center was designed to weaken the US economically so that the US economy and government would eventually collapse altogether. The Pentagon attack was a symbolic strike on our military might.

I quickly learned that what the media was leaving out was Islam and jihad. Sure, they told us that the 9/11 hijackers thought of themselves as jihadis, but they claimed those terrorists were a tiny minority who practiced a twisted form of Islam. Having just familiarized myself with the Internet, I found myself spending more and more time online. Websites that specialized in jihad terror became my obsession: *TheReligionofPeace.com, Jihad Watch, Little Green Footballs*, and others. I read the writings of Ibn Warraq, Bat Ye'or, Robert Spencer and other experts on Islam.

The more I learned, the more I understood. This was not some one-off. This was twenty-first century jihad and the opening salvo of a long war.

As I familiarized myself with the enemy and his motives and goals, I began to see truths that I believed should be stated, and courses of action that I thought should be taken. But few people, if any, were stating these things, and no one was taking these actions. So I began to write and I began to act.

One day, a very bright university student sent me the template on the Google blogger platform. He and I regularly conversed online about Ayn Rand, political philosophy and such, and I enjoyed his comments enormously.

"Blog template? What the hell is that?" I said.

"Shut up and start writing," he shot back.

And so I did. I started a website, naming it *Atlas Shrugs* after Ayn Rand's towering novel, *Atlas Shrugged*, and began offering my own commentary on news events. It seemed to me to be the perfect moniker. Those familiar with the masterwork would immediately understand my political philosophy and sense of life. Those who hadn't read *Atlas Shrugged*, I hoped would be encouraged to. For those unfamiliar with the book, the blog title would serve as a warning. What happens if Atlas shrugs? The world would fall down.

Initially, I only updated two or three times a day. That changed quickly the more I pored through the news and became obsessed with sharing my take on the day's events, pushing stories I felt hadn't received adequate attention in the media, and sharing my historical and philosophical musings. Every day I covered news that the media increasingly did not cover.

And from the very beginning, there was pushback—ugly, vile pushback. I quickly discovered that for anyone who took up this battle, there was already a machine in place.

Even when I had only a handful of readers and was essentially unknown, a parody website, *Atlas Juggs*, was established, mocking me and the positions I took. They photoshopped pictures of me with senior Bush officials in sexual positions. One gif had Instapundit's Glenn Reynolds's head popping out of my ass. It was disgusting. Most people would recoil from such attacks and back away from the keyboard. Which was and is the very mission of these campaigns of personal destruction. I, on the other hand, thought that they just didn't understand. They were so wedded to their dogma. They only needed to educate themselves and then they, too, would see the grave threat to freedom we faced. Naïve? Yes. After years of doing battle, I would later come to understand the evil of the left and its dogma of superiority of feelings over reason.

It was not until years later that I understood that the left was as big a problem, perhaps bigger, than the jihad. For the left it was all about control, which is why they are aligned with the jihad force. There is no better system of control than sharia.

It isn't Democrat versus Republican. It is the eternal struggle of mankind. Individualism versus collectivism. The state versus the individual. The left despises the individual, which is why they are so deeply at odds with America, and why they stand with Islamic supremacists. There is no unique soul under Islam, no "individual." America, on the other hand, was the first moral government in history to be based on individual rights.

Ayn Rand wrote,

It took centuries of intellectual, philosophical development to achieve political freedom. It was a long struggle, stretching from Aristotle to John Locke to the Founding Fathers. The system they established was not based on unlimited majority rule, but on its opposite: on individual rights, which were not to be alienated by majority vote or minority plotting. The individual was not left at the mercy of his neighbors or his leaders: the Constitutional system of checks and balances was scientifically devised to protect him from both. This was the great American achievement—and if concern for the actual welfare of other nations were our present leaders' motive, this is what we should have been teaching the world.[4]

The left has been fighting Americanism for most of the 20th century. Cozying up to the communists and now the jihadists.

So they came after me. I wasn't offended by the vile attacks. I was mystified. Why would anyone care so much about taking down someone who was then an insignificant blogger? Of course, it was to squash dissent in its infancy. I was called things such as "neo-kike-ess." James Wolcott, one of the signature columnists at *Vanity Fair*, wrote a series of columns about me. In one, he wrote: "In a scene sadly reminiscent of those titty-flashing *Girls Gone Wild* videos without which no bachelor's personal library is complete, a female blogger fondles her breast while rubbing up against 'globally influential' content provider Glenn Reynolds in the orgy room of the OSM launch party. She's wasting her rubbing energy, I fear. He's hardly that influential."[5]

I was the "female blogger" he was writing about, and I wasn't fondling my breast, I was giving the thumbs-up sign. It was a taste of what the Southern Poverty Law Center's Mark Potok said later: "Sometimes the press will describe us as monitoring hate groups, I want to say plainly that our aim in life is to destroy these groups, completely destroy them."[6] When they target you in that way, fairly or not, who can emerge unscathed?

I once did a video blog at the ocean; I never imagined it would go viral. I became the "bikini blogger." It was quite by chance that I made the now infamous bikini vlog. I had just landed in the USA—I had been covering the recent flare-up of the jihad war against the Jews in Israel—in the summer of 2006.

I was on the road in Ashkelon and Sderot, visiting kindergartens, schools, and homes that had been hit by the terrorist group Hamas. They had been firing an endless barrage of rockets into Southern Israel when I got word that my mother had suffered a stroke. I headed to the airport immediately, flew back to the States and went directly to the hospital. I was devastated. Anyone who has had a loved one stricken by a debilitating stroke understands how harrowing those day-long vigils by the bedside are. So after hours upon hours of waiting, worrying and praying that my ma would regain consciousness,

I went directly to the beach. I needed succor. Having gotten off a plane not twelve hours before, I had so much I wanted to share with readers. So I started talking to the camera while standing in the ocean, waist up in the water. Hence the bikini video. It was downloaded hundreds of thousands of times, with leftists removing my audio and inserting music, such as Kelis's "Milkshake:" *"My milkshake brings all the boys to the yard..."* One very inventive troll downloaded the audio and animated an inflatable doll mouthing my words. You get the picture.

But instead of driving me away, all this only fueled the fire. I began to grasp the enormity of what we were up against.

The left has enormous resources, and the evil will, to go after anyone and everyone who gets out of line. And most people have no idea that it is even happening.

This is why we're losing. This is how they're doing it. Most people don't even know they're losing, the greatest gift, the most precious gift ever that humanity has ever received outside of the idea of God: freedom. And people don't even know what is happening.

The Tea Party got a taste of it. When good, decent Americans stood up to bailouts and socialized medicine in 2009, the media and cultural establishment went after the movement like sharks on chum. They were vicious. Racists! Supremacists! Bigots! Nancy Pelosi used photos that had been cropped by the *Huffington Post* to defame Tea Party members as Nazis, claiming they were making the Nazi salute (they were actually holding signs, but the signs were cropped out). Good, decent folks didn't know what hit them. And the left has doubled down on Trump and his supporters in exactly the same evil way.

I was not surprised. I had been living it for years.

I began documenting my intellectual journey on *Atlas Shrugs* in late 2004. I would rant against the creeping sharia which I saw growing every day. I would cover the vicious anti-Bush and anti-Israel protests, vicious demonstrations of hatred against America and Jews. I saw what few would, that "Palestinianism" was a marketing term for Jew-hatred. And the left embraced it. Despite the monstrous anti-gay policies of sharia-ruled nations or the gender apartheid inherent in Islam, the left joined forces with the jihad.

These scenes were life-altering. Most especially the anti-Israel protests. My friend and colleague, Pamela Hall, would photograph them all. In a rational world, her work might win her the Pulitzer Prize, but in a left-wing auto-cratic media, her most searing images remained unseen except on websites like mine. One of Hall's powerful images was in 2008. She has a photo of an angry Muslim holding a sign, "Death to the Juice" (that is, "Death to the Jews," rendered in such a way as to retain some deniability in the sign-holder's mind, should he ever be challenged). Years later, the Muslim holding the sign, Carlos Almonte, pled guilty to trying to fly to Somalia to join the jihad terror group al-Shabaab.[7]

When establishment media outlets such as the *New York Times* were reporting on Carlos Almonte's arrest and conviction, no one used Hall's iconic image. That's how deep sharia self-enforcement goes. In fact, in many ways sharia censorship was already in place even before 9/11. Islamic suprem-acists worked through the 1990s and before that to silence criticism of Islam. In 1991, Tom Clancy's novel *The Sum of All Fears* featured "Palestinian" ter-rorists as villains. But after CAIR protested, when the book was made into a movie the villains were changed to neo-Nazis. The Muslim Brotherhood project was already well underway by the time of 9/11—so much so that CAIR was able to get Bush to a mosque to proclaim that Islam was a religion of peace within a week of 9/11.

The Muslim influence was all-pervasive. Compare the *Standard Reference Encyclopedia* from the late 1960s with the *World Book Encyclopedia* from 2001—both standard reference encyclopedias representing the assumptions of their times. In the 1960s encyclopedia, the editors actually included a draw-ing of Muhammad, something they would never, ever do now. Underneath it was this description: "Muhammad, founder of Islam, with the sword and the Koran, symbols of his faith." In the *World Book Encyclopedia* from 2001 (pre-9/11), I was shocked to find that the crime of whitewashing and propa-ganda was already in full practice. No depictions of Muhammad. No mention of jihad wars, land appropriations, cultural annihilations or enslavements. No mention of the sword. Instead, Islamic propaganda was provided by *Ali Hassan Abdel-Kader*, with additional sourcing by the best-known apologists of Islam, Karen Armstrong.

They actually printed this: "He [Muhammad] banned war and vio-lence except for self defense and for the cause of Islam." Whitewash. "Muhammad brought a new message to his people. ... He taught them there was only one God."

Actually, the Jews did that.

"He preached against the injustice of the wealthy classes in Mecca, and tried to help the poor."

I kid you not.

"He limited polygyny (marriage to more than one wife)." But *World Book* never tells us that a Muslim man is limited to four wives.

It goes on and on, and this was before 9/11. This process only accelerated after 9/11. Most Americans have no idea how infiltrated we are by these moles for Moe, and how entrenched they are.

In the early days of my—how shall we say it—apprenticeship, I wanted to cheerlead for Americanism, for freedom. I went to all these leftist/Islamic demos, largely because the media wouldn't and the protests were horrible but very newsworthy. I wanted people to understand what was going on under their noses—which they neither saw nor knew. It was shocking, and it foretold of what was to come. And it wasn't good.

I remember that I got very close to the action at one protest in Central Park organized by the notorious Cindy Sheehan, the far-left, anti-war agitator who built an anti-American career on the death of her son, Casey Sheehan, who was killed while serving in the US Army during the Iraq War. In one photo of Cindy and me, I am smiling and giving her the finger. That photo was featured in what became my first viral blog post.

There was just a handful of us protest warriors. We went to every ugly demo, and I decided that we had to counter-protest against this evil movement.

The work overtook my life. I wanted to learn everything. In February 2005 I went to see Bat Ye'or speak at Columbia University (something that would never happen today with the blacklist now firmly in place). Bat Ye'or is the pioneering historian of *dhimmitude*, the institutionalized harassment of and discrimination against Jews and Christians (and some other groups) under Islamic law. Although this mandated persecution is a key element of Islamic history and explains much of what is going on in the world today, it had been largely ignored by historians—until Bat Ye'or.

On that day in Columbia, she was brilliant, clear, and unflappable in the face of incessant heckling from Muslim students. Even back then they were organized. My takeaway from the evening was the time I spent talking to Bat Ye'or herself. After much commiseration, I said, "What's to be done?" And she said, "Learn everything first."

It's the best advice I ever got. It's what I tell readers and supporters when they ask me the same thing.

Many of us bloggers had a huge stake in the 2004 election. It was the bloggers who unearthed the fraud Dan Rather and *60 Minutes* tried to pull off to bring down President Bush in 2004. Rather pushed a series of memos purporting to be from Lt. Col. Jerry Killian, Bush's commanding officer during his service in the Air National Guard in 1972-73, describing Bush as disobeying orders and shirking his duties, while being protected by powerful people who were pressuring Killian to whitewash Bush's failings in the service.

The *Powerline* blog discovered that the memos were forgeries, and clumsy ones at that. I joined others in publicizing the forgery and CBS's lack of journalistic integrity. CBS ignored us and pretended the smoking gun memo didn't exist. But the shock troops were on the march. Our readers and commenters made sure that the American people discovered the truth. Rather's career was left in ruins. I loved being a part of history

The left never got over that devastating shot across the bow. To their credit, they redeployed their enormous resources and manpower and tackled the "interwebs" that had up to that point largely been left to us. The left didn't need it—they controlled the establishment media, the network news, and virtually all other means of communication. But David hit back at Goliath, and a new era was upon us. Mind you, the left's denial is impenetrable. Eleven years after Dan Rather's fake news story about President George W. Bush's time in the National Guard, the subject was made into a condescending self-righteous movie called *Truth*. It was anything but, which is not surprising, since the left is always on the opposite side of the truth.

Though outed as false, these "journalists" stood by their story. In a scathing review of *Truth*, Jeff Baker of *The Oregonian* noted: "The obvious lesson—if you're going to accuse the president of ducking active duty during a war in which more than 58,000 Americans died, you'd better have your facts nailed down and your documents authenticated—has been lost on Rather and Mapes."[8] Indeed.

The Bush victory was owed, in large part, to the blogosphere. Bush's Democratic opponent John Kerry had been ahead before the release of the smoking gun memo. As conservative pundit Jonah Goldberg noted: "The conservative blogs are the shock troops of a decades-long battle to seize back the culture."

In March 2005, I attended a symposium entitled *The Program for Middle East & Academic Integrity*, organized by Charles Jacobs, founder of the American Anti-Slavery Group and the David Project. It was a seminal event, where I met fighters with whom I would form lifelong relationships, most notably the leader of the Freedom Movement in Sudan, Simon Deng.

There was no turning back for me now.

Despite the daily horrors I would write up, I never lost sight of why I was fighting: for art, music, and love. For freedom. I always tried to make it clear that this was not just a great civilizational struggle *against* Islamic jihad savagery, but *for* humane values, and to the astonishing and unparalleled achievements of the Western world in art, music, and everything that exalts the human spirit. This was why, no matter where I was and what I was doing, by hook or by crook, I always featured at *Atlas Shrugs* (which I later renamed the *Geller Report*, and continued these features) music selection on Friday night, and a classic movie from Hollywood's golden age on Saturday night. And even now, 15 years later, I still relish making these selections every week. Sarah Vaughan or Leonard Cohen, film noir or something from the Archers, Powell and Pressburger. The glorious gifts of the West.

Cartoon Jihad: A Defining Moment for the Blogosphere

The cartoons of Muhammad were first printed in September 2005. The uproar that ensued was not about some drawings; it was about imposing the speech laws under Islam on the West. And it worked.

The controversy began when the Danish newspaper *Jyllands-Posten* reported that an author named Kåre Bluitgen was looking for artists to illustrate his book on Muhammad, but couldn't find anyone who would dare draw the prophet of Islam. In response to what it perceived as the erosion of the freedom of speech in the face of violent intimidation from Muslims, *Jyllands-Posten* asked forty artists to draw cartoons of Muhammad and published twelve of the drawings.

The cartoons ran in Denmark without incident in September 2005. They even ran in an Egyptian newspaper without incident the following month. There was no reaction either time. I, of course, covered the cartoons, because the idea that folks in Denmark were afraid to draw or publish a silly cartoon was astounding and inexplicable to me. But at that time, I was one of the few.

Cartoons only became an issue after the Organization of Islamic Cooperation, the multinational Muslim organization composed of fifty-seven governments (which also constitutes the largest voting bloc at the United Nations) convened in Saudi Arabia in December 2005 and decided to make the cartoons a flash point in Islam's conflict with the West. The OIC issued a communiqué at this meeting in which it "condemned the recent incident of desecration of the image of the Holy Prophet Muhammad in the media of certain countries," and warned against "using the freedom of expression as a pretext to defame religions."[9]

The OIC, Bat Ye'or explains in her book *Europe, Globalization, and the Coming of the Universal Caliphate*, is nothing less than a "would-be, universal caliphate."[10] It might look different from the caliphates of the Ottomans, Fatimids, and Abbasids. It might resemble, instead, a thoroughly modern trans-national bureaucracy. But, already, the OIC exercises significant power through the United Nations, and through the European Union, which has been eager to accommodate the OIC while simultaneously endowing the U.N. with increasing authority for global governance. Among the other organizations Bat Ye'or says are doing the OIC's bidding are the U.N. Alliance of Civilizations, the U.N. Commission on Human Rights, and the European Parliamentary Association for Euro-Arab Cooperation (PAEAC).

In the eyes of OIC officials, no problem in the contemporary world is more urgent than "Islamophobia," which Turkish President Recep Tayyip Erdogan calls "a crime against humanity" that the U.N. and the EU must officially outlaw.[11] Even discussing why so much terrorism is carried out in the name of Islam is to be forbidden. The OIC insists, too, that international bodies ban "defamation of religion," by which it means criticism of anything Islamic. Defamation of Judaism, Christianity, Bahai, Hinduism, and even heterodox Muslim sects such as the Ahmadiyya is common within the borders of many OIC countries, a fact the OIC refuses to acknowledge. The OIC exists to spread and impose Islam, and never acknowledges any of its repulsive aspects: honor killings, female genital mutilation, gender apartheid, creed apartheid, jihad violence, and the rest.

Muhammad el-Sayed Said, deputy director of the Ahram Centre for Political and Strategic Studies in Cairo, observed that the publication of the cartoons were "no big deal until the Islamic conference, when the OIC took a stance against it."[12]

The outcome of their outrage was attacks on Danes in Saudi Arabia, the bombing of churches in Iraq, and a declaration by an Iraqi terrorist group of jihad on any Danish or Norwegian target in the world. There were riots in most Muslim countries and in many other countries that had significant Muslim minorities; at least 200 innocent people were killed.[13] An Islamic political party in Pakistan offered a reward of 50,000 Danish kroner (just under $8,000) to anyone who would murder one of the Muhammad cartoonists. All this happened despite the fact that the newspaper had apologized over and over again.

They should never have apologized, but no Western media stood with them. No American media outlet would run those twelve innocuous cartoons. And innocuous they were.

An imam from Denmark who toured the Middle East trying to stir up outrage over the cartoons distributed the only truly offensive cartoons. Evidently he didn't think the original cartoons were offensive enough, so he added three more that never ran in the paper. In 2010, at the height of the Ground Zero Mosque controversy, I was ambushed with this during an interview on *Russia Today*: the interviewer demanded to know why I had published offensive images of Muhammad on *Atlas Shrugs*. The one that most offended her was one of the fake Muhammad cartoons the Danish imam had fabricated.

The Western media had a chance to stand in solidarity with *Jyllands-Posten* and reprint the Muhammad cartoons, showing that they were determined to defend the freedom of speech. But instead, with very few exceptions, publications in Europe and North America cowered in fear, claiming that they weren't going to publish the cartoons out of "respect" for Muslims.

The war on free speech had come to the West, and Western elites, without so much as a hint of resistance, surrendered. Calling for death to America, death to Israel, that's ok. Incendiary anti-Semitic cartoons that run on a daily basis against the Jews in the Arab Islamic press? Fine. Accusations of blood libel against the Jews? Part of the school curriculum. But cartoons of Muhammad? For most of the Western media, that was too far.

We held rallies in New York City in support of free speech. The media didn't cover them either. Because the only media outlets that would run the Danish cartoons were the counter-jihad blogs and websites, the Muhammad cartoon controversy became a watershed moment for us. I call it our Gutenberg moment. We took the next great leap in communication over the corpses of dinosaur media. Almost overnight I had tens of thousands of new visitors. Americans and freedom-loving people everywhere had not agreed to accept the punitive and barbaric speech laws under Islam. The media elites had, but not us.

The Danish cartoon jihad and Rathergate showed me how critical the role of new media was in the war on our freedoms in the twenty-first century.

In April 2006, I attended a panel discussion at New York University on the controversy over the Muhammad cartoons. It was then that I began to see just how the Islamization of the culture was having a deleterious effect. This was a panel discussion on the jihad violence that had followed the publication of the cartoons and on the importance of the freedom of speech. Each of the cartoons had been set up on an easel so that the audience could view it. Yet to my shock and dismay, NYU officials had decided to shroud these innocuous cartoons in black cloth (like a burka) so that no one could see them.

The Muhammad cartoon controversy was about whether the West would stand up for the freedom of speech or submit to violent intimidation and adopt sharia blasphemy laws. NYU was capitulating even in the act of discussing what the controversy was all about and what was at stake. It foreshadowed even worse things to come.

At that event I met Dr. Andrew Bostom. He too became a colleague and friend. Dr. Bostom knows everyone, and he would introduce me to more than one of the great warriors in this fight. In 2006, through Dr. Bostom, I met Robert Spencer and Ibn Warraq at a conference in Las Vegas I went to cover. Dr. Bostom insisted that I introduce myself to Spencer and to tell him Bostom sent me.

And so it went. Wonderful friendships were born, and spending time with this eclectic group would come to feel like family: warm, safe, bound by a solidarity of purpose.

– Three –
Muslim Girls

It became my daily custom—wake up, rub my eyes, flip open the machine, and blog. No matter where I was in the world this was my ritual. Hundreds of daily emails became thousands. Readers were my best source of news and information. My readers were awake and loaded for bear. Their eyes were open. They would tip me off to things happening in their towns, their villages, their schools, universities, and so forth.

The website became the mother ship of all ideas, activism, conferences, and ad campaigns, merely from the news I reported daily—24 hours a day, seven days a week, 365 days of the year.

This is how my activism began. What I was chronicling demanded action. This became clear in 2007 when Jason Mattera, then a spokesman for the Young America's Foundation , invited me to speak at a YAF conference alongside Scott Johnson of the *Powerline* blog on "Advancing your conservative ideas in New Media."

This was the first invitation of its kind. I was taken aback, but thrilled. The blog was having an impact, which was the whole of my mission—educate, educate, educate. And while YAF never had me back—so very green was I— my path was clear. (I was a little too freewheeling, and called somebody on the right a real putz—I don't remember who. But I do remember overhearing one of the organizers say, "I'm glad she didn't call me a putz.")

In any case, as I began a daily practice of tracking news of jihad activity, I began to hear about honor killing. Few Americans today are aware of the barbaric practice of Islamic honor killing, in which a girl or woman is murdered, usually by her father and/or brothers, in order to cleanse the family of the "dishonor" she has supposedly brought. This dishonor usually stems from not following Islamic laws regarding veiling or by having some contact with men, real or imagined, that the men in her family find intolerable. The first thing that must be done to counter this barbaric practice is raise awareness of it among Americans who have no idea that it is happening.

The Aqsa Parvez memorial, which I initiated, was the very first occasion on which non-Muslims began to notice the victims in North America and Europe of Islamic honor killing, and to proclaim publicly to their killers that the victims would not be forgotten or their murders ignored. Memorials to Aqsa Parvez were planned in the Canadian town of Pelham, Ontario, as well as in Jerusalem.

Aqsa Parvez was brutally murdered by her father and brother in December 2007 for refusing to wear the hijab, the traditional Islamic headscarf. They lured her home and killed her there. But that was only the beginning: the abuse of this girl continued. She was buried in an unmarked grave. Her family refused to acknowledge her life, as she had "dishonored" them. In defiance of her devout father and brother, she had refused to live under the suffocating dictates of Islamic law. The eleventh-grade student began taking off her hijab when she went to school, and would put it back on when she returned home. Her dad would go to her school during school hours and walk around trying to find her, trying to catch her not wearing Islamic garb, talking to boys, or hanging out with "non-Muslims." "She wanted to dress like us," said one friend of Aqsa, "to be normal."

The *Toronto Star* recounted:

> She first refused his demands to wear the hijab and the traditional Pakistani clothing her four older sisters always wore. She hung out with girls outside her own culture, and when things became intolerable at home, she opted to live in a shelter.
>
> She told officials she feared she would be beaten, perhaps even killed, if she told her father she didn't want to wear traditional clothing anymore to school, especially her hijab.
>
> Aqsa was murdered around 7:30 a.m. on December 10, 2007 at her home on Longhorn Trail in Mississauga.[1]

She was murdered by her father and brother for not wearing the hijab. The whole family knew—but also knew they had to keep quiet. The *Star* continued:

At the time of her death, 12 people were in the house. Her two sisters, Irim and Shamsa, slept in the bedroom across the hall from Aqsa's bedroom, but they told police they didn't hear a sound that morning.

They said they learned about Aqsa's death when they heard their mother crying hysterically and their father told them what he had done.

While the family claimed otherwise, they must have known of the ongoing tension between Aqsa and her father. Aqsa's friends certainly did:

> She contemplated leaving home again but told a couple of her close friends in November that if "she ever messed up again," her father would "kill me."
>
> She began to cry. "No, he swore on the Koran," Aqsa said. "He said he'd kill me if I ever ran away again."

Aqsa's mother, Anwar Jan, knew.

> "Oh God, Oh God. . . Oh my Aqsa, you should have listened," Anwar Jan said in a police interview room. "Everyone tried to make you understand. Everyone begged you, but you did not listen. . ."

Meanwhile, Aqsa's father made no secret of what he had done. He called 911 after he killed Aqsa, and told them: "I killed my daughter. . . with my hands." He told Anwar Jan, "This is my insult. My community will say you have not been able to control your daughter. This is my insult. She is making me naked."

The *Star* continued: "Parvez was also worried about Aqsa's future. All of his children had married their first cousins through arranged marriages. And the plan was for Aqsa to be married in the same way when she was old enough, to a boy in her brother's wife's family."

When it became clear that this plan was not going to work, Aqsa's father and brother hatched plans to murder her:

According to testimony, Waqas [her brother] had discussed with friend and fellow tow truck driver Steve Warda, about the tense situation at home and the plan to kill her. He asked him if he could get him a gun.

In a recorded conversation months later, Waqas told he had choked her sister…

For this, her family prefers to this day that she be forgotten—unknown, unloved, unmourned. After his father and brother murdered his sister, Aqsa's brother Muhammad Shan said, "We are with them"—that is, with the killers.

In December 2008, when I read in the *Toronto Sun* that Aqsa lay in an unmarked grave, I got sick.[2] I could not let that stand. The girl died in the cause of freedom; she would not lay in an unmarked grave. I started a memorial fund to get her a headstone. Nothing political or controversial. A simple headstone. I had no idea how difficult and ugly it would be simply to honor a teenage girl in Canada who just wanted to live free—and how eagerly Western non-Muslims would aid and abet the family's efforts to dishonor her in death as they did in life.

Atlas Shrugs readers opened their hearts and their wallets. Robert Spencer called me and said he wanted to help support the initiative. I, of course, agreed. It was the first of many mutual efforts to come.

Readers and supporters contributed $4,000 for a headstone for Aqsa. Not a political statement, not a brouhaha, just a headstone that read, "In loving memory of Aqsa Parvez, Apr. 22, 1991-Dec. 10, 2007—Beloved, remembered, and free." Others contributed ideas for a garden, a memorial and such. I contacted the Meadowvale Cemetery in Brampton, Ontario where Aqsa was buried and we proceeded to buy the headstone.

All was going according to plan until, after much silence, the cemetery advised me that the family (yes, the family that murdered her) had refused to "sign off" on the headstone. The director of the cemetery said, "The family wants changes and is planning on coming in to see me. They did not book an appointment yet but I hope to see them soon."

Of course, the family never came, and after a period of weeks, no word was forthcoming. I contacted the cemetery and asked them what the hold up was. The family would not move forward. I asked if I could contact the family and work with them. The cemetery gave me the number, and I called Aqsa's home. I introduced myself and explained that we wanted to help. We had a budget of $4,000 and would be happy to install whatever the family wanted. The voice on the other end of the phone said, "We don't speak English." Click. They hung up on me.

After that, of course, the family never came back with any information about what kind of headstone they would approve, and when we inquired as to purchasing a plot near Aqsa's body, we could not. I asked to buy the plot next to Aqsa. I asked if we could buy a plaque. A tree. A rock. A bench. I was told categorically, no. You see, all the plots were owned by the Islamic Society of North America. The family refused to allow the headstone to be put on Aqsa's grave, and according to the cemetery, could remove it if it were placed there by others.

But those of us who had contributed to the Aqsa Memorial Fund were determined to make sure that Aqsa would be memorialized. We checked into other locations and made plans, only to see them canceled at the last minute out of... fear. I explained the problem on *Atlas Shrugs* and Canadian readers suggested other ideas. So many readers were enormously helpful in scouting for a place for Aqsa.

Of all the many wonderful suggestions, the arboretum at the University of Guelph in Ontario sounded perfect. I contacted and began making plans for a small memorial garden. One reader, a horticulturalist, designed a garden. Others suggested trees and blooming plants that would add color all year round. It was going to be an exquisite tribute to a brave Muslim girl. That is, until a university official wrote me to say that "no matter how worthy, a memorial to Aqsa Parvez would draw much public attention and would thus be inconsistent with current use of The Arboretum."

A spokesman for the University of Guelph, Chuck Cunningham, said that my blog was "politically charged." According to an article in the *Guelph Mercury*, he also noted that I enunciated "strong views against Islam," and that "the university was leery that a memorial could be seen as an endorsement." Cunningham said: "We don't want the Arboretum to become a vehicle for someone's political agenda. The Arboretum serves many purposes in the community—it's a place for quiet reflection and contemplation. We will not let our Arboretum get caught up in controversy."

Cunningham claimed that in the wake of its decision, the university had received some critical phone calls and emails "calling us spineless cowards and worse. It's upsetting our staff here. But it confirms that we made the right decision."[3]

It does?

Not everyone was ready to cower before Islamic anti-woman violence. The town of Pelham, Ontario, responded to the outcry at *Atlas Shrugs* and passed a resolution honoring Aqsa, and the Aqsa Parvez Memorial was erected in Pelham in the summer of 2009, featuring a granite bench inscribed, "In loving memory of Aqsa Parvez, Beloved, Remembered, and Free." This was placed in the Aqsa Parvez Peace Park.

Scott McLeod, fire chief for the town of Pelham in the Niagara region of Ontario, was a wonderful man who contacted one of his Municipal Councilors regarding the Aqsa memorial. The Councilor, Sharon Cook, presented a motion to offer an area in the Pelham Peace Park for a suitable memorial. On February 11, 2009, Councilor Cook made a "notice of motion" regarding the memorial for Aqsa to be placed in Pelham Peace Park.

That was how *Atlas Shrugs* worked. And it was good.

But still the *Atlas* donor memorial languished. We could not find an appropriate place in Canada that was willing to stand in defense of freedom.

And then it hit me. Why not a grove of trees in Independence Park in Jerusalem not just for Aqsa, but for victims of honor killings worldwide? It cost more than the 5,000 dollars we had and I asked readers what they thought. Almost immediately the donations poured in and we took the monies raised and planted the Aqsa Parvez Grove in American Independence Park in Jerusalem. The plaque reads, "In Loving Memory of Aqsa Parvez and All Victims of Honor Killings Worldwide."

The memorials in Pelham and Jerusalem were the first indication that we were not going to stand by silently in the free world while the Islamic world brutalized women and treated them as worthless trash. These were two small steps toward widespread resistance against honor killing in the West and elsewhere. But they were important steps. The individual can make a difference. The individual can change the course of human events.

Rifqa Bary's Fight for Freedom

In the wake of the Aqsa Parvez memorial initiative, a story came across the local newswire in July 2009 about a teenage girl who ran away from her home in Ohio after she reported that her father threatened to kill her upon discovering her conversion out of Islam. One of her friends sent me the link to a small news story. When she disappeared, many of her friends, and those of us who had heard of her plight, thought she had met the worst of fates (as almost all of these cases end the same horrible way). Imagine our joy when she emerged alive.

Who can forget the case of Rifqa Bary, which caught the attention of the entire nation and shone unprecedented light on Islam's death penalty for apostates?

Here was a little girl—a little American girl in Ohio who rejected the oppressive and brutal dictates of Islam and left that religion for Christianity. When her father found out, he threatened to kill her. The local mosque had spied on her and told her parents. Her father threatened to kill her, so she fled Ohio, and ran to the only safe haven she knew.

Reliable reports informed us that members of the Islamic supremacist Noor mosque in Columbus, Ohio, which Rifqa's parents had attended, spied on her and found out that she had converted out of Islam. This, plus the reported threat from her father, was the occasion of her fleeing from her home. Islamic supremacists, Rifqa's parents, and the Hamas-linked Islamic supremacist group the Council on American-Islamic Relations, or CAIR, then subjected Rifqa to a shameful campaign of intimidation and persecution, advising her parents behind the scenes and even demanding that the Christmas cards she received be confiscated.[4] Their objective was to shut her up and return her to the hellish home that she fought so desperately to escape.

The pressure on Rifqa Bary was intense, the fatwas calling for her death were numerous. Readers of *Atlas Shrugs* fought hard for Rifqa. On November 16, 2009, I held a rally for Rifqa in her hometown of Columbus. Hundreds of people showed on that cold, bitter day. Simon Deng, leader of the freedom movement in Sudan, joined me, as did former Muslim Nonie Darwish, Virginia Anti-sharia Taskforce chair Jim Lafferty, Jamal Jivanjee—a former Muslim, now a Christian pastor and Rifqa's friend—and others.

Rifqa fled to Florida to the only safe place she knew she could go—a pastor's home. When she was discovered, she was taken into custody by Florida child welfare authorities. Hearings were held to return Rifqa to her home. I flew to Florida to cover the hearings. My reportage was wildly mischaracterized and vilified by the mainstream press, particularly by Meredith Heagney of the *Columbus Dispatch*. Press conferences outside the courthouse were contentious. Go to YouTube, search Rifqa Bary Press Conference: Pamela Geller. It's a circus.

The Florida courts sent Rifqa back to Ohio.

Fox News reporter Phil Keating and I crossed swords in the parking lot. As we exited the courthouse, Keating went up to the news crews stationed outside and gleefully exclaimed with both thumbs raised high before him: "She's going back to Ohio, boys!"

Imagine being happy about sending a girl to certain death.

When she returned to Ohio, I continued to cover Rifqa's struggles. Because her home was a dangerous place for her, she was placed in the Franklin County Juvenile Detention Center. For what crime? They allowed inmates to receive Christmas cards so I began a huge Christmas card drive on *Atlas Shrugs*. A devout Christian, Rifqa was all alone on Christmas day, denied visitors and unable to return home for fear of being murdered. My readers sent her hundreds of Christmas cards and gifts in a holiday campaign. Her parents' lawyer, Omar Tarazi, tried to have them seized and censored—unsuccessfully, I might add.

Imagine what kind of people would try to stop and seize Christmas cards from a traumatized young girl who was all alone in the care of the state. She had been gagged by the state, so communication had been restricted.[5] The reader outpouring of support and affection for Rifqa was overwhelming. I asked Big Fur Hat (BFH) of the blog *IOTWreport.com*, my long time art collaborator, to create Christmas cards that people could download and mail. BFH worked with me on creating iconic posters of Rifqa's plight that went viral on the web, which further increased awareness of the young girl's plight. The outpouring of love and support from folks across the country was what you would expect from Americans.

Despite terror-tied CAIR, the court ruled that Rifqa would be allowed to keep her Christmas cards and gifts. I received this message from one of the key people who was fighting to keep Rifqa safe and free:

> Dear Pamela,
> Rifqa wanted me to convey to you her great appreciation for your wonderful effort to encourage people to send her cards and to

thank you and the over 500 people from all over the world who sent her Christmas cards and gifts.

She was so grateful for the love and support she received when she needed it. She wished she could thank everyone personally but in her situation she cannot do that.

They truly blessed her and encouraged her when she needed support during that intense isolation. God bless you and thank you for all you have done for Rifqa. You are in our prayers as you fight the good fight.

We continued to contact politicians and officials in Florida and Ohio to keep Rifqa safe from her Islamic supremacist home and mosque. And, ultimately, the Islamic supremacists lost.

The media was vicious. The *Orlando Sentinel*, along with Meredith Heagney of the *Columbus Dispatch*, who wore a hijab when she visited a Columbus mosque, and Michael Kruse of the *St. Petersburg Times*, among others, consistently filed slanted, anti-Rifqa stories, actively attacking Rifqa and working hard to smear and discredit her—in submission to Hamas-CAIR and sharia. Freedom be damned.

In July 2014, the *Orlando Sentinel* did a story on Rifqa Bary. At that time I had known for some time that she was safe, but I didn't write about it so that she may remain that way. In contrast, the *Sentinel*'s Rene Stutzman reported her whereabouts, making her an easy target for devout Muslims in a town that covered up the honor killing of another Muslim woman, Fatima Abdullah. According to the Florida Family Association:

> The Hillsborough County Medical Examiners ruled that a Palestinian woman [Fatima Abdullah] killed herself by repeatedly beating her face against a coffee table.
>
> An insider's observations may prove to be very important to reopening this mishandled case. A member of the Hillsborough County Medical Examiner's staff has informed several people that the medical examiner's finding of this death as an accident caused great controversy and distress among many staff members because they could not believe that this case was ruled an accident.[6]

It ultimately was revealed that police covered up the honor killing in order to preserve the peace in heavily populated Muslim areas.[7]

As for Stutzman, she was one of the most vicious of the many media jackals who actively sought to garner sympathy for the parents and provoke animus towards Rifqa.[8] Stutzman spun the story this way: "Mohamed Bary is a doting Muslim father, intent on giving his daughter the best education he can. But he says he made a terrible mistake last October: He bought her a laptop computer." Of Mohamed Bary's death threat to his daughter, Stutzman wrote: "Mohamed Bary said, 'I still cannot believe she would think that.'"[9]

Nonetheless, the lovers of freedom and those who were determined to defend it were victorious: Rifqa was not forced to return home, and went free when she turned eighteen in August 2010.

But no good deed goes unpunished. Much less well known than Rifqa's plight and her fight for freedom of conscience was the campaign of intimidation that Omar Tarazi, her parents' Islamic supremacist lawyer, continued to wage after her case was over. In September 2010, Tarazi filed a federal lawsuit against me and one of Rifqa's lawyers for defamation. Tarazi was enraged that I had identified him, using material readily available on the Internet, as having ties to Hamas-linked CAIR, and demanded $10 million in damages.

All of us know what the real objective of this litigation jihad was. This lawsuit by Omar Tarazi was yet another attempt to impose sharia prohibition against blasphemy on the free marketplace of ideas. He lost, and I was unbowed. I will not be silenced; nor will my colleagues. This is free speech. Period.

Jessica Mokdad Human Rights Conference

On April 29, 2012 I hosted the first-ever human rights conference dedicated to exposing the plight of women under Islamic law in Dearborn, Michigan. I chose the date because it was the first anniversary of the honor murder of Jessica Mokdad, a young woman in Michigan who was killed by her father. The event was titled *The Jessica Mokdad Human Rights Conference*.

The Jessica Mokdad Human Rights Conference was held at the Hyatt Hotel in Dearborn. After bowing to Muslim pressure and canceling a speech by me that had been scheduled for a Hyatt in Nashville, Tennessee, the Hyatt reversed its stance, recovered its understanding of the American principle of free speech, apologized, and offered us space in a Hyatt for a future Conference to make it up to the human rights organization. I chose the Hyatt in Dearborn to stand in solidarity there with girls who were in danger of being victimized, like Jessica Mokdad.

Jessica Mokdad was a 20-year-old Muslim woman in Warren, Michigan, who was brutally murdered in May 2011. *Fox News Detroit* reported, "Authorities say a Minnesota man killed his 20-year-old stepdaughter in Michigan because she left home and wasn't following Islam." Jessica's stepfather, a devout Muslim, tracked his stepdaughter over four states to murder her for bringing dishonor on her family.

We named the conference after her as part of our ongoing campaign to raise awareness and bring a stop to the phenomenon of Islamic honor killing. These girls have rights, too, they're human beings, and yet they're completely forgotten in our politically correct culture, in which speech that is offensive to Islam is increasingly forbidden. We were standing for the human rights of girls like Jessica.

I tried to place ads on Detroit-area buses offering help to people wishing to leave Islam and threatened by their families. SMART, Detroit's transit authority, refused the ads, and we sued on free speech grounds. We won, and the ads were scheduled to run, yet SMART still refused to post them. The same week they were scheduled to go up, Jessica Mokdad was murdered. Perhaps if she had seen one of our ads, she would be alive today. This underscored the cowardice of Detroit-area officials and the need for our conference in Dearborn.

The speakers included ex-Muslim human rights activist Nonie Darwish; Sudanese ex-slave and freedom fighter Simon Deng; and James Lafferty of the Virginia Anti-sharia Taskforce, co-host of the conference. Also speaking was David Wood of Acts 17 Apologetics, a Christian group that was suing the city of Dearborn for covering up Islamic honor killings performed in the area, and others.

A 2010 *Middle East Quarterly* report noted:

> In 2000, the United Nations estimated that there are 5,000 honor killings every year. That number might be reasonable for Pakistan alone, but worldwide the numbers are much greater. In 2002 and again in 2004, the U.N. brought a resolution to end honor killings and other honor-related crimes. In 2004, at a meeting in The Hague

about the rising tide of honor killings in Europe, law enforcement officers from the UK announced plans to begin reopening old cases to see if certain murders were, indeed, honor murders.[10]

Muslims are responsible for 91% of honor killings worldwide.[11] Islamic law specifies that "retaliation is obligatory against anyone who kills a human being purely intentionally and without right," but "not subject to retaliation" is "a father or mother (or their fathers or mothers) for killing their offspring, or offspring's offspring."[12] Muslims who kill their children are not subject to the penalty for murder, and Jordan, Syria and several other Muslim countries have reduced penalties for honor killings.[13]

Until the free world faces this, many, many more young women are going to suffer and die the way Aqsa Parvez and Jessica Mokdad did.

– Four –

The Ground Zero Mosque: Second Wave of the 9/11 Jihad Attacks

And the hits just kept coming.

In early December 2009, the *New York Times*—on its front page—heralded the arrival of a fifteen-story mega-mosque going up at Ground Zero. I, of course, began writing it up for *Atlas Shrugs*. It was shocking. I don't know what was more grotesque: the jihadists' triumphal mosque or the *New York Times'* preening of it. The *New York Times* ran a piece entitled "Muslim Prayers Fuel Spiritual Rebuilding Project at Ground Zero;" the title was later changed to "Muslim Prayers and Renewal Near Ground Zero."[1]

The *Times* was enthusiastic:

> The location was precisely a key selling point for the group of Muslims who bought the building in July. A presence so close to the World Trade Center, "where a piece of the wreckage fell," said Imam Feisal Abdul Rauf, the cleric leading the project, "sends the opposite statement to what happened on 9/11."[2]

The *Times* article contained no quotes at all against the project.

Imagine: a triumphal mosque built on the site of an Islamic victory, one no less unmistakable than the Dome of the Rock and the Al-Aqsa mosques on the Temple Mount in Jerusalem, which both assert the victory of Islam over Judaism. There are thousands of triumphal mosques marking the site of Islamic victories all over the Islamic world. The Ground Zero Mosque would be yet another. These triumphal mosques are either converted from churches, synagogues, and Hindu temples, or built over churches, synagogues, and Hindu temples that were destroyed in jihad attacks.

These mosques were designed to mark Islam's victory over and superiority to the religions that Islam views as rivals. Everywhere jihad attacks have been successful, triumphal mosques have been established. The most famous are the Dome of the Rock and the Al-Aqsa Mosque on the Temple Mount in Jerusalem, and the Aya Sofya Mosque in Istanbul, formerly the Hagia Sophia Cathedral, which, for one thousand years, was the grandest church in the Christian world.[3] Historian Sita Ram Goel has estimated that over two thousand mosques in India were built on the sites of Hindu temples.[4]

There are, by contrast, no mosques of healing and reconciliation built at the site of previous jihad attacks in order to reach out to those targeted by these attacks. The Ground Zero Mosque was supposed to be the first, but how could Muslims worldwide see it that way with no historical precedents? If Muslims worldwide had seen the Ground Zero Mosque go up, they would have viewed it in light of the victory mosques around them—and this victory mosque would have emboldened jihadists worldwide as no other victory mosque ever had.

The location was no accident. The imam Feisal Abdul Rauf, the cleric leading the project, said in that *Times* article, "New York is the capital of the world, and this location close to 9/11 is iconic." And even that was deceptive. The building slated to be torn down to build the mega-mosque, the former Burlington Coat Factory at 45 Park Place, was partially destroyed on 9/11. A piece of the landing gear from one of the planes that hit into the World Trade Center crashed through its roof. Interestingly enough, when the controversy heated up, Rauf's comment was scrubbed from the *Times* article. I caught the quote right away and wrote about it, and soon afterward it vanished, even from the Wayback Machine.[5]

I was appalled, and blogged on it, as did several other counter-jihad blogs. The media virtually ignored it. As the months passed, the powers behind the Ground Zero mosque proceeded to host horse-and-pony shows for the clueless and complicit politicians and various puppets on lower Manhattan's Community Board One, which did not have to approve the project, but would serve the propaganda campaign of the stealth jihadists. In one of the news articles, when it was reported that the financial committee, a small subcommittee of Community Board One, had unanimously approved the project, it was time for action. I didn't even know such a meeting was held. I hunkered down and began working the phones to find out the next such clandestine meeting. This was not going to happen in a vacuum. America deserved no less than transparency. "Sunlight is said to be the best of disinfectants," as Louis Brandeis said.

On *Atlas Shrugs,* I called patriots and freedom-lovers to attend the community board hearing scheduled to discuss the project. Hundreds showed up ready to defend freedom and have their say as to why the mosque must not be built. As soon as they began to speak, those who were in favor of the mosque started to smear their foes as racists and bigots. The room was noisy and the atmosphere grew tense. Margaret Chin, the local city councilwoman, said that all opposition to the mosque was "bigotry," and supporters of tolerance and pluralism had to support the mosque.[6] She issued a statement calling upon people to "speak out against hate and bigotry," and declared that "Lower Manhattan has no room for bigotry."[7] A couple who lost their son on 9/11 wrote in to the *New York Times* that Chin "accused opponents of being prejudiced or anti-immigrant."[8]

The hearing organizers distributed a written statement from Manhattan Borough President Scott Stringer that stated, "I for one never want to see our country or our city abandon religious tolerance as the result of an act of violence, even one as unspeakable as the 9/11 attacks."[9] Later, Manhattan's Community Board 7 issued a statement in favor of the mosque project that said: "Should we become haters and bigots in reaction to hatred and bigotry? We must not."[10]

Each person who wanted to address the board had to fill out a form in order to speak. And on this form, the speakers had to give the topic of their remarks. In order to be heard early on I wrote "outreach" as the reason for my being there and wanting to speak. I wrote my name down as Pam Atta (after the ringleader of the 9/11 attacks, Mohamed Atta). Sure enough, I was called third after two speakers in favor of the mosque and long before any other opponents were given an opportunity to say anything. Imagine that. But that's how they stack the deck.

I made my way through the hot, crowded room, amid too large a crowd for that space, and I understood in that moment that I had two minutes to right the wrong narrative that Islamic supremacists and their media shills were trying to lay on the American people, guilting them into submission, trying to shame their rational reactions to so monstrous a proposal. I also knew that given the way they were "selecting" people to speak I would be the only one heard on our side for hours maybe.

And while my remarks and the remarks of my peers never made it onto the media newscasts, they did go viral in the only place left for us—the Internet— and the movement was born. Here are my remarks at the Community Board meeting:

> First, I'd like to say that it's interesting to me that the elected officials do not represent all of the people. Every elected official has one perspective. Also: Cordoba Initiative [the name that the Ground Zero Mosque organizers had given to their project]. It's important to remember that Cordoba is symbolic of the Islamic conquest of Spain, where Christians and Jews lived as *dhimmis*, where they lived under a sub-class status, and that is the message in the word "Cordoba." I want also to say that the opposition to the mosque is against bigotry, against racism, against Islamic anti-Semitism, and against kafirophobia. We too want outreach with the Muslim world. We too are sensitive to the sensibilities of the Muslim world. We ask that Muslims be sensitive to our sensibilities. This is an insult, this is demeaning, this is humiliating, that you would build a shrine to the very ideology that inspired the attacks of 9/11. We feel that an Islamic Center dedicated to the hundreds of millions of victims of over a millennium of jihadi wars, land appropriations, enslavements, and cultural annihilation would be more in order. An Islamic Center dedicated to expunging the Koran of its violent texts would be appropriate on the hallowed ground of 9/11. I encourage all infidels, kafirs, and non-Muslims to join me—and Muslims with a conscience—decent Americans on June 6 to protest the mega-mosque going up on sacred ground. Thank you.

The largely anti-Cordoba crowd cheered, as they did when 9/11 family members were eventually given the opportunity to speak. A black Coptic Christian priest from Egypt would blow the shofar when people made good points against the mosque project. But the fix was in. After the lopsided vote in favor of the mosque, defying the crowd that was easily 75% against the mosque, printed remarks were distributed from Stringer congratulating the board for its vote. He must have known before the hearing how the board would vote. How did he know how the board would vote? Was the fix in from the start?

And the pushback began. So loud and fierce was the opposition that the media could no longer ignore the story—especially when thousands showed up at my American Freedom Defense Initiative/Stop Islamization of America rally in lower Manhattan on D-Day, June 6, 2010, to protest the Ground Zero mosque. Free people came from Washington state, California, Texas, Ohio, Michigan, Pennsylvania, Connecticut, New Hampshire, Maine, South Carolina, Florida, and elsewhere. They were Christians, Jews, Hindus, Sikhs, Buddhists, atheists, and Muslims of conscience. They were lovers of freedom.

Both of our rallies were attended by tens of thousands of people and featured speeches by me, Dutch freedom fighter Geert Wilders, former U.N. Ambassador John Bolton, the late conservative journalist Andrew Breitbart, popular talk show host Mike Gallagher, Sudanese ex-slave Simon Deng, courageous military vet Ilario Pantano, and many 9/11 family members and first responders.

At our first rally, police estimated that 5,000 people were there, and other estimates ranged as high as 10,000. The crowd carried signs expressing their love for freedom, their contempt for sharia, and their anger at Islamic supremacism and the insult to the memories of those murdered on 9/11 that this mosque represents.

Even more people showed up for our second rally. Tens of thousands attended the Rally of Remembrance for the 9/11 victims and against the Ground Zero mega-mosque on September 11, 2010. The crowd was so large, it stretched as far as the eye could see; you could not see the horizon from our stage.

Yet the bias was relentless. The *Associated Press* reported that the pro-mosque counter-demonstration drew around a thousand "activists," while "a smaller group of opponents rallied nearby, chanting, 'USA, USA.'" The *New York Post* was only marginally more honest, numbering our rally attendees at 2,500: "The estimated 3,000 pro-mosque demonstrators outnumbered the mosque opponents by about 500."

NY1 did a story on the rallies, but only showed footage of the small pro-mosque rally. The *Post* likewise only published pictures of the pro-mosque rally. *AP* ran an aerial photo of the rally, but one that was so poorly framed that one-third of it was dominated by a large gray building, and the crowd was cut off on the other side.

No one ran accurate photos of the rally, showing the full size of the crowd stretching beyond the horizon. Why didn't anyone think to take aerial shots of both rallies? That would have settled all questions. The pictures don't lie, but the media does. *AP* and the *Post* were not alone in their depiction of our rally and the pro-Islamic supremacist one as "dueling rallies." Their coverage of our immense rally versus the tiny counter-protest is dangerous and absurd.

The media operate under the narcissistic assumption that if they don't report it, it didn't happen. The Ground Zero mosque story shattered this fundamental belief of theirs. The Ground Zero mosque story is the first news of not only national but international proportions that dominated the headlines day after day, week after week, month after month, without the propulsion of the mainstream media. They scrambled to cover it late. They were playing catch-up, and then tried to force it, shape it, and destroy it.

The people were having none of it. The people drove that story. The people came to be heard. The media favored the construction of a 15-story mega-mosque at Ground Zero and, like the activists and politicians, charged that those who opposed it were racists and bigots—a claim as absurd as their suggestion that the 70% of Americans who opposed the building of the mosque did so out of hatred of Muslims.

The mainstream media began to blame me for the conflict, as if millions of Americans didn't know right from wrong and had no mind of their own. *Salon* said that, "the controversy was kicked up and driven by Pamela Geller, a right-wing, viciously anti-Muslim, conspiracy-mongering blogger."[11] CNN blamed me also—as did Rauf's wife, Daisy Khan, Hamas-linked CAIR's Nihad Awad, and others. They consistently ignored the fact that the vast majority of Americans were against this mosque. Americans didn't want a victory mosque marking the site of the 9/11 attacks. They didn't want an insult to the 3,000 Americans who were murdered there by Islamic jihadists and for whom Ground Zero is a cemetery.

From the media's perspective, the Ground Zero mosque was an historical phenomenon. For the first time, a major news story became the most important national and international news story without the media. They were forced to cover it when almost 15,000 people showed up at my first rally. The little coverage there was about the mosque before this was all sweetness and light. The puff piece in the *New York Times*, all about how wonderful a mosque at Ground Zero would be for "spiritual rebuilding," was typical of the coverage. There was little else. But I was not having it, and began writing about it regularly. When I heard a Community Board vote passed with no notice, I vowed we would be at the next meeting and we were. Were we ever. Once we packed the Community Board meeting and then showed up fifteen thousand strong at my June 6 Ground Zero mosque protest, the story took on a life of its own. Then we had roughly 20,000 people at Ground Zero on September 11, 2010. The story could not be written or controlled by the mainstream media.

Think about that. The Ground Zero mosque was not shaped by the media, not covered by the media—not at first anyway. The media scrambled to cover the story. They had no narrative, at first. They would put me on and let me speak. Of course, they always had some Islamic supremacist liar on to destroy me, but they never could. And, despite all the handicaps, I had the opportunity to present America with concretes on Islam.

Fox had me on with Nihad Awad, and CNN had Ahmed Soliman debate me.[12] I got in the ring with Ibrahim Ramey on CNN, and again with Ramey on the Canadian Broadcasting Centre.[13] There were lefty apologists like Nicole Neroulias, faculty member of the Columbia School of Journalism, who got into the ring with me on *Fox and Friends*.[14]

"Palestinian" hip-hopper Will Youmans spewed pure fiction in our debate. I also debated with Robert Salaam on RLTV and other hostile talking heads, including a nasty Bill O'Reilly who *had* to have me on to refute what Nihad Awad had said on his show the night before. He didn't say "Kill Pamela Geller," but he held up a cartoon of Muhammad with urine on his head, saying that I had depicted Muhammad on my website. This was a clear incitement to violence.[15] Joy Behar took her best shot (and missed), joined by Daisy Khan and Roy Sekoff, founding editor of the *Huffington Post*.[16] That panel was thus stacked with three mosque supporters against me alone, but even that was still not skewed enough for them.

I faced off against David Lane and Michael Gross, ACLU and civil rights lawyers who took their shots at me on *Hannity*.[17] And there were classic moments with Ibrahim Hooper of CAIR.[18] CNN's *Anderson Cooper 360* show went so far as to do a whole segment accusing me of ginning up the Ground Zero mosque controversy, saying that if it hadn't been for me, there would have been no issue. (Talk about condescending to the American people.)[19]

There were skirmishes with Safaa Zarzour, Secretary General of the Muslim Brotherhood-front Islamic Society of North America, and Hussam Ayloush of Hamas-tied CAIR's Los Angeles chapter.[20] Not to mention a brisk brush with Michael Ghouse.[21] Across the pond I debated Shahed Amanullah on the BBC.[22] Geraldo did a hit piece on me.[23] I took on Malik Shabazz of the New Black Panthers.[24] I went head-to-head with leftist misogynist Bob Beckel and hate sponsor CAIR-Chicago's Ahmed Rehab.[25]

It is also instructive to contrast these battles to the kid gloves, fawning treatment the media accorded to Rauf and the Ground Zero Mosque project developer, Sharif El-Gamal. Rauf even claimed credit for "training" a particularly compliant *New York Times* reporter.[26]

I was not deterred. Each appearance was "a teachable moment." And I was glad of it.

The Sunday magazine of the UK's *Independent* ran a cover story under the headline, "Pamela Geller, The Most Dangerous Woman in America?"

As if....

Still, it was a unique opportunity for counter-jihadists. Right after 9/11, the media didn't have its story straight either, and there were moments where you heard and saw things you would never hear or see now. The media was surprised and wasn't ready for that terrible act of war against America. But they dusted the human remains off their jackets and began to shape a suicidal narrative about how the West was ultimately responsible for the conflict. We have gone so far down the rabbit hole, 9/11 images are embargoed and not shown. They are trundled out but once a year and then secreted back into the vault of things the media won't talk about.

The dirty smear merchants over at Media [anti-]Matters understood what was happening and issued a directive to the left-wing lemmings: "Do not have Geller on national television."[27] The very same day that Goebbels-inspired post ran, Chris Matthews canceled my TV appearance for that evening.[28] And with the exception of breaking news stories (i.e., historic landmark First Amendment rulings, the jihad attack on our free speech event in Garland or jihad beheading plots to kill me), I haven't been on ever since, with the rare exception of a few appearances on the *Hannity* show.

The media, both left and right, has generally fallen into lockstep. They will only have me on if they have no choice. If I make news vis-a-vis a lawsuit or rally or some other newsmaking event and they are forced to, they do so reluctantly. If they can get my lawyer instead, they will because they have become so fearful of the truth.

Despite this, the left could not contain the story. The American people would not back down.

In the continuing Ground Zero mosque story, the media hoped the "opposition would just melt away," to quote Matt Lauer in his puff piece on thug Ground Zero mosque developer El-Gamal. The media tried to play catch-up. They settled on the tired "racist–Islamophobic–anti-Muslim–bigot" narrative, but it didn't fit. The 9/11 families, like all Americans, were entitled to their pain and their grief. The *ummah* couldn't cry about sensitivity to Muslims when their leaders showed such callous heartlessness towards the pain and sensitivity of non-Muslims and Muslims of conscience. The more they tried to destroy the opposition, the more intolerant they looked.

The alphabet networks stayed out of it for as long as they could without looking completely out of touch. And when they finally weighed in, the heavyweights like *60 Minutes* shilled for Islamic supremacists, and consequently came under enormous fire from the American people, the blogs, and talk radio.

The mosque story has been a game-changer. The media is now working on preaching Islam, spreading the historically inaccurate whitewash of Islam. That is how they are using their considerable power to disarm the American people against a mortal enemy that seeks our destruction. They ask, why are we fighting? That is the role the media has chosen and it's no accident. Beware, America.

There were numerous reasons to oppose the mosque. Even the name of the initiative—Cordoba—spoke volumes. While Islamic Spain is held up today as a proto-multiculturalist paradise, in reality non-Muslims there suffered under the discrimination prescribed in Islamic law for *dhimmis*, non-believers who were subjugated as inferiors and denied equality of rights. When we started calling attention to the true meaning of the name Cordoba, the name of the mosque initiative suddenly changed to Park51—with the media lapdogs immediately falling into line. They never mentioned Cordoba again, just like that.

These mega-mosques are making a supremacist statement. Most people assume they're just like synagogues or churches. They don't realize that Islam has political goals that are expressed through the mosques, and that the mosques often symbolize that Muslims are claiming a particular territory as their own.

For the Muslim Brotherhood, mosques aren't just houses of worship. They're centers of political power, from which plans are made to increase that power in various ways.

When you hear Muslims speak of tolerance, you should understand that Islamic notions of "tolerance" arise out of Koran 9:29, where tolerance means that non-Muslims are to be tolerated only as those who submit to Islam as inferiors, without equality of rights with Muslims. Many oppose the Ground Zero mosque for just this reason. After all, we do know that this is what is taught in mosques that are designated "Islamic Centers"—the ones that some people ignorantly claim are not mosques. Certainly the Muslim Brotherhood in America's goals in outreach have nothing to do with successful outreach or achieving Western standards of tolerance, but rather with bringing over converts and getting us to subvert our way of life—primarily by working with them.

Is it really "racism" and "bigotry" to oppose the mega-mosque because of all this? Of course it isn't. It's just common sense—common sense and love for America.

One might think that the Muslim community would have been capable of some sensitivity, considering how maniacally sensitive they are about any perceived insult to Islam. Every time there is a jihadist attack, which is happening with increasing frequency, the *ummah* (global Muslim community) starts wailing on us infidels about Muslim sensitivities and anticipatory and imaginary affronts and insults. Yet what could be more insulting and humiliating than a mosquestrosity (as I called it) sold to us as a multicultural Islamic community center in the shadow of what once was the greatest multicultural community center in the world, the World Trade Center buildings?

Imam Rauf and Daisy Khan, along with the Ground Zero mosque developer Sharif El-Gamal, said it was a mosque of healing. Yet Rauf, Khan, and El-Gamal could not control the perception that Muslims worldwide will have of this mosque. That perception would be guided by Muslims' own cultural context.

If this mosque really were about healing, why wouldn't the self-declared Muslim leaders build an Islamic Center dedicated to expunging the Koran and Sunnah of their prescribed violent teachings that inspired the attacks of

9/11? There have been over 17,000 Islamic jihad attacks since 9/11, each one with the imprimatur of a Muslim cleric. What is being done about this?

Sadly, New York City officials were avid to help the Ground Zero mosque organizers get their victory mosque built. The *New York Daily News* reported in December 2010:

> Mayor Bloomberg's top deputies went to great lengths to help those trying to build a mosque at Ground Zero—even drafting a letter to the community board for them, newly released documents show. City Hall on Thursday released a flurry of emails between its brass and Feisal Abdul Rauf, the imam pushing to build a mosque near the sensitive site, and his supporters.

Another instance of the New York City government colluding with the mosque organizers was the Metropolitan Transportation Authority's refusal to allow SIOA's anti-mosque, pro-freedom ads on New York City buses. They said that the ad's images of the burning World Trade Center towers were offensive. As I said at the time, "What's more insulting and offensive—that image of truth, or a fifteen-story mega-mosque looking down on the sacred ground of Ground Zero?"[29]

We threatened a lawsuit. The MTA backed off and allowed the ads. But the episode illustrated two things: the city government's strong pro-mosque stance, and the necessity to keep fighting until attaining victory. The fact that we even had to fight this battle shows the grave threat to freedom of speech in the US today, and how anxious authorities are to kowtow to Islamic supremacism.

We called attention to the mosque organizers' dishonesty. We galvanized the opposition to the mosque and used every means at our disposal to make our voice heard. And we were heard. The mosque remains wildly unpopular with the American people, despite relentless media propagandizing for it. And so by the spring of 2011, it was likely that the organizers would not make their initial goal of breaking ground for the mosque on September 11, 2011. And we would keep up the pressure to make sure that it would never be built at all.

The people were awake.

And that mosque was never built.

Despite all the opposition and abuse they faced, the people stood up and fought against the Ground Zero Mosque, and *won*. An army of Davids.

The Ground Zero mosque battle is a story of ordinary Americans defeating powerful and moneyed elites. Our acclaimed documentary, *The Ground Zero Mosque: Second Wave of the 9/11 Attacks*, tells the whole story, gives highlights of the rally speeches, exposes the sinister forces behind the mosque, and strikes back against the media liars. This was the first and only documentary that told the whole truth about the Ground Zero mosque. We premiered it in Manhattan's Theatre District before a standing-room-only crowd of freedom-lovers. It was after our AFDI 9/11 Freedom Rally celebrating our victory over the sinister forces behind the Ground Zero mosque.

By far our greatest victory was the defeat of the Ground Zero mosque. Despite overwhelming odds, President Obama, Mayor Bloomberg, legions of craven politicians and a sharia-compliant, jackbooted media intent on getting that cultural obscenity built, it was soundly and roundly defeated. We did that. Our rallies and our patriots did that.

In May 2017, Ronda Kaysen of *New York Times*, still licking her wounds that a 16-story mega-mosque on hallowed ground was not going to be built, asked me for comment about Sharif El-Gamal's new project: pricey condos combined with a hagiographic museum of Islam. How many condo projects in New York get written up in the *Times*? The *Times* has a real estate section, so development projects do often get written up, but this was treated as a news story, not in the development section, but on the front page.

The *Times* was still reeling from their defeat in the Ground Zero mosque controversy.

I opened my laptop and fired off a response.

> The 16-story mosque that El-Gamal initially planned to build there has not been built. [The exact number of stories the mosque was slated to have changed in various reports; some said 13, some 15, some 16.] Our efforts in showing what an insult it was to the American people and to the victims of 9/11, and how many Muslims worldwide would inevitably view it as a triumphal mosque built on the site of a jihad attack, defeated it. Now El-Gamal plans an Islamic Museum, which is just as much of an insult; it will be like having a Museum touting the glories of the Japanese Empire at

Pearl Harbor. A genuine Islamic Museum that detailed the 1,400-year history of jihad warfare, cultural annihilation, land appropriation and enslavement would be appropriate at that location, but El-Gamal's museum is certain to be a whitewash of the doctrine and history of jihad and a paean to imaginary Muslim contributions to various important inventions and achievements.

We will never surrender.

– Five –
Fighting for Truth

Stealth Turkey Jihad

The activism I engaged in took many forms. I fought for the rights of Muslim women and girls for whom no one, neither Muslims nor feminists, was standing up. I fought against sharia encroachment into the public sphere and one of the most memorable instances of my work in that arena was an unlikely controversy regarding... Thanksgiving turkeys.

The turkey you enjoy on Thanksgiving Day is probably halal. Butterball says of itself: "Butterball is the largest vertically integrated turkey producer in the United States and accounts for 20 percent of total turkey production in this country."[1] And for years, although Butterball ended the practice in 2012 after I called national attention to it, if it was a Butterball brand turkey, then it certainly was halal—whether the consumer wanted a halal turkey or not.[2]

It is a cruel means of slaughter. Where are the PETA clowns and the ridiculous celebs who pose naked on giant billboards for PETA and "animal rights"? They would rather see people die of cancer or AIDS than see animals used in drug testing, but torturous and painful Islamic slaughter is O.K.

Halal meat is slaughtered according to Islamic ritual. According to Islamic law, Muslims should eat only halal meat, which is slaughtered in a particular way, as the words "Bismillah allahu akbar"—in the name of Allah the greatest (the same prayer made when beheading infidels)—is pronounced. Halal slaughter involves cutting the trachea, the esophagus, and the jugular vein, and letting the blood drain out. Many people refuse to eat it on religious grounds. Many Christians, Hindus or Sikhs and Jews find it offensive to eat meat slaughtered according to Islamic ritual (although observant Jews are less likely to be exposed to such meat, because they eat kosher).

Many others understandably object to eating halal meat, for humanitarian reasons (since halal slaughter is especially brutal to the animal), or religious grounds, or because they simply object to certification from Muslim groups. The same Islamic law that mandates that animals be cruelly slaughtered according to halal requirements also teaches hatred of and warfare against unbelievers, the oppression of women, the extinguishing of free speech, and much more that is inimical to our freedom.

In 2010, a citizen activist and reader of *Atlas Shrugs* wrote to Butterball, one of the most popular producers of Thanksgiving turkeys in the United States, asking them if their turkeys were halal. A Butterball spokesperson responded: "Our whole turkeys are certified halal."

In a little-known strike against freedom, millions of Americans and Europeans were unwittingly forced to consume meat slaughtered through a torturous method: Islamic ritualized killing. Even if the method isn't troublesome, there's the matter of principle. Why should consumers and families gathered around the Thanksgiving table be forced to conform to Islamic norms? It's Islamic supremacy on the march, yet again.

Non-Muslims in America and Europe don't deserve to have halal turkey forced upon them in this way, without their knowledge or consent. I wouldn't knowingly buy a halal turkey—would you? Halal turkey, slaughtered according to the rules of Islamic law, is just the opposite of what Thanksgiving represents: freedom and inclusiveness, neither of which are allowed under that same Islamic law. Also, Thanksgiving is explicitly not a religious holiday. The most inclusive and quintessentially American holiday was being quietly dedicated to Islam.

In November 2011, I penned an article that caused a firestorm across the political spectrum, revealing that Butterball turkeys were all halal, but were not labeled as such.[4] Heads exploded on the left—not over Butterball's deception, but over my having the audacity to reveal it. And the clueless and compromised on the right were enraged as well: writer John Podhoretz tweeted, "I'd tell Pamela Geller to put a sock in it, but the sock might be halal."[5]

I was, of course, excoriated as a racist, Islamophobic, anti-Muslim bigot. In reality, however, we have no objection to halal meat being sold, as long as it is clearly labeled as such, and as long as non-halal meat is available. Meat that is halal must be labeled as such.

Our petition regarding ritual slaughter was posted on the FSIS website on February 14, 2012. It was a "ritual slaughter" petition that applied to all types of ritual slaughter: kosher, halal, etc. Every type of ritual slaughter holds some type of concern for some segment of the consuming public. We were not asking the USDA to single out a specific type of slaughter when dealing with this issue; our petition did not single out one type of ritual slaughter over another, nor did it wish to discriminate against a specific religious group.

We just wanted all meat that had been ritually slaughtered to be clearly labeled to that effect. Kosher meat is routinely marked accordingly; why not halal meat?

Butterball backed down, but the meat industry's halal scandal is little noted but ongoing. Most producers have an established practice of not separating halal meat from non-halal meat, then not labeling halal meat as such. In October 2010, I reported some explosive revelations: that much of the meat in Europe and the United States was being processed as halal without the knowledge of the non-Muslim consumers who buy it.[6]

I discovered only two plants in the US that perform halal slaughter kept the halal meat separated from the non-halal meat, and they only did so because plant managers felt it was only right to do so. At other meat-packing plants, animals were slaughtered following halal requirements, with only a small percentage of the meat actually labeled halal. It's a cost-saving measure: most of the meat is halal, then the meat packers package some halal meat as such, and the rest is sold as regular meat. People don't know it has been prayed over with Islamic prayer. It's cheaper that way: rather than have separate operations for halal and non-halal meat, many producers simply make all meat halal and then sell some of it without noting that it is halal.

A veteran of the meat-packing industry explained to me:

Meat and poultry is being slaughtered under halal but only a small portion of the meat is being labeled halal. The rest is sold without being identified as halal in the meat department of your local grocery store or fast food chain. The exact same situation as in the UK, Australia, and New Zealand.

After asking lots of questions, I discovered that the two plants I worked with that did halal slaughter kept the meat segregated only because the employees of the plant thought it was the right thing to do. Many others are slaughtering an entire shift worth of meat under halal but only selling a small portion under a halal label."[7]

This industry insider also informed me:

> I started digging into this a bit further, talked to colleagues in other plants, etc. What I found out was pretty astonishing. Evidently the facilities I was familiar with that did the halal slaughter were the exceptions and not the rule. Because they only sold whole chickens that were halal, everything was segregated. Plants that sell further processed product commingle the halal slaughtered stuff in with everything else because only certain parts are exported to the halal market.
>
> While slaughter establishments have to request an exemption from the humane slaughter rules for religious slaughter of any sort and meat carrying either the kosher or halal label must actually be slaughtered in that manner, there is no requirement that halal slaughtered meat or poultry be segregated from conventional product. There is currently no list of establishments that have requested a religious exemption that is accessible to the public. I have submitted a FOIA request for that information.
>
> I have also discussed the issue with the former FSIS administrator who now works for industry as well as the head of FSIS's office of policy development at a small committee meeting this morning. The former administrator had the same concerns that I did and promised to make sure that I was given a list even if the FOIA request was denied or delayed. The current policy director admitted that he had never thought about the issue in the way I had described. I asked him to either note on the establishment directly which plants had a religious slaughter exemption or to make the list of such readily available.
>
> By sorting through the limited number of lists of establishments exporting to countries that require Halal slaughter, I was able to identify some establishments. Almost all of the large beef plants in the country perform halal slaughter based on these export documents (see link below for example). I am also combing through the 850+ page establishment directory to determine the best I can which plants do halal slaughter of at least some product. The first 200 pages of that is attached with plants that

slaughter halal at least some of the time highlighted. It is not complete but the best I can do without a list from the agency. I will work on the rest of the directory and get that to you as I can. I was disheartened to find at least one slaughter establishment that produced both kosher and halal product. When you buy meat or poultry at retail, the establishment number is in the middle of the USDA inspection shield. Armed with the establishment directory, consumers can check it against any product in the grocery store.

From the looks of it, most of the beef sold in the US comes out of a plant with some halal slaughter. The chicken picture is less clear so far, though the following processors are known : Allen's Family Foods-Seaford plant; Perdue Farms-Dillon, SC plant; Amick Farms-Hurlock, MD & Saluda, SC plants, Gerber Poultry-Ohio plant, Harrison Poultry-Bethlehem, GA plant.

This industry veteran had long exchanges with the USDA about what could be done to give enough information regarding ritually slaughtered products that would allow consumers to make informed purchasing decisions. Several options were suggested, but in the end, it was decided at USDA that the only way to effectively do so was through a labeling petition. But the government kept putting up roadblocks, as the insider recounts:

Not wanting to put a burden on industry, I made an effort to find out which establishments did ritual slaughter and which of these sold to the school lunch program through FOIA requests so that I could avoid purchases based on establishment number. My FOIA requests were ignored by USDA until October of 2011 (one year after the request). When I got them, they did not include any red meat establishments and the list of poultry facilities was incomplete. At that point, it became clear that the only choice was to petition to require labeling because if I as an industry insider could not find complete and accurate information, there was no way that Suzie Q Homemaker would be able to do so.

This industry expert also told me: "The choice to label is strictly up to the processor and therefore a free speech issue."

Labeling laws in the US require that, "The Labeling and Program Delivery Division (LPDD) develops policies and inspection verification methods and administers programs to protect consumers from misbranded and economically adulterated meat, poultry and egg products such that all labels are truthful and not misleading."

We attempted to right this wrong. But the US Department of Agriculture has for years now ignored, shelved, or just plain refused to rule on our petition.

As many Americans do not, for a variety of reasons, wish to eat halal meat, in February 2012, AFDI filed a citizen petition with the USDA's Food Safety and Inspection Service, asking that a regulation be enacted to ensure that all halal food be clearly labeled as halal. That April, we agreed not to publicize our petition in order to give the agency some space to review the document without any pressure from the public.

A month later we had a face-to-face meeting in the USDA offices with top FSIS officials. We discussed this petition and the need for halal meat to be clearly labeled. Dan Engeljohn, a longtime USDA official who is now Assistant Administrator for the Office of Policy and Program Development in the FSIS, was present at the meeting. He's responsible for FSIS regulations.

Engeljohn and company will have had six years as of February 2018 to rule on our petition. They've done absolutely nothing.

This is strictly a false labeling and consumer choice issue. Religious people—Jews, Muslims, and others—should have the freedom to have meat and poultry products produced in a way that meets their needs. Conversely, consumers who *don't* wish to consume ritually slaughtered products have a right to sufficient labeling information.

Labeling is untruthful when key facts are omitted. Consumers have the right to choose for themselves if they want to eat ritually slaughtered products. Some Christians see the New Testament prohibiting the consumption of meat sacrificed to idols, and would view halal meat as meeting that definition. But under current law they have no way to avoid eating it.

Just as those who buy meat and poultry products labeled halal or kosher should have a reasonable expectation that the meat they're buying was actually produced in that manner, so also those of us who don't want to eat halal meat for whatever reason should have a reasonable assurance that meat not labeled halal was not actually slaughtered in accordance with sharia rules. As halal slaughter continues to be practiced in the US, and will increase with the rising Muslim population, the likelihood of unknowingly buying meat sacrificed under the present system also increases.

This is a matter of simple justice and common sense. So why did the USDA stonewall on our petition?

The Tennessee Protest

In June 2013, Obama's Justice Department warned against using social media to spread information considered offensive to Muslims, threatening that it could constitute a violation of civil rights. I had warned of such consequences of an Obama presidency in my first book, *The Post-American Presidency: The Obama Administration's War on America*. And here it was.

The DOJ's top federal prosecutor, Bill Killian, announced he was headed to Manchester, Tennessee for a sharia outreach meeting with Muslim leaders, declaring "federal civil rights laws can actually be violated by those who post inflammatory documents aimed at Muslims on social media."

Obama's DOJ was working in earnest to impose Islamic law on our First Amendment rights—in other words, crushing our basic freedoms.

On Facebook, Twitter, and *Atlas Shrugs* I called for a protest of speech restrictions aimed at coddling sharia. AFDI board members Robert Spencer and James Lafferty joined me in Manchester, where thousands of patriots and freedom-lovers, all happy warriors, converged to oppose a seminar led by an Obama-appointed US attorney on how to use civil rights laws to shut down speech deemed "inflammatory" against Muslims (a label used before to shut down truthful speech about jihad and Islamic supremacism).

This was a fight for the very soul of America in a very small town: Manchester has no more than 10,000 people and almost 2,000 people were at my event. It was a small American town, much like thousands of other small American towns. Beautiful, green, with lots of American flags and pickup trucks. Patriotism abounds. A tired cliche? Only to the jaded and the lost.

This was the perhaps unlikely venue for a seminar led by a US attorney and an FBI special agent on how "inflammatory" speech against Muslims violated civil rights laws. It was held there because a local official had sent around a tongue-in-cheek photo that many regarded as threatening to Muslims. But nowhere was it ever explained how there could be honest examination of Islam's teachings of jihad that wouldn't be "inflammatory"—and that was just the point.

Numerous speakers addressed the roaring crowd before the anti-free speech seminar began, including me and other freedom fighters. Then when the Muslim-pandering event began, there were close to 800 people filling the small room to way beyond capacity. The lines were three deep along the wall, with folks spilling out into the hallways.

When the event started more than 600 people couldn't even get in, but they stayed outside and held a freedom rally. The large number of freedom-lovers was beautiful. And those outside weren't missing much—unless they were in the mood to be admonished and hectored as xenophobes, bigots and racists by an Islamic supremacist spokesman and two Obama officials who steadfastly refused to address the elephant in the room: the reality of jihad terror and Islamic supremacism, no matter how many times the boisterous crowd called them on their nonsense.

Killian gave a PowerPoint presentation on hate crimes and hate speech. From beginning to end it was full of condescension, smears, charges that the crowd was racist, and thinly veiled threats that truthful speech about Islam could be prosecuted. Never once did he address the fact that people aren't concerned about Muslims because of racism and xenophobia, but because of the reality of jihad terror and the uniform denial, obfuscation, and victim-hood-posturing in Muslim communities that follow every jihad attack.

Killian even stooped so low as to claim a sharp rise in "religiously moti-vated hate crimes," without ever informing the crowd that he was lumping in anti-Semitic hate crimes (which are at worldwide record levels, largely due to Islamic anti-Semitism) with anti-Muslim hate crimes. FBI special agent Kenneth Moore was little better. Both echoed the opening remarks by Zak Mohyuddin of the American Muslim Advisory Council, all about how the people of Tennessee had to learn to be welcoming of people who were different.

The media coverage of both our free speech rally and the anti-free speech seminar was deceptive and typically mendacious. One would think the industry that has the most to lose from restrictions on free speech would fight the fascism. But you would be wrong. These tools were so in the bag for the Obama regime that the knaves attack the patriots (and there are many of us) who stand between freedom and tyranny.

The headline of every news story should have been "Obama's Department of Justice seeks to criminalize free speech." Instead, the headlines spun the Muslim victimhood myth narrative that a Muslim outreach program was disrupted by racist, Islamophobic, anti-Muslimbigots. Nothing on the constitutional putsch. They didn't bury the lede; they never recovered the body.

"Tenn. Muslim group's forum disrupted by protesters," declared *USA Today*. Newswires went with, "Protesters, hecklers disrupt Muslim forum in Tennessee." Knoxville's WBIR-TV's headline read, "Protesters disrupt Tenn. Muslim group's meeting." Nowhere in the coverage did the media deign to mention why folks were there. People came to protest Killian's vow to criminalize criticism of Islam on social media. Folks were boisterous and well they should have been. Does anyone think we ought to go quietly into the night?

Taking their orders from Islamic supremacist groups, the DOJ and FBI said the meeting would be an open forum. It was even titled "Public Discourse." But they changed the rules. Instead of an open forum we were told to write questions on index cards. Yeah, uh-huh. And, of course, after hours of condescension and accusations of racism, they only read two questions.

Yes, people called them on it. Yes, people grimaced and moaned when Holder's name was mentioned. As we saw it, he was second only to Obama in greatest threats to our freedoms.

I was there. It was a great American moment. Americans aren't going to sit quietly while our freedom of speech is taken away. We are never ever going to submit and stop telling the truth about the jihad that threatens us all. We are an army.

But telling the truth came at an increasingly great price.

Banned in Britain

On June 25, 2013, I was banned from entering Britain.

I planned to be there on June 29 for an event I organized with British activist Tommy Robinson, at that time of the English Defence League, or EDL, an anti-sharia organization. I was going to be among a group of freedom fighters—a true rainbow coalition of human rights activists from all over the world (even a Hindu princess had been set to join us)—to honor the memory of Lee Rigby, a British soldier murdered on a London street in broad daylight by an Islamic jihadist on May 22, 2013.

We planned to pay our respects to Lee Rigby by placing a wreath at his memorial, in his memory and in memory of his service. We planned to bring the Stars and Stripes, as well as British and Danish flags, and participate in Armed Forces Day memorial commemorations at the Royal Artillery Barracks in Woolwich, where Rigby served. We called on all freedom-lovers to join us.

But the day before I was to board the plane to London, I received a letter from the British Home Office, then headed by Theresa May, the future Prime Minister, saying I was not going to be permitted to enter the country as my presence was not "conducive to the public good."

Who would have imagined that twelve years after 9/11, patriots and freedom-lovers dedicated to opposing the ideology behind those attacks on the homeland (and over 21,000 deadly Islamic attacks worldwide since) would be demonized, dehumanized, and the object of a campaign to get us banned from an allied nation. It could only be the result of insanity or... defeat.

That was the mentality of the Board of Deputies of British Jews, the main representative body, which issued a statement saying it shared "the very strong and longstanding concerns about the views of people like Pamela Geller." The board's vice president, Jonathan Arkush, said, "our community has no need of their presence here and they would be better advised to have nothing to do with the EDL."

This action was an enormously sad commentary on Jewish lay leadership and, worse, a stunning indictment of their culpability. It mimicked the inadequate and ill-conceived political action of the Jewish Councils in Germany in the late 1930s and 40s, hoping to appease the Nazis into granting the Jews some breathing room. We are not supposed to say such things, but it is true.

The brilliant German-American political theorist Hannah Arendt was cast out of the Jewish intelligentsia and various academic circles when she made similar statements in her historic coverage of the Eichmann trial in Jerusalem.[8] But Arendt's reportage was accurate, and her observations were meant to serve a cautionary purpose, lest the horrors be repeated under different historical conditions.

These are those conditions.

If the Jewish councils had not collaborated to various degrees with Nazis like Eichmann, the number of those who were slaughtered might very well have been less. How much less? *A life is a life.*

How scared and cowed they are. I understand that conditions were difficult in Britain at the time I was banned, but their zealous collaboration was ill-conceived. These were the German Jews of the 30s.

Europe has learned nothing from the Holocaust. The same can be said of that continent's Jews. What were they thinking? They knew what was going on in Europe; they knew what was going on in their neighborhoods. If they couldn't or wouldn't fight, then why attack those of us who would?

As the author Richard Bernstein wrote, we Jews must be very mindful of the "role of the Jewish leaders in the destruction of their own people."[9]

In December 2013, the whole truth came to light about why I was banned from the country, and it made the Board of Deputies of British Jews look even worse. In my court battle to overturn the ban, I have received a new cache of documents that revealed a principal reason why I was banned from the country was because I was pro-Israel.

An official (name redacted) in the Foreign and Commonwealth Office wrote in a May 7, 2013 letter: "We do have concerns with some of the reasoning in the sub," that is, the "subject profile" that had been prepared on me, "particularly citing pro-Israeli views." The official explained that "pro-Israeli views (and also support for waterboarding) apply to a large number of Americans, including former presidents," and said that if I were to ask for details under Britain's Freedom of Information laws about why I was banned from the country, "that being pro-Israeli is cited as a reason may be problematic," and I could "argue publically" that I was banned from Britain on the basis of my "support for Israel."

To avoid this, the writer advised, "removing references to being pro-Israel from the main body of the sub, as this is not grounds for exclusion." Presumably this advice was followed, as there is little information about my pro-Israeli views in all this material, but my "subject profile" still says, "She strongly supports Israel and is an ardent Zionist." And also: "Pamela Geller's outspoken support for Israel may also attract pro-Palestinian groups to attend, further complicating the policing operation on the ground and making it harder to keep opposing groups apart."

So now the real reason why I was banned was clear. The letter writer noted that being pro-Israel was not grounds for exclusion, but clearly it was part of the Home Office's reasoning, or this letter would not have had to have been written.

The move to ban me, meanwhile, was a massive operation. At the first hint that I might be speaking at a freedom protest in the UK, numerous British government and law enforcement agencies sprang into action. Although I had not decided to go and speak in the UK until June 2013, various government agencies began working to ban us as early as February 2013.

There were numerous documents from the Office of Security and Counter-Terrorism, or OSCT. That's right, we were banned with the collusion of the office of counter-terrorism. These were supposed to be legitimate government organizations, and they were just tools of nefarious forces. How was the UK government preventing a terror attack on the UK, which is the objective of the OSCT? By banning counter-terror activists. Why was the OSCT spending enormous sums of a bankrupt nation investigating a "character" (me, in the words of an unnamed British official whose correspondence on my case I received through a freedom of information request) who opposed terror, as they supposedly did also?[10]

Another, among a multitude of agencies investigating my case, was a Casework and Operations Red Team for Special Cases. That's right: the Home Secretary employed a Red Team on our case. Red Teams are designed to devise new strategies and approaches to deal with a threat. Now I ask you: is spending their time and money on seeking reasons to ban a human rights activist like me from the country in any way going to constitute a new strategy for effectively fighting the jihad terror threat against Britain?

The amount of time, money, and human resources devoted to this Kafkaesque exercise was breathtaking. These venerable agencies begin their in-depth and comprehensive research at—wait for this—Wikipedia. From there, they cited to each other such notorious and reputable smear machines as *Loonwatch* and *Islamophobia Today*. Senior analysts from Asia, the Middle East and Europe were part of the research and information team. My case, according to this British official, had "very senior scrutiny," as there was a "need to push" on this research.[11]

Mind you, much of the material in these documents was redacted. Wouldn't the unredacted documents have made interesting reading?

All references to the identities of those who asked that I be banned were blacked out. A British government representative, writing "for the Treasury Solicitor," explained to my lawyers that, "The documents provided have been redacted to remove references to information which is not relevant to the claims." No, clearly the documents were redacted to conceal who was behind the ban and what their motives were, and to conceal the conspiratorial nature of the exclusion.

But their black marker missed one reference, revealing that one of the groups complaining about me was Faith Matters. Faith Matters was founded by a Muslim named Fiyaz Mughal, who also headed up Tell Mama, a group dedicated to tracking "Islamophobia." Tell Mama lost British government funding in June 2013 after making false claims of waves of attacks considered to be "Islamophobic incidents."[12] Tell Mama is the British counterpart of the Southern Poverty Law Center, except that it is run by Muslims, not leftists. Their made-up hate crimes are notorious, as are their misleading claims. The *Telegraph* reported in 2013: "Tell Mama confirmed to the *Sunday Telegraph* that about 120 of its 212 'anti-Muslim incidents'—57 per cent—took place only online. They were offensive postings on Twitter or Facebook, or comments on blogs: nasty and undesirable, certainly, but some way from violence or physical harm and often, indeed, legal. Not all the offending tweets and postings, it turns out, even originated in Britain."[13] Yet they are still used by the British government and media as a reliable source of data, even though they've been defunded.

The Home Secretary assured Fiyaz Mughal, the discredited liar, that all decisions to exclude were based on sound evidence. How are the wild defamations of *Loonwatch* and *Islamophobia Today* sound evidence? In many of the documents, they didn't even spell our names correctly, or get our birthdates right. Is that sound evidence?

My "subject profile" said that I displayed "a picture of the Prophet [Muhammad] with a pig's face superimposed on it on her blog." The Muhammad pig cartoon they were referring to was one that a Danish imam added to the infamous Muhammad cartoons printed by the Danish newspaper *Jyllands Posten*, in an attempt to gin up anger among Muslims against the Danes. The imam presented the Muhammad-as-pig cartoon as if it were one of the original Danish cartoons, which it wasn't, and then the British government presented it as something I created, which wasn't true either. The caption on the Muhammad-as-pig photo at *Atlas Shrugs* read: "Supposed to be [Muhammad] as half pig, but actually an altered photograph of a guy at a French pig-squealing contest."[14] So they took a photo that I showed was clearly marked as not Muhammad at all, and presented it as if I were depicting Muhammad as a pig.

They had teams of people spending untold amounts of money researching me, and they couldn't even get these basic facts right. This crack research team had one eureka moment when one of the redacted names "has discovered circa 120 articles written by Geller on one website alone[!] In order to go through this properly, we need another week to conduct our research." More time. More money. More people.

"The government," one document says, "is clear that it opposes extremism in all forms." Did it oppose extremism in pursuit of truth? Did it oppose extremism in pursuit of justice? Of liberty?

The ban was never lifted and in December 2016 Prime Minister May even bragged about it. Speaking at a Conservative Friends of Israel event attended by over 800 people and over 200 parliamentarians, May said she had banned me from entering the UK because "Islamophobia" was just as harmful as anti-Semitism.

This was an extraordinary statement for May to make. We already knew that, according to documents released under Britain's duty of candor, a good part of the reason I was banned was because of my support for Israel, as well as the fact that anti-Semitic hate crimes were far more common than anti-Muslim ones, and Jews presented no terror threat.

May had become utterly ridiculous, tying herself into knots at the behest of her nation's would-be executioners. There is no doubt that she will eventually regret taking the course she and her colleagues have so recklessly chosen for Britain—but by then it will almost certainly be too late.

– Six –
CPAC and What's Wrong with the Right

Bringing Geert Wilders to CPAC 2009

There were a handful of brave and vocal defenders of freedom in the West who stood against the onslaught of jihad terror and advancing sharia. Foremost among them was Geert Wilders, the Dutch parliamentarian and producer of the film *Fitna*, which shows simply and clearly how jihadis act upon the Koran's calls for violence.

I began to see what I was up against when I wanted to bring Wilders to the annual Conservative Political Action Conference in Washington, D.C. and expose him to a much larger American audience, one outside the echo chamber of the counter-jihad movement.

For months, I fought fiercely to get Wilders on the official CPAC 2009 roster. They should have been clamoring to have him. He represented, and still represents today, the fight for the idea of American freedom, our unalienable rights as endowed by our creator.

After much conversation, David Keene planned to give the Charlton Heston Courage Under Fire Award to Wilders at CPAC for his fight for free speech (the very bedrock of conservative principles). Yet within 24 hours of the decision to give Wilders the award, it was withdrawn. Keene canceled the decision to honor Wilders because of an article in *Newsweek* in which David Horowitz and Robert Spencer criticized CPAC for its Norquist-mandated refusal to deal with the jihad or Islamic supremacism in any meaningful or effective way.[1] It would have been redemptive for CPAC to give Wilders the award after criticism, but CPAC wasn't looking for that kind of redemption. Jihad and sharia were the political third rail. I had to fight tooth and nail to get him there—why wouldn't they welcome him? Indeed, why wouldn't they welcome my colleagues and me?

Upon their refusal, I raised the funds and I brought him myself. Imagine having to battle with the head of the American Conservative Union to have the leader of one of The Netherlands' largest political parties, who continues to be persecuted for speaking the truth, address an audience at CPAC. Meanwhile, they featured a circus of clowns—freak-show gay bashers, Birchers and Paulian hordes.

We proceeded as an independent event, but that didn't stop CPAC attendees from coming. The evening with Geert Wilders exceeded even our wildest expectations. Having not done anything like this before did not stop me from seeing that the over 8,000 attendees (according to my cabbie) were clueless about what the critical, most damaging issues of the day are—freedom of speech, Islamic supremacism, the global jihad—none of which were being addressed at CPAC.

I was unaware when planning the Wilders event that there would be such a dearth of real issues discussed at CPAC—so the evening with Wilders was kismet. *Wilders would be at, not of, CPAC. And was he ever!*

I had no idea if I would have 50 or 200 patriots—this was *just a blog* event. *Just a blog* event indeed. I hardly expected the line (six feet deep) to grow and grow and snake out through the promenade—down and through the main lobby. If you are familiar with the Omni Shoreham Hotel, you know what I am talking about.

I understand well over 200 people or more were turned away at the door. I did not know. They stopped letting folks in after 500, which was the max the room could take. If I had known, we would have opened up another room.

I was working inside the ballroom setting up the space, making my makeshift posters using the poster board from an expired event, when, like the roar of an approaching train, the crowd started to cheer outside the doors. I knew what was happening—Wilders had gotten off the elevator. The ballroom was electrified.

We turned a corner on that Friday night, February 27, 2009. Something really big happened. Something historic. In the face of a complacent, lethargic conservative leadership we seized the moment. The individual took up the mantle for the freedoms we hold so dear. The astounding success of our event told us a good deal about how we could, and should, mobilize our forces in the future.

The place was packed with shiny, happy people. My menu was quintessential Geller: chocolate, strawberries, fresh fruit, sushi, a chocolate fountain (don't ask), and open bar.

It was pandemonium.

When I kicked off the evening's program, the place was packed. People were hanging from the rafters. The speakers gave rousing talks and we screened *Fitna*, Wilders's groundbreaking film about how jihadi terrorists work from the directives of the Koran. Afterwards I asked folks to please consider donating to the Geert Wilders legal defense fund; he has been brought up on spurious "hate speech" charges in The Netherlands several times for speaking the truth about Islam and jihad. Many asked the price of admission and I declined to charge—but if you had something extra in these harsh financial times, please give something.

The response was moving. Lots of folks gave something. One woman took the watch off her arm and said, "Take it, it was my mother's."

I overheard another say, "It felt like a revival meeting."

This event was unprecedented. I have lived... a lot, and this is one of the most memorable evenings of my life—a sentiment shared privately to me in many emails with readers who attended and expressed the same thing. The individual can make a difference.

But the conservative elites didn't see it or didn't want to see it. This issue would remain contentious, controversial and eventually verboten in powerful conservative circles—until President Trump's candidacy, that is.

The following year I returned to CPAC and launched my organization, the American Freedom Defense Initiative, with an inaugural event entitled "Jihad: The Political Third Rail—*What They Are Not Telling You*," featuring some of the premier American and international voices of resistance to global jihad and Islamic supremacism.

The conference was designed to educate Americans about the Muslim Brotherhood's infiltration at the highest levels of the US government, as well as its war on free speech and attempt to silence those who speak up against jihad and sharia encroachment in the West. Speakers emphasized the international nature of the jihad against the West and on how the Islamic war against free speech (and the media's self-imposed blackout on this issue, as in the Fort Hood jihad massacre, which had taken place the previous November) was part and parcel of the same jihad against the West that terrorists were pursuing by violent means.

The principal speakers were Steve Coughlin and Wafa Sultan. Coughlin was a former Islamic law specialist with the Pentagon who was making his first public appearance since he was fired after pressure from Islamic infiltrators; a Defense Department official named Hesham Islam objected to his work (without offering any refutation of it).[2] He presented startling information about Islamic infiltration in our government, including the Brotherhood ties of Hesham Islam and other high-placed US officials.

Wafa Sultan was the courageous ex-Muslim who stood up for human rights against sharia on Al-Jazeera in a debate with an Islamic cleric on a famous viral video. She was the author of a blistering indictment of Islam's denial of rights to women and non-Muslims, *A God Who Hates*.

A number of people questioned my choice of venue for this historical counter-jihad event. Many felt, and rightly so, that the American Conservative Union (ACU)—the political Right's largest and most influential grassroots umbrella organization and sponsor of the Conservative Political Action Conference (CPAC)—had abandoned conservative principles and morphed into some fleshy, ambiguous, compromised political machine doling out money and favors for cronies, when it was doing anything at all.

I agreed then and I agree even more now. Wholeheartedly. CPAC had been co-opted. Conservative kingmaker and power-broker Grover Norquist was for years a member of the Board of Directors of the American Conservative Union, which hosts CPAC. From the looks of CPAC's covered topics and omitted discussion of jihad year after year, it looked as if he exerted enormous influence over CPAC.

But we could not cede the field. The army of activists who came across the country, from near and far and far and wide, had no idea that the American Conservative Union (ACU) had been infiltrated and co-opted by Islamic supremacist forces, as Norquist's activities showed. We needed to reach the twelve thousand strong activists.

We had an enthusiastic standing-room-only crowd at our AFDI event. But as in 2009, the event was *at* CPAC, not *of* CPAC. This was likely because of the influence of Norquist.

How did CPAC come to this?

Grover Norquist's ties to Islamic supremacists and jihadists have been known for years. He and his "Palestinian" wife, Samah Alrayyes—who was director of communications for his Islamic Free Market Institute until they married in 2005—are very active in "Muslim outreach." Just six weeks after 9/11, *The New Republic* ran an exposé explaining how Norquist arranged for George W. Bush to meet with fifteen Islamic supremacists at the White House on September 26, 2001—to show how Muslims rejected terrorism. Wrote *TNR* author Franklin Foer:

> On the afternoon of September 26, George W. Bush gathered 15 prominent Muslim- and Arab-Americans at the White House. With cameras rolling, the president proclaimed that "the teachings of Islam are teachings of peace and good." It was a critically important moment, a statement to the world that America's Muslim leaders unambiguously reject the terror committed in Islam's name.
>
> Unfortunately, many of the leaders present hadn't unambiguously rejected it. To the president's left sat Dr. Yahya Basha, president of the American Muslim Council, an organization whose leaders have repeatedly called Hamas "freedom fighters." Also in attendance was Salam Al-Marayati, executive director of the Muslim Public Affairs Council, who on the afternoon of September 11 told a Los Angeles public radio audience that "we should put the State of Israel on the suspect list." And sitting right next to President Bush was Muzammil Siddiqi, president of the Islamic Society of North America, who last fall told a Washington crowd chanting pro-Hezbollah slogans that "America has to learn if you remain on the side of injustice, the wrath of God will come."[3]

It was Norquist who ushered these silver-tongued jihadists into the Oval Office of an incurious president after the worst attack ever on American soil. Instead of Hamas, Hizballah, and the Muslim Brotherhood, the president's advisors should have been Ibn Warraq, Bat Ye'or, and Wafa Sultan. Rather, at that September 26 meeting, Bush declared that "the teachings of Islam are teachings of peace and good." It was a critically important, historic incident. What should have been the most important teaching moment of the long war became a propaganda tool for Islam. A singular opportunity was squandered, and the resulting harm is incalculable.

Bush did this because he trusted Norquist, who vouched for these Muslim leaders. Yet, "The record suggests," wrote Foer, "that [Norquist] has spent quite a lot of time promoting people openly sympathetic to Islamist terrorists."[1] And this continued for years. In December 2003, David Horowitz wrote that Norquist "has formed alliances with prominent Islamic radicals who have ties to the Saudis and to Libya and to Palestinian Islamic Jihad, and who are now under indictment by US authorities. Equally troubling is that the arrests of these individuals and their exposure as agents of terrorism have not resulted in noticeable second thoughts on Grover's part or any meaningful effort to dissociate himself from his unsavory friends."[5]

Horowitz wrote this in an introduction to a detailed exposé by Frank Gaffney showing how Norquist had given Muslims with jihad terror links access to the highest levels of the US government.

Norquist was on the Islamic payroll before and after the carnage of September 11; Abdurahman Alamoudi, who is now serving twenty-three years in prison for financing jihad activity, wrote checks to Norquist's Islamic Institute.[6] Gaffney revealed Norquist's close ties to Alamoudi. And according to the Investigative Project on Terrorism:

> Grover Norquist hoped to... harness votes from the country's growing Muslim population by creating the Islamic Free Market Institute in 1998. He did so with significant financial help from Abdurahman Alamoudi, then one of America's most influential Muslim activists and head of the American Muslim Council. Today, Alamoudi is serving a 23-year prison sentence after admitting to illegal transactions with Libya and being part of a plot to assassinate the then-Crown Prince of Saudi Arabia. Alamoudi was also found to be a long time secret financial courier for Al Qaeda while at the same time being routinely invited to the Clinton White House for receptions and meetings.[7]

In 2000, Alamoudi said at a rally, "I have been labeled by the media in New York to be a supporter of Hamas. Anybody support Hamas here? ... Hear that,

Bill Clinton? We are all supporters of Hamas. I wished they added that I am also a supporter of Hizballah."[8]

Alamoudi was at that time head of the now-defunct "moderate" group known as American Muslim Council (AMC), and he was active in other Muslim groups in the US that showed sympathy to or support for jihadists. And Alamoudi, according to Gaffney, gave $50,000 to the lobbying group Janus-Merritt Strategies, which Norquist co-founded.

Alamoudi's money bought influence. Gaffney wrote in 2003: "It seems unlikely that even in Alamoudi's wildest dreams he could have imagined the extent of the access, influence and legitimacy the American Muslim Council and allied Islamist organizations would be able to secure in Republican circles, thanks to the investment they began in 1998 in a relationship with Norquist."[9]

Alamoudi also helped found Norquist's Islamic Institute with a $10,000 loan and a gift of another $10,000.[10] The founding director of the Islamic Institute was Khaled Saffuri, a "Palestinian" Muslim who had previously been active in Islamic groups in Bosnia, where Islamic jihadists from all over the world gathered "to establish," says Gaffney, "a beachhead on the continent of Europe." Gaffney adds that Saffuri "has acknowledged personally supporting the families of suicide bombers—even though, in public settings, he strenuously denies having done so." Saffuri also denounced Bush's shutdown of the Holy Land Foundation, which was funneling charitable contributions to Hamas.

Norquist also carried water for Islamic supremacist attempts to weaken anti-terror efforts. Gaffney revealed:

> Norquist was also a prime-mover behind efforts to secure one of the Islamists' top pre-9/11 agenda items: the abolition of a section of the 1996 Anti-Terrorism and Effective Death Penalty Act that permits authorities to use what critics call 'secret evidence.' ... Norquist was an honoree at an event held by Sami Al-Arian's National Coalition to Protect Political Freedom in July 2001, two months before 9/11. The award was for being a 'champion of the abolishment movement against secret evidence.'[11]

Al-Arian in 2006 pleaded guilty to "conspiracy to make or receive contributions of funds to or for the benefit of Palestinian Islamic Jihad."[12] The group that calls itself Palestinian Islamic Jihad, a Sunni jihad group like Hamas, is actually even worse than Hamas: it celebrates the killing of Israeli civilians and calls repeatedly for the destruction of Israel.

Scott Johnson of the *Powerline* blog noted shortly after Gaffney's article appeared that Norquist's response to this exhaustively documented exposé was "personal and evasive. He attacks Gaffney as racist and bigoted; not a trace of evidence in the public record supports these charges. I heard Norquist respond to Gaffney in this manner at the Conservative Political Action Conference in Washington this past January [2003]. He did not deign to respond to Gaffney's remarks in substance."[13]

Norquist also introduced Nihad Awad, co-founder and executive director of the Council on American-Islamic Relations, to President Bush. CAIR is one of the foremost Islamic supremacist hate sponsors in the US The Investigative Project on Terrorism (IPT) wrote that, "CAIR, which touts itself as America's premier Muslim civil rights organization, was named as an unindicted co-conspirator in the Holy Land Terror trial." IPT noted that CAIR co-founders Nihad Awad and Omar Ahmad attended "a 1993 Philadelphia meeting where the HAMAS members and supporters discussed a strategy to kill the Oslo Peace Accords, which threatened to marginalize HAMAS. The group also discussed ways to improve HAMAS fundraising in America."[14]

The IPT also revealed that according to the testimony of an FBI agent, "CAIR was listed as a member of the Muslim Brotherhood's Palestine Committee." The Palestine Committee is dedicated to jihad for the destruction of Israel. IPT reveals that a 1992 memo seized from a jihadi's home explains that "Palestine is the one for which Muslim Brotherhood prepared armies—made up from the children of Islam in the Arab and Islamic nations to liberate its land from the abomination and the defilement of the children of the Jews and they watered its pure soil with their honorable blood which sprouted into a jihad that is continuing until the Day of Resurrection and provided a zeal without relenting making the slogan of its children 'it is a Jihad for victory or martyrdom.'"[15] Omar Ahmad and Nihad Awad were also listed as members of the Palestine Committee.

Were these Norquist's bedfellows? Abusing his power and access, he introduced Islamic supremacists who advocate the stealthy overthrow of the government to those who have sworn an oath to protect and defend the Constitution and advocated for their cause. The enemy's strategy for winning is to subvert our senior leaders. Norquist made that possible. Bush was incurious, and he may not believe that he was subverted. In fact, he was.

Norquist continued his activities on behalf of the Islamic supremacists. In 2008, journalist Paul Sperry revealed Norquist's sponsorship of Muslim candidates with shadowy ties to terrorists and wrote that Norquist had a "wicked project to dress Islamists up as patriotic Republicans so they can infiltrate the government."[16] Norquist sponsored Kamal Nawash's unsuccessful bid to become Republican Party leader in Virginia; Nawash was Abdurahman Alamoudi's attorney. Norquist also aided previous failed political runs by Nawash—including Nawash's 2003 Virginia state Senate bid, to which Saffuri gave money.

So it is no surprise that CPAC, year after year, had nothing to address the war we were and continue to be engaged in. This was due not only to the influence of Norquist, but to that of Suhail Khan, another CPAC board member. According to Discover the Networks, an online resource for tracking the agenda of the left, Khan "has repeatedly been a featured speaker at MSA, ISNA and CAIR events"—that is, the Muslim Students Association, Islamic Society of North America, and Council on American-Islamic Relations, three groups linked to the Muslim Brotherhood, the international Islamic organization dedicated to establishing the rule of Islamic law and the subjugation of infidels worldwide.[17]

Norquist almost singlehandedly ushered Islamic supremacist leaders into America's highest levels of government—subversives, the Islamic fifth column. He gave them unparalleled access. Why didn't Gaffney's revelations, and those that preceded and followed his exposé, end Norquist's influence among conservatives? Why does he still have so much power, even to this day?

Norquist had great influence over the toothless, amorphous "Mount Vernon statement" issued at the time of CPAC 2010. This statement said nothing about national security or the war against the global jihad. It was a tactic to rein in the independent and truly grassroots Tea Party movement with a pat on the head, because the establishment right is desperate to control it—and no one is more desperate to do so than Grover Hiss.

Norquist should have been a pariah, not a kingmaker. If we can't get obvious enemies removed from conservative positions of leadership, we won't get elected the kind of men—honorable men—that we need to turn the tide.

That was exactly why I held the 2010 event at CPAC and returned for several years afterward, and did not criticize the Islamic supremacists and infiltrators who seemed to have enormous influence over the CPAC show. In 2010, it was too important that the presentation be made in order to educate everyone. The story of a cancellation might have made good blog fodder, but it would have served no other purpose.

The public wasn't going to find out the truth about the jihad threat at any other event at CPAC. In fact, they were fed misinformation. Take, for example, this 2010 panel: "You've Been Lied To: Why Real Conservatives are Against the War on Terror." At this event, Jacob Hornberger of the Future of Freedom Foundation (FFF) said that there were four reasons why real conservatives should be against the war on terror: because it was too costly, because it made us less safe (arguing that Americans were less secure because our troops killed children and mothers and people who were simply defending their country against invaders), because it violated Constitutional principles, and lastly because it was a threat to liberty.

Nothing was said about the Islamic doctrine that showed that jihadists would be waging war against the US even if we did end all actions in Afghanistan and Iraq. The panel agreed with then-President Obama, that Muslims were angry with us because of our actions, and would stop being angry with us if we changed our foreign policy.

This view was naïve and reflected ignorance of Islamic doctrine. There was, and remains, nothing conservative about soft-pedaling jihad. This was CPAC? Or was it the Islamic repackaging of the conservative movement?

Every year CPAC got progressively worse.

In 2011, our AFDI event at CPAC focused on the Ground Zero mosque debate. And unlike the left, we really did want to have a debate: we invited mosque leaders Sharif El-Gamal, Daisy Khan and Imam Rauf to join us at CPAC for "inter-faith dialogue."

All of them ignored the invitation, of course. Islamic supremacists and their leftist lapdogs aren't interested in debate. They only want to shut down their opposition and not allow their opponents any hearing at all. We went ahead at CPAC 2011 without them, and we told the truth about the Ground Zero mosque.

It was the most difficult and heart-wrenching event I have put together in all my years in this fight. We featured speakers who had lost family members on 9/11: Nelly Braginskaya, the mother of 38-year-old Alex; Joyce Boland and Vince Boland, who lost their son Vincent; Eileen Walsh, who lost her firefighter son Michael E. Brennan; Dr. Rosaleen Tallon, who lost her firefighter brother Sean (USMC) and is Family Liaison for Advocates for 9/11 Fallen Heroes; and Sally Regenhard, who lost her firefighter son, Christian. They all took the train in from New York to Washington in order to testify and be heard. Their stories and their opposition to the mosque had been embargoed by the media, just as images from the bloody, black day have been embargoed by that same enemedia.

What they said was devastating. Their accounts of that day and of the ensuing eight years were chilling. But for the enemedia, predictably, the story was not them nor the hard truths they told. The notorious left wing blogs' heads exploded over my remarks on the corruption of CPAC leadership. Justin Elliot over at *The War Room* at *Salon* turned on his camera only after my Ground Zero mosque event. In his article, Elliot wrote, "At Geller's insistence, one of the 9/11 family members who she brought to the event stood by her during the interview." Elliott, in accordance with left wing "journalism" standards, was being patently dishonest. I was just emerging from an emotionally draining two hours with many 9/11 family members, and Rosaleen Tallon was with me. When Elliot wanted to do his guerrilla interview, I agreed, and said he ought to interview Rosaleen about why she came to CPAC. He haughtily refused.

Contemptible.

In his article, "Pamela Geller Versus CPAC," Elliott identified me as "the notorious blogger" and focused on my exposure of Norquist: "There have been tensions between Geller and the leadership of CPAC, particularly American Conservative Union board member Grover Norquist, the anti-tax activist. Norquist has been a target of Geller and her cohort for years because of his friendly ties to Muslim leaders. In my interview with Geller... she accuses Norquist of actually being a Muslim Brotherhood stooge."[18]

But in his sneering account Elliot did include some of the searing words of the 9/11 family members: "Each family member told their Sept. 11 story and then denounced the plans to build the Islamic center near ground zero. One woman said, 'This is like spitting on the grave of my son.' Another: 'If we have to stand there and protect that building physically—with Pam Geller first—we will.'"[19]

Politico quoted Norquist's cohort Suhail Khan saying that my colleagues and I were "not part of the conservative movement. Everywhere they turn, the conservative movement is turning their back on them."[20]

Khan and his allies were working hard to make that a reality.

Nevertheless, we were back at CPAC the next year in 2012 with an event entitled "Islamic Law in America." I decided on that topic because, at that time, the Obama Justice Department was not just tolerating but actively aiding the assertion of Islamic law in the US and the primacy of sharia over US law. Our explosive conference gave the details of that effort and showed Americans what we do to preserve our Constitutional freedoms.

Speakers included J. Christian Adams, the election lawyer and former Department of Justice official who blew the lid off the Obama DOJ's racial bias and corruption. Adams resigned from the Justice Department over the Obama administration's refusal to pursue charges of voter intimidation against the New Black Panther Party.[21] Other speakers included Robert Muise, the nation's leading legal authority on laws banning the use of Islamic law in American courts, and Ilario Pantano, a war hero and Congressional candidate in North Carolina.

The *Critical Post* reported that my colleagues and I continued to "decry the attempts of CAIR's stealth jihad upon America by showing up at this year's CPAC 2012 conference. Relentless in their pursuit for awareness and pursuit for concerned Americans, the work is nonetheless a thankless effort because, for the most part, except for a minority it falls on deaf ears." Their report continued:

> Our publication has been steadily standing firm behind the maligned Geller. We have been waging an email campaign to synagogues to wake up and come to her aid, with no success. Hundreds of emails have been sent thus far all over the nation, and not one Jewish organization has stepped up to the plate to ask her to speak.
>
> Apparently the liberal Jewish community is struck by the same antipathy Jews felt in early Nazi Germany. The phrase "It can't happen here," comes to mind.
>
> Here's the truth, it can happen here. Libertarians are out there calling the Jewish lobby AIPAC, Zionist thugs and blatantly blaming FED activity on the Jewish people as a whole. This is unacceptable. It's also grossly false.[22]

It was true. The Jewish diaspora was once again failing miserably. If one comforted oneself that the failure of the American Jews during the Holocaust was an aberration, what was happening in 2012, and is still happening today, is proof of just the opposite. This is the same "Stephen Wise" Jewish mentality that sold us out and delivered us into the hands of the Third Reich during World War II. It was the appeasing Wise who prevailed among the American Jewish community, not the brave, forthright and true Peter Bergson, who urged action for the rescue of European Jewry during the Holocaust.

By this time, David Horowitz, who had helped AFDI get rooms for earlier CPAC conferences, was no longer a sponsor of CPAC: the Norquist/Khan cabal was deeply problematic to many others besides me. So we partnered with the Tea Party. Yet despite our being under the official umbrella of the Tea Party, CPAC put that event in a tiny, windowless, sweltering room—which was packed to the rafters with people, as CPAC knew it would be, given the urgency of the subject and the fact it wasn't being discussed in any official CPAC event. It was openly vengeful, and yet another indication of how petty the ACU leadership is.

One bright spot: at that conference, I received the Anti-Jihad Blogger of the Year award from *TeaParty.net*.[23] This was lovely, considering how CPAC had gone out of its way to ignore my work and the fruits of those labors.

The following year, I wanted to hold an event entitled, "The War on Free Speech." I had just won historic free-speech legal battles in Washington, D.C. and New York over our pro-freedom bus ads and the ongoing fight to run our counter-jihad ad campaign. (More on those battles later.) So what could have been more timely than a panel on the importance of the freedom of speech and how it was imperiled?

I applied to CPAC and was met with their signature wall of silence. I tried to partner with the Tea Party (as I had done in 2012), but no dice.

CPAC continued to get progressively worse. Silly, even. In 2013, the leadership blamed its past controversies with me for forbidding me to hold an event. The head of CPAC at the time, Al Cardenas, told the *Washington Post*: "This year we decided not to invite Pamela Geller for comments she made at CPAC critical of our officers. In each of these cases, their ad hominem attacks denigrate the debate and distract from the real point of CPAC."[24]

As is clear from the evidence I set out above, what I exposed about Norquist was not "ad hominem." But he wielded enormous power over CPAC. I learned in 2013 that the Tea Party had come under enormous pressure the previous year when they helped me hold our event. A confidential source told me that the pressure upon them to cancel was ongoing. Suhail Khan also bragged that he had successfully prevented my colleagues and me from being invited to speak. He went so far as to warn people not to attend our events or read our books. And so it was no surprise when in 2013 I wasn't allowed space to hold an independent event.

Also, at that time my column was carried at *Newsmax* every week—until I dared to write about Norquist's unsavory ties to Islamic supremacists. As soon as I published my *Newsmax* column concerning Norquist's pernicious influence at CPAC, my *Newsmax* column was taken down, and my name and picture were removed from the *Newsmax* page. It had been two slots away from Grover's. My weekly column never appeared at *Newsmax* again. It was axed.

I might add that every AFDI event at CPAC had been *standing room only*. We turned people away every year.

How did CPAC come to this?

Commentator Jennifer Rubin, who is not often right, was right about CPAC 2013 when she said: "If you weren't convinced before that CPAC—the organization, not the pols and conservative activists trying to speak to others and solve the movement's problems—is a symbol of what must change on the right, this might do it. I have to cover it, but I can't imagine why any well-meaning conservative would want to give the event credence by attending."[25]

And so it was particularly delicious that I was invited to speak at CPAC after all, at the invitation of the Breitbart organization. The Breitbart event, "The Uninvited," was a special two-hour session of hot button issues, including Global Jihad, the ongoing global persecution of Christians, and the gutting of the American military.

The theme of my remarks was "The War on Free Speech." Since the story broke of Grover Norquist's and Suhail Khan's successful Geller ban, good and decent freedom-loving folks were up in arms. Because it was not about me. It was about the subject matter—that discussion of sharia and jihad had been effectively banned at the largest conservative gathering in the country.

My wrestling and wrangling with CPAC, cajoling CPAC organizers to allow me the same privilege they routinely extend to other conservative groups—the right to host events at the largest gathering of conservatives in the country—went on year after year. Every year, I faced roadblocks, delays, and lame excuses—all stemming from the crippling cowardice of the CPAC leadership and its adamant refusal to grapple honestly with the jihad threat. Year after year, even as the jihad threat to the whole world became ever harder to deny, it didn't get better—it got worse.

During CPAC 2013, I met with Al Cardenas, who was then the ACU's chairman. He admitted to me that I had been banned by the ACU board and apologized for this, assuring me that I would be on the official CPAC roster of speakers the following year. On June 1, 2014, however, Cardenas resigned—so he almost certainly knew when he made that promise that it was an empty one. Matt Schlapp took over, and when I applied in January 2015 to secure a space, I was told that I had asked too late. "If only I had asked earlier," they said.

So for CPAC 2016, I inquired in October 2015. I contacted Schlapp and informed him that AFDI wanted to be a full-fledged sponsor of CPAC, so that I could host an event, "How Liberal Ideology Is Crippling National Security Capability." Being a CPAC sponsor is not some honor that CPAC organizers confer; any conservative group can buy sponsor status.

Thinking our money was as good as anyone else's, we invited Geert Wilders, who had just won the "Politician of the Year" award in a poll of voters in The Netherlands.[26] We also invited Swiss freedom fighter Oskar Freysinger; Israeli political analyst Caroline Glick; DHS whistleblower Philip Haney; and British politician Paul Weston of the LibertyGB party, who had been arrested for publicly quoting Winston Churchill's words about Islam. Churchill wrote this in his book *The River War*:

> How dreadful are the curses which Muhammadanism lays on its votaries! Besides the fanatical frenzy, which is as dangerous in a man as hydrophobia in a dog, there is this fearful fatalistic apathy. The effects are apparent in many countries: improvident habits, slovenly systems of agriculture, sluggish methods of commerce, and insecurity of property exist wherever the followers of the Prophet rule or live.
>
> A degraded sensualism deprives this life of its grace and refinement, the next of its dignity and sanctity. The fact that in Muhammadan law every woman must belong to some man as his

absolute property, either as a child, a wife, or a concubine, must delay the final extinction of slavery until the faith of Islam has ceased to be a great power among men.

Individual Muslims may show splendid qualities, but the influence of the religion paralyses the social development of those who follow it. No stronger retrograde force exists in the world. Far from being moribund, Muhammadanism is a militant and proselytizing faith. It has already spread throughout Central Africa, raising fearless warriors at every step; and were it not that Christianity is sheltered in the strong arms of science, the science against which it had vainly struggled, the civilization of modern Europe might fall, as fell the civilization of ancient Rome.[27]

Today, Churchill, like Weston, would be excoriated as a racist, Islamophobic, anti-Muslim bigot.

I followed up with Schlapp, ACU Executive Director Dan Schneider, and the ACU's Director of Events & Conferences, Carin Walters, regularly. I was put off, put down, jerked around, and made to go jump through hoops—which I did. I followed up for months while they "studied the issue."

They were concerned about security because of the death threats I have received since my free speech conference in Garland, Texas in May 2015 had been attacked by jihadis. I assured them that my entire security apparatus, a seasoned team of the top professionals in their field, would be in place (at our expense, not CPAC's), and that several of my speakers who were European politicians would also be coming with their own secret service protection.

This should have been adequate. I hardly would have been the first person to be at CPAC after receiving death threats. And even after receiving death threats in the past, I had been at CPAC many times. There was a time I was asked to speak, or at least introduce, notables at CPAC. At CPAC 2008, I introduced Mark Steyn. I also once introduced David Horowitz. But once I started to criticize CPAC, the ACU's David Keene, along with members of the ACU board such as Norquist and Khan, those invitations quickly stopped coming.

During the many long-winded discussions we had after that about security, I had to promise that if I came to CPAC, there would be "no cartoons." So I had to surrender on the point where free speech is most challenged in order to speak out there for free speech.

They also told me I could not publicize my event beforehand. My past events at CPAC were always SRO, but if I couldn't publicize it, how would people know to come? Nevertheless, I agreed to every request.

They told me for months that they were concerned about security despite the extensive arrangements I planned to have in place. They delayed until there was almost not enough time for me to put together the event. Then Dan Schneider, Executive Director of the American Conservative Union, finally told me that they were not allowing AFDI to be a sponsor—not because of security concerns, but because I have criticized them in the past for not paying adequate attention to the jihad threat.

When Schneider told me that I was being denied because of the "negative press coverage" I had previously given them, after months of saying that they were hesitating because of something else, I responded that I had reported on what happened. I reported what was true and accurate. Back on our first phone call, Schneider had even admitted that I had been right about CPAC, that in previous years the conference had gone to great lengths to avoid the subject of jihad and sharia. And yet now that was why they denied me an opportunity to host an event. It was clear: Schneider's new and improved CPAC was the same as the old, broken CPAC.

The ACU was so small and thin-skinned over the negative publicity that I gave them in the past for ignoring the jihad that they were doing it again, and barring what would have been a significant discussion of the most important issue of our time. For that is what I did for years, and would have done again this year: I have done what CPAC refuses to do and given CPAC attendees opportunities to become knowledgeable about covering the issues that ought to have been center stage, prime time at CPAC.

Apparently it is official CPAC policy, at this point, to avoid and ignore the greatest national security threat to our country—or at best to feature speakers whose analysis is hamstrung by political correctness and ignorance of the subject.

The Middle East is on fire. ISIS has vowed to commit a jihad attack larger than 9/11 and called on Muslims to murder American civilians. The country is deeply concerned about the jihad issue, and yet it is never a significant presence on the CPAC schedule, and they do not allow me space because I criticized their weakness and flabbiness on this very issue in the past.

The work my organization and I do is critical and singular. It addresses the most serious issue of our time. CPAC should have been inviting us, not banning us.

CPAC doesn't deserve the name "Conservative." It should be called the "Cowards Political Action Conference."

His Own Private Islam

While I was unacceptable by CPAC standards, so-called moderate Muslim Zuhdi Jasser was—he was eventually even put on the CPAC Board, in order to camouflage their adamant refusal to cover the jihad threat adequately.

But Jasser and I had had our own controversies.

In January 2011, Congressman Peter King (R-NY) told *Politico* that in the hearings he was planning to hold on radicalization among American Muslims, he was "not planning to call as witnesses," people such the Investigative Project on Terrorism's Steve Emerson to whom Muslims objected.[28]

Based on this, it appeared that the hearings would be a charade. Representative King seemed a wee bit over his head. I was filled with dread and sorrow at another lost opportunity. Didn't King know he was going to be smeared and defamed for these hearings no matter what? (And he was.) So why not achieve something? Why not have the courage of your convictions?

King called Zuhdi Jasser. To what end? Jasser's Islam does not exist. He does not have a theological leg to stand on within Islam. Whatever he is practicing, it's not Islam, and he speaks for no one but himself. Also, Jasser has done some strange things: in May 2009, he made a last-minute effort to quash Geert Wilders' appearance on Capitol Hill under the aegis of Arizona Senator Jon Kyl, calling Kyl's office the morning Wilders was supposed to appear and stating that while Jasser had been in the Netherlands, Wilders refused to meet with Jasser because Wilders "doesn't meet with Muslims." That never happened, according to Wilders.[29]

When I interviewed Jasser for *Atlas Shrugs* back in 2007, he referred to Israel as occupied territory in the last five minutes of the interview.[30] He blew his cover. Further, Jasser claimed in that interview that Islamic anti-Semitism did not exist. He may be well-intentioned, but his approach and theology are just plain un-Islamic. Jasser has no following among Muslims and doesn't represent any Islamic tradition. So what's the point?

King probably thought that Jasser was the voice of reason in our cause of educating Americans about the threat of radical Islam. But in this, Jasser fails miserably. First off, there is no "reason" in Islam. There is only Islam. You cannot question, reason, or go off the reservation in any way. Hence, Jasser cannot educate about the threat, because he obfuscated the truth and has invented the Islam he follows.

What a waste.

After I wrote an article about this in the *American Thinker* in January 2011, Jasser responded the following month with an extraordinarily lengthy article in the same publication.[31] Methinks Jasser did protest too much. The objective was bigger than just responding to me. Rather, it was an attempt to validate and advance his own preposterous narrative.

Jassers article was entitled, "American Islamists Find Common Cause with Pamela Geller." Equating me with Islamic supremacists was like saying that General Patton found common cause with the Nazi General Erwin Rommel, the Desert Fox, because Patton criticized the British Field Marshal Bernard Montgomery. My criticism of King's capitulation and CAIR's attempt to impose sharia in America by silencing and punishing those exposing the hidden war had nothing in common with each other.

So here Jasser was intellectually dishonest and deliberately misleading. He undoubtedly knew this, and stood behind an article headlined with this false premise. He was being at the very least disingenuous, and was attempting to marginalize me in the most debased and dishonest fashion (as did CAIR). Placing me on the same moral playing field as those who are working toward "eliminating and destroying Western civilization from within" and annihilating the Jews was very stealthy jihad. It was propaganda of a kind I was by then very familiar with. Not good, Mr. Jasser.

Expanding on this outrageous claim, Jasser said that my comments in my "echo chamber" showed I was "against any solutions from within the 'House of Islam.' This only aids and abets all Islamists. But, then again, that doesn't matter if the target includes all Muslims and their only viable solution is conversion of one-fifth of the world's population."[32]

Echo chamber? I was by then reaching just under two million people a month on my blog. That and book sales, regular TV and radio appearances, speaking engagements, conferences, and additional 50,000 "friends" on my various Facebook pages, Twitter and SIOA group, etc., made for quite a cacophonous echo chamber. I submit that it was Jasser's chamber that was empty. Where are all the Jassers?

Jasser mentions "many Muslim reformers." Where are they? Where are the Muslims who take to the streets when another girl is killed for honor, or another apostate is murdered under sharia? Where were all the Muslims taking to the streets after Mumbai, London, Madrid, Beslan, Bali, Times Square, Fort Hood? But they take to the streets by the hundreds of thousands, light embassies on fire, and slaughter innocents when a cartoon offends them.

Even the title of Jasser's article, "American Islamists Find Common Cause with Pamela Geller," plays into this false narrative. Islamist? What is that? What is a Christianist? A Judaist? A Hinduist?

Simply his use of the word "Islamist" here predetermines the futility of Jasser's enterprise. It's not Islamism, it's Islam.

But the fact that Islam teaches violence and supremacism doesn't mean that I am against all Muslims, as Jasser implied. This was patently untrue. Through my work with "Refuge from Islam," we helped Muslims here in America who wanted to leave Islam and were under threat from their families and communities. Escaping their mosque, their "faith community," and their families to safe houses was dangerous. People did not begin to know the difficulty, although Amina and Sarah Said, the girls who, in a notorious case, were murdered by their father in Texas on January 1, 2008 for dating non-Muslim boys, gave many Americans a graphic window into the lives of these girls.

The safety network was covertly established, and required utmost secrecy and security. Did Jasser do this kind of work? Did he even acknowledge it? I was raked over the coals for this work—for my campaign to save them. Did Dr. Jasser come to my defense? He was strangely silent. He lived near the spot where a Muslim woman, Noor Almaleki, was murdered by her father for honor. He should have talked more about that, and about why women suffer so under Islam. I am glad his wife is safe, but the world was bigger than Jasser's home.

Jasser said that neither I nor any other non-Muslim should be allowed to speak about this question. He apparently thought that only Muslims should be permitted to speak about what Islam may or may not be, despite the fact that anyone can read the Koran and Hadith, and the statements of Islamic jihadists and supremacists who read and quote them. Jasser says that non-Muslims have to shut up and have no right to read such documents and think about them. "Frankly," Jasser wrote, "it takes a lot of *chutzpah* for any non-Muslim, let alone one who has never met me, to insist that I am not practicing Islam."

Nevertheless, Jasser acknowledged in that article, "American Islamists Find Common Cause with Pamela Geller," that he did see a "valid debate as to the prevalence and intellectual underpinnings of the Islam I and my family practice, and whether it constitutes a minority or majority of Muslims. It is an important national conversation whether most Muslims can be counted upon to lead any type of genuine, lasting reform toward modernity."

It was a valid debate, only non-Muslims couldn't participate. Got it?

Despite Jasser's wishes, I continued to participate. What I wrote was true: *Jasser's Islam really does not exist.* When I interviewed him, he spoke about moderate Muslims, saying that they should be judged by "how devout they are, how they treat other people, the Golden Rule, how honest, what their integrity is, what their character is." That sounds good, but in reality, Islam has no Golden Rule. In the Koran, Muslims are told to be "merciful to one another but harsh to unbelievers" (48:29). That's a far cry from "do unto others as you would have them do unto you."

In that same interview, Jasser claimed that the Koran has "passages where God tells Muhammad if I wanted everyone to be Muslim or believe in God I could have made them but I did not." Jasser makes this sound like an expression of tolerance and pluralism by Allah. Actually it is something quite different. Here's the full verse: "And if We had so willed, We could have given every soul its guidance, but the word from me concerning evildoers took effect: that I will fill hell with the jinn and mankind together" (Koran 32:13). So actually, Allah is saying that He decided not to guide some people, but instead to send them to Hell, apparently for no reason at all.

Jasser also claimed in that interview that "there are passages that say 'your affairs are up to you.' That's the only passage actually in the entire Koran that refers to government. There is absolutely no passage that talks about how citizens should form their government. So to me it is completely consistent that one modern interpretation is that you can separate religion and government."

But the Koran also says this: "If any do fail to judge by (the light of) what Allah hath revealed, they are (no better than) unbelievers" (5:44). And unbelievers can be killed (2:191, 4:89, 9:5). So the society the Koran envisions is a coercive one in which people who do not "judge by what Allah has revealed" may be killed—this is hardly a pluralistic vision.

Jasser tried to blame the anti-Semitic passages in the Koran on faulty English translations: "I am not sure I agree with that translation. You have to remember that a lot of the translations that are currently being used are coming out of Wahabist interpreters." Would he have us believe that there is some possible translation of the Koran that doesn't say that the Jews are the Muslims' worst enemies (5:82) and are under Allah's curse (9:30)?

In my interview with him Jasser even claimed, "The passage that is being interpreted by most translation as being permission to beat your wife actually does not mean that in Arabic. Those that are experts in classical Arabic will tell you that that means... it actually means whenever you have an argument step away, take a timeout, etc. It doesn't mean to beat them."

Nonsense. This is a false statement. The overwhelming majority of English translations translate this passage as "beat them," or "strike them," or something similar. The only ones that don't are those that have been published in the last few years with the clear intention of whitewashing this passage.

Of the Islamic law that Muslim men can marry non-Muslim women, but Muslim women cannot marry non-Muslim men, Jasser said, "Most of the sharia interpretations are that Muslim women need to marry Muslim men because of protecting their rights and because of the way the faith is transmitted paternally rather than maternally." He made it sound so benign. In reality Muslim women can't marry non-Muslim men because if they did, the non-Muslim communities would grow instead of perpetually declining.

Jasser in the interview characterized Islam as "a completely personal faith between me and God. There is no institution for excommunication or communication." Yet, historically, Islam has never been this way. All sorts of authorities excommunicate Muslims they consider heretical (*takfir*). Islam has never taught that the Muslim is on his own as an individual before Allah—instead, he is part of the *umma*. He also says that Islam "accepts all of the same moral constructs" as Judaism and Christianity. But it doesn't: Polygamy, wife-beating, honor killing, clitorectomies, suicide bombing, on and on. None of this is justified by Judaism or Christianity. Only by Islam.

So does Zuhdi Jasser have his own private Islam? You be the judge.

Jasser also wrote: "Between the two of us, I certainly more than Geller have a far more credible perspective coming from a lifetime as a practicing Muslim from within diverse Muslim faith communities," but the record of those "Muslim faith communities" was clear. It needs pointing out that wherever Muslims live in non-Muslim countries, there is a level of agitation and conflict, the level of which is directly tied to the size of the Muslim population. That says a great deal about which brand of Islam—Jasser's or, say, Anwar al-Awlaki's—is more mainstream among Muslims worldwide. Aside from those Muslims in non-Muslim countries, the rest of the world's Muslim population is already living in one of 56 Muslim nations, so the only conflict there is between differing Muslim groups, i.e., Sunni vs. Shia.

Jasser said, "To dismiss me as having a 'private Islam' is absurd for anyone let alone an outsider." But could he point to "Muslim faith communities" that do not practice violent jihad or pursue the Islamic supremacist imperative to impose sharia? Muslims may refrain from waging jihad or pursuing the supremacy of sharia for a variety of reasons, but do these "moderates" also reject jihad and sharia in theory? Do they have a version of Islamic theology that rejects them, as does Dr. Jasser?

Jasser went on: "During the twenty-four month period between our interview and this libelous assault, she conducted many more radio programs, and wrote hundreds of blog articles—yet *never once* mentioned this allegation. To the contrary, she posted instance after instance of positive references to my efforts to fight radical Islamism—yet not a word about how I supposedly 'blew my cover' on anything."

Yes, because I do not hate all Muslims. Because I too wanted to believe. Those "positive references" are years old—prior to my continued reading of Ibn Warraq, Wafa Sultan, et al, and earlier in my study of Islam in the West and in the Muslim world. Who doesn't want to believe Jasser? Yes, I was more supportive when I was less informed on Islam. We all want to believe in Santy Claus. But avoiding reality is not an option. You can avoid reality, but you cannot avoid the consequences of avoiding reality.

Jasser claimed that my "target includes all Muslims" and that the "only viable solution" I offered was "conversion of one-fifth of the world's population."

Here again Jasser echoed the stealth jihadists, in adding some implied threat against 1.5 billion Muslims into the pot. Conversion? Was he saying that the Muslim world would not reject the violent teachings of the Koran and work to expunge it of its violent texts? I never suggested conversion of one-fifth of the world's population. But any ideology that calls for violence and oppression of those outside the fold must be defeated.

Jasser insisted he had been "one of the most outspoken American Muslims against the toxic and potent linkage of our Muslim faith community to the goals and propaganda of the 'Palestinian' lobby in the United States." But where was he ever outspoken against the virulent Jew-hatred in the Koran, which is the source of and motivation for everything the "Palestinian" lobby does? The hatred against the Jewish homeland is not a "Palestinian" invention ("Palestine" itself, incidentally, is a Latin word for the Jewish State). *No, it is rooted in Islamic teaching that encourages Jewish genocide.* If Jasser strongly supports Israel, he must fight to expose and expunge Islamic teachings of this hate. Instead, he obfuscates this key issue.

Jasser must know that in Islam he is a hypocrite, and under sharia that is punishable by death. He advances the idea of separation of mosque and state, but even he must know that in Islam, mosque is state.

So when Jasser wrote that he wanted Americans to "see the stark difference between Muslims who are part of the problem (promoters of Islamism) and Muslims who are part of the solution (anti-Islamists who promote reform and modernity)," forgive me, but who was he talking about other than himself?

I understand everyone wants moderate or secular Muslims to be the silent majority, and Jasser gives them a much-needed face. But in order for Islam to reform itself, the truth about Islam must be made known, and the genocidal, racist aspects of Islamic teaching must be rejected (like Nazism) and those who hold those teachings must be forced under the weight of international pressure to reform.

So the answer is no, Dr. Jasser, I am not aiding the "Islamists." But it is not at all certain that you aren't. Years went by and Jasser never modified his views. Instead, he clung to them all the more tenaciously.

Then in one fell swoop in March 2017, "moderate Muslim" Jasser dropped a MOAB on the most effective counter-jihadists in the West. The Grand Mufti of the Stealth Jihad devoted an entire episode of his show on The Blaze Network, *Reform This!,* to smear me and many of my colleagues as "alt-jihadists." He even said, "there are no greater jihadists than the alt-jihadists when it comes to living in the land of freedom. Because they seem to be wanting to kill us and knock us off at the knees."[33]

That's right: "No greater jihadists" than me and my colleagues.

"Alt" means Nazi. He knew exactly what he was doing.

Who even knew he had a show on The Blaze? No one. Why did The Blaze founder, Glenn Beck, give this vicious saboteur a platform? Jasser did this deliberately, knowing it would blow up—that spoke volumes about his character and his true motives.

But some people are endlessly eager to be fooled. Frank Gaffney immediately wrote to a group of us whom Jasser targeted, telling us to hold off in the interest of peacemaking! It was striking how quickly Gaffney jumped to Jasser's defense. (I've never seen him jump to my defense like that.)

What a step-and-fetch-it boy Gaffney was for Jasser. This epitomized how much people who recognize the jihad threat have been fooled into thinking they have to have moderate Muslims on board or their efforts will be criticized by the left as "Islamophobic." The left is going to say that anyway, no matter what they do.

As for me, I didn't start this war, and I wasn't going to let Jasser's lies sit out there unchallenged. It was Jasser who had thrown down the gauntlet (again)—the idea that he was defending himself against attacks, as journalist Patrick Poole claimed on Twitter, was nonsense.

I was right about Jasser all along. When I interviewed him in 2007, he was unable to answer my questions about how the "immutable" word of the Koran could be radically reinterpreted. He was completely dumbfounded about the simple fact that such "reformation" or "reinterpretation" is punishable by death. In other words, you can't have your private little Islam. Period.

And then when he referred to Israel as occupied territory in the last five minutes of the interview, he blew his cover. Further, in the interview Jasser claimed as well that Islamic anti-Semitism didn't exist.

In this new attack, Jasser's whole premise was false. We were "alt-jihadists" for pointing out how jihadists use Islamic teachings as their motivation and impetus? So those who told the truth about the Nazis were just like the Nazis, because they were reinforcing the Nazis' message? He admitted that Islamic government and the most respected Islamic institutions did not reflect his interpretation of Islam, but then he hit us for noticing the same thing. He wanted us not to believe reality and instead to embrace a fantasy that has failed catastrophically post-9/11.

Why did not one, but two mosques throw him out? Jasser said of me:

> She peddled lies that I was kicked out of my mosque and that when
> I confronted her on it in the piece she blamed Andrew Bostom.

And now she just last month retweeted again, saying that I was kicked out of my mosque twice now. When in fact I've talked about pieces in which the clerics at our imam called me up from the pulpit and I then responded publicly with editorials in our state newspaper, pushing back into the face of the cleric at our Scottsdale mosque the sermon that called me out because of my criticism of Hamas. Yes, I've taken them on. But I've never been kicked out of my mosque.

Lies? My source was an Arizona physician who knows Jasser personally. Jasser was able to sidestep this because he may have been affiliated with several mosques. If the information I received was inaccurate, he should have said so, but he didn't precisely do that, and my source is trustworthy. But, desperate to defame, Jasser made this about me lying.

Here is another truth that Jasser doesn't want aired: his organization is minuscule. Where is his invisible giant movement? And why has he not prevailed and gained a huge Muslim following in the wake of the unfathomable bloodshed caused by jihadis, if that bloodshed were so very un-Islamic? He has no significant following among Muslims, and is not going to get one. He is much more popular among non-Muslims who are just aching to be fooled.

Jasser and his ilk are not moderates. They are liars. There's a difference. Jasser proves that on his show when he cites former Bosnian president Alija Izetbegovic as an example of a Muslim reformer. In his 1969 *Islamic Declaration*, Izetbegovic wrote :

Muslim nations will never accept anything that is explicitly against Islam... He who rises against Islam will reap nothing but hate and resistance... The first and foremost of such conclusions is surely the one on the incompatibility of Islam and non-Islamic systems. There can be no peace or co-existence between the 'Islamic faith' and non-Islamic societies and political institutions... The Islamic movement should and must start taking over the power as soon as it is morally and numerically strong enough to not only overthrow the existing non-Islamic, but also to build up a new Islamic authority.

90

Izetbegovic a reformer? Just like Jasser is one. The day after I called Jasser "the Grand Mufti of the Stealth Jihad," more evidence for the accuracy of this title came along.[34] A convert to Islam named Courtney Lonergan was one of Jasser's close associates—she works for Jasser's American Islamic Forum for Democracy (AIFD). AIFD's website contains biographies of just two people: Jasser himself and Lonergan, who has the title of AIFD's "Community Outreach Coordinator."[35]

But she also knew the Garland, Texas jihadi Ibrahim Simpson. She knew all about him. The distinction between "moderates" and "extremists" is not as large as many non-Muslims imagine it to be.

The Garland jihadis Ibrahim (formerly Elton) Simpson and Nadir Soofi were members of the Islamic Community Center of Phoenix.[36] Not long after the Garland attack, the *Arizona Republic* quoted Courtney Lonergan saying that, "Simpson would never waver from the teachings he picked up in the mosque and elsewhere." Lonergan also said, "He was one of those guys who would sleep at the mosque. The fact that he felt personally insulted by somebody drawing a picture had to come from the ideological rhetoric coming out of the mosque."[37]

That *Arizona Republic* article also said that Lonergan "met Simpson at that mosque about 10 years ago." So Lonergan, a "moderate Muslim" who works for the "moderate" Jasser, knew the "extremist" Simpson for years, and apparently knew him well.

I have long argued against the false arguments of Jasser. But people cling to the idea of Jasser because the alternative is unthinkable. I understand better than most that everyone wants moderates or secular Muslims to be the silent majority, and Jasser gives them a much-needed face. *But in order for Islam to reform itself, the truth about Islam must be made known* to the civilized.

– Seven –
The Ad Wars

Leaving Islam?

In 2010, I was in Florida to attend a court hearing in the Rifqa Bary case. While waiting for a red light at an intersection, I saw in the next lane a bus bearing a huge ad calling people to Islam. It made me think: what about the people who want to leave Islam, like Rifqa, but have no help doing so and know their lives would be threatened if their apostasy were made known?

This gave me the idea for AFDI's first ad campaign. On April 13, 2010, our "Leaving Islam" ads rolled out on the streets of Miami in response to the misleading CAIR *dawah* (invitation to Islam) bus campaign that I had seen that day in Miami. Our ad read, *"Leaving Islam? Fatwa on your head? Family threatening you? Got questions? Get answers."* That's all it said. It offered a life-saver for those who were completely and utterly alone with no system of support or help.

This was the first time anyone had offered public help to those who were threatened under Islam's apostasy law. In the Land of the Free, government and law enforcement should have been on this. But they weren't. So we were. It was time for free citizens to stand for freedom—or lose it.

The ads ran without incident in Miami, New York City, and San Francisco. But in a notable assault on the freedom of speech, in the spring of 2010 Detroit's SMART public transportation system refused to run the ads.

Despite the total lack of resources for Muslims under threat for leaving Islam, and the large number of Muslims in the Detroit area, which meant the potential of more people wanting to leave Islam safely, the city of Detroit refused to run our campaign on the Dearborn and Detroit buses. Dearborn is over 40% Muslim, and authorities there have shown a disturbing eagerness to be sharia-compliant.

In June 2010, Acts 17 Apologetics, a Christian evangelistic group, was banned from passing out fliers at Dearborn's Arab Festival. They went to the festival anyway and ended up getting arrested simply for preaching Christianity, which is not illegal in the US, but is illegal under sharia. Eventually Acts 17 won an apology from Dearborn authorities, but it was clear where their loyalties lay.[1]

AFDI sued Detroit. Detroit SMART's guidelines for bus ads stated:

> As a governmental agency that receives state and federal funds, SMART is mandated to comply with federal and state laws. First Amendment free speech rights require that SMART not censor free speech and because of that, SMART is required to provide equal access to advertising on our vehicles.[2]

But they didn't. In our AFDI motion to compel SMART to run our ads, we explained, "the fact that society may find speech offensive is not a sufficient reason for suppressing it. Indeed, if it is the speaker's opinion that gives offense, that consequence is a reason for according it constitutional protection."[3]

I flew to Detroit to testify in the suit back in July 2010.[4] David Yerushalmi and Robert Muise represented me. I had with me hundreds of pictures of honor killing victims, the testimony of Rifqa Bary, and screenshots of fatwas calling for apostates to be killed, including one from Al-Azhar, the foremost institution in Sunni Islam.

The judge who ruled on this case, Judge Denise Page Hood, was hardly a Clarence Darrow acolyte, but she understood the law and ruled in favor of our free speech rights. She understood the First Amendment. She was clearly not sympathetic to us, which I could tell from her questions, her cross examinations, and the way she handled the courtroom. But she had to rule in our favor. She was not partisan, she was following the law, which may sound matter of fact and, "Well, yeah, of course," but this is not generally the case with partisan judges.

This was a huge win, not just for us, but for the First Amendment, and a defeat for all those who claim that I am a hater because I am willing to talk about what is wrong in Islam—including, as in this case, honor killings and fatwas for apostasy. But then these enemies of freedom *appealed*. SMART was refusing to run outreach ads that might help Muslims living in dangerous households. You might have thought that the Muslim Brotherhood was running SMART Detroit. It was astounding. And considering Detroit's bankruptcy, it was astonishing sharia adherence appeared to be more important to Detroit officials than the freedom of speech and fiscal responsibility.

SMART claimed that this ad offering help to people in fear for their lives was "political," and hence outside their guidelines. The Sixth Circuit heard their appeal and agreed that our religious-based ads were political. It was ridiculous to say that saving lives was a political act, but that was what they claimed.

The case went on. In May 2013, I spent a grueling six hours in the kindergarten sandbox with the neighborhood bully: SMART's attorney, Christian E. Hildebrandt. You would have thought this was a criminal case and I was the defendant. In reality, I was the plaintiff, being deposed in what was by then a three-year legal battle for free speech against SMART transit over their refusal of my ads offering help and in some cases a lifeline to survival for Muslim girls (and any Muslims) living in dangerous and violent households: *Geller vs. Detroit.*

Hildebrandt was supposed to question me about the case. Actually, in the course of my deposition, he attacked me and my brilliant counsel, Robert Muise, with a profanity-laced tirade at the top of his voice. It was a vicious cross-examination. It was as if I was on trial for murder. Hildebrandt was rabid. He actually spewed "sh*t" all over the transcript in his aggravation at Muise's adherence to American law in American courts. I never knew "sh*t" was a legal term.

The case continued. In August 2013, we filed a motion for summary judgment in the United States District Court for the Eastern District of Michigan, asking the court to rule that the refusal of our ads violated the US Constitution. And the legal battles dragged on and on.

Bottom line, everyone has the same right to a free life. And for a government agency to use taxpayer dollars to do the bidding of Islamic supremacists was treasonous. We are still fighting Detroit over this. It's not over.

Civilized Men vs. MTA Savages

In September 2011, AFDI filed suit against the New York City Metropolitan Transit Authority's restriction of free speech and sanctioning of Jew-hatred in the city's subways.

It all began when I was waiting on a platform for the New York subway when I saw that Jew-haters were running ads suggesting that Israel's self-defense was the obstacle to "peace." I knew I had to counter these lies with the truth, and on the same platform where the anti-Israel lies ran. We designed ads calling terrorism against innocent civilians "savage." They were banned by the MTA, deemed "demeaning" and "insulting" to savages. Our ad simply quoted Ayn Rand followed by a message of solidarity with Jews. "In any war between the civilized man and the savage, support the civilized man. Support Israel. Defeat jihad, " it read.

In January 2012, in response to our discovery motion, we received highly revealing documents showing how the MTA acted inconsistently and out of political bias in rejecting our ads. What was so unnerving about the MTA emails we received was the apparent casual acceptance among MTA staffers of anti-Semitism, their unhesitating approval of the anti-Israel ads, and their knee-jerk negative reaction to my simple and true ad.

And on a not unrelated note, the emails between the mainstream press and the MTA were very cozy. Jennifer Fermino of the *New York Post* reassured the MTA in a September 20, 2011 email that a story about our pro-Israel ads had been set to be on the front page, but was moved off the front page and reduced: "Now it's only [a] 7 inch story, very short."[4] I wondered, who killed it and why?

Why was my use of the word "savage" inaccurate? The relentless 60-year campaign of terror against the Jewish people is savage. The torture of Israeli soldier Gilad Shalit, taken hostage by Hamas in 2006 and detained for five years, was savage. The 2011 bloody hacking to death of five members of the Fogel family, in their beds, by two "Palestinians" was savage. The 1972 Munich Olympic massacre of 11 Israeli team members and one German officer by "Palestinians" was savage. The unspeakable torture and eventual murder of Israeli soldier Ehud Goldwasser in 2006, which sparked the Lebanon war, was savage. The tens of thousands of rockets fired from Gaza into southern Israel (into schools, homes, etc.) were savage. The vicious Jew-hatred behind this genocide was savage. The endless demonization of the Jewish people in the "Palestinian" and Arab media was savage. The refusal to recognize the state of Israel as a Jewish State was savage. The list was endless.

Instead of acknowledging any of this, MTA officials tried desperately to justify their anti-Israel position. They did not, in fact, run both sides. The haters' side was presented, and the defenders of Israel presented the apologists' side, but Israel's right to self-defense was not presented. Who did these MTA bureaucrats think they were, sanctioning jihad and prohibiting truth and the voices of freedom? How did these clerks dare to normalize anti-Semitism while enforcing the blasphemy laws under sharia? That seemed exactly what this amounted to.

It was all so arbitrary. So we sued. In July 2012, in a case with vast free speech implications extending well beyond our own campaign, we won.

Federal Judge Paul Engelmayer wrote a wonderful, brilliant opinion, establishing a precedent that will do much to protect free speech all over the country. The money quote from the ruling was when Engelmayer explained that, "the AFDI ad is not only protected speech—it is core political speech. The ad expresses AFDI's pro-Israel perspective on the Israeli/"Palestinian" conflict in the Middle East, and implicitly calls for a pro-Israel US foreign policy with regard to that conflict. The AFDI ad is, further, a form of response to political ads on the same subject that have appeared in the same space. As such, the AFDI ad is afforded the highest level of protection under the First Amendment."[5]

Indeed, this was a great victory for the First Amendment. Judge Engelmayer struck a huge blow against the left's sinister authoritarian effort to curtail speech and stood up for that freedom which is the cornerstone of all others.

It was a super opinion. Illustrating the MTA's inconsistency, Engelmayer noted that "under MTA's no-demeaning standard, an advertiser willing to pay for the privilege is today at liberty to place a demeaning ad on the side or back of a city bus that states any of the following: 'Southerners are bigots,' 'Upper West Siders are elitist snobs,' 'Fat people are slobs,' 'Blondes are bimbos,' 'Lawyers are sleazebags,' or 'The store clerks at Gristedes are rude and lazy.'"

Engelmayer concluded: "Whatever weight might be assigned to the governmental interest in banning demeaning speech on the exterior of New York City buses on an even-handed basis, there is no good reason for protecting some individuals and groups, but not others, from such abuse. MTA's no-demeaning standard, as currently formulated, is, therefore, inconsistent with the First Amendment."

He was right. Disallowing a pro-Israel ad was clearly a politically correct, politically motivated denial of free speech. "At the heart of the First Amendment," wrote Engelmayer, "is the recognition of the fundamental importance of the free flow of ideas and opinions on matters of public interest and concern." That free flow of ideas is just what the left and Islamic supremacists want to suppress, and the tools in the MTA eagerly did their bidding.

Judge Engelmayer's decision was crucial not just for AFDI and the MTA but for the freedom of speech in general. The AFDI case set a key legal precedent for the freedom of speech and won a great victory for the First Amendment.

The enemedia's response was predictable. The *Huffington Post*'s headline was "Anti-Islam Bus Ads OK'd by Judge," even though neither Muslims nor Islam were ever mentioned in the ad. The reaction from Islamic supremacists was equally predictable. One report noted: "Most Muslim-Americans have lashed out at proposed advertisements to be placed on New York City buses that call enemies of Israel 'savages.' Muslims argue this is hate speech and they should be removed immediately."[6]

One Muslim took that to heart. On September 25, 2012, CNN "journalist" Mona Eltahawy was arrested after spraying pink spray paint over one of my Civilized Man/Savage ads in the New York subway. On that day at 12:42 p.m. Eltahawy tweeted: "Meetings done; pink spray paint time. #ProudSavage #F–kHate." Shortly thereafter, she was about to spray paint over AFDI's pro-Israel ad in a subway station when longtime pro-freedom activist and blogger Pamela Hall stood between her and the ad. As she vandalized the ad, Eltahawy also spray-painted Hall and broke her glasses.

This criminal behavior and fascism was immediately lauded in leftist circles. Her vandalism caused an international brouhaha—her spray-painting made the front page of the *New York Post* and headlines in national and international newspapers.

Eltahawy's behavior was all the more ironic in light of the fact that she was viciously sexually assaulted by "protesters" in Cairo's Tahrir Square in 2011, and subsequently wrote a searching piece about the misogyny that is inherent in Islamic law.[7] But she was roundly attacked by her fellow Islamic supremacist writers for that article, and I believe her vandalism of my ad was her attempt to get back into their good graces. Now, in a classic case of Stockholm Syndrome, she was defending the same savages who brutally attacked her in Tahrir Square.

Eltahawy was carrying water for those who advocated a new genocide of the Jews and who celebrated the murders of innocent civilians. She sprayed our ad because she objected to the word "savages" being used to refer to Islamic jihadists who murder Israeli civilians then celebrate those murders by passing out candy, as they did in Gaza in 2014 after a jihadi murdered four people in a Jerusalem synagogue, and on many other occasions.[8]

Eltahawy described herself as a "liberal Muslim," and everyone assumed that meant she was worlds away from the Muslims who committed such savagery, and only "Islamophobes" would consider the two to be in the same camp. But then, in the criminal case against her for destroying my ad, Eltahawy retained Jewicidal leftist lawyer Stanley Cohen, who had represented savages such as Mousa Abu Marzouk of Hamas and Sulaiman Abu Ghaith, Osama bin Laden's son-in-law.[9]

Six degrees of separation? This was no degree of separation. Eltahawy hated that I called the jihadis "savages," and then retained the savages' lawyer. Cohen once said: "If I don't support the politics of political clients, I don't take the case."[10] So, Eltahawy was a "liberal Muslim" who was outraged that I called jihadis "savages," and she had a lawyer who supported jihad terror against innocent Israeli civilians, the bloody murder of the Fogel family, the mass murders of Israeli civilians in buses and restaurants, etc.

Cohen said in 2001, "If Osama bin Laden arrived in the United States today and asked me to represent him, sure I'd represent him."[11] Mona Eltahawy would have to do.

The case against Eltahawy dragged on for over two years. In December 2014, she declared victory, tweeting: "My attorney @StanleyCohenLaw just wrote to tell me that my spray painting case has been dismissed in the interests of justice. #ProudSavage." Not surprisingly, Eltahawy was lying. The case wasn't dismissed outright "in the interests of justice."

The Assistant District Attorney in charge of prosecuting the case told Hall that what Eltahawy actually got was an adjournment in contemplation of dismissal, which means that the case will be dismissed in six months if she stays out of trouble. Although this was not a conviction, Eltahawy had to complete two days of community service and pay restitution of $794.60 to Hall for her broken glasses. Hall remarked in a statement, "Mona has thrown in the towel, giving up on her bogus claim to free speech, and finally agreed to do her community service as required for spraying graffiti in the subway."[12]

In a piece for *The Guardian,* justifying her vandalism, she wrote, "I broke the law, yes. So what?" Eltahawy went on about her "love of the First Amendment," while demonstrating her abysmal lack of understanding what the freedom of speech is, how it works, and why it is important.[13] If Eltahawy wanted to exercise her freedom of speech she could have bought her own advertisement and expressed herself any way she wished. Attacking people with toxic spray paint and destroying property is not freedom of expression or any legitimate form of protest.

We fought another war for the freedom of speech in Boston. We submitted our now-famous Civilized Man/Savage ad in response to a vicious anti-Israel ad that was pulled after complaints but then re-posted despite those complaints.

In fighting for free speech in Boston, we exposed the inconsistency and self-contradictions of those who would limit our freedom of speech and the truth about jihadist savagery.

Our ad was again rejected as "demeaning" and we sued. We did not succeed in our motion for a preliminary injunction. US District Court Judge Nathaniel Gorton ruled against us.

But in reading his thorough, well-written opinion, it appeared that he did so reluctantly. We knew going in that overcoming the Ridley decision, which upheld the Massachusetts Bay Transit Authority's right to reject ads it considered "demeaning" to some group, would be an enormous hurdle. The Ridley case is the Dred Scott of free-speech decisions. This landmark case "involves the rejection of one advertisement from a religious group on the grounds that the ad violated the MBTA's guidelines prohibiting advertisements which demean or disparage an individual or group of individuals."[14] During our hearing, Judge Gorton specifically stated that, being a district judge, he did not have the authority to rule on or alter the decision in that case.

Here is the most interesting part of his opinion:

> Nevertheless, the Court agrees with the plaintiffs that the most reasonable interpretation of their advertisement is that they oppose acts of Islamic terrorism directed at Israel. Thus, if the question before this Court were whether the MBTA adopted the best interpretation of an ambiguous advertisement, it would side with the plaintiffs. But restrictions on speech in a non-public forum need only be reasonable and need not be the most reasonable. See Ridley, 390 F.3d at 90.[15]

He did not want to hold against us, even going so far as to say that he personally viewed jihad as violent war but, in his view, Ridley tied his hands as a binding precedent.

We filed an appeal, and would fight to the Supreme Court if necessary. But we also decided to test the MBTA's "demeaning" standard. We submitted a new ad, identical in appearance to the first but read, "In any war between the civilized man and those who commit savage acts, support the civilized man. Support Israel. Defeat violent jihad."

The MBTA approved this version immediately. Its acceptance of this ad and not the first ad shows the absurdity of its position and exposes how it had subjected the First Amendment to its capricious whims. The fact that "savage" was a noun in one ad and an adjective in the other, and one ad was approved and the other wasn't, was ridiculous and served only to make our case stronger. Now advertisers had to hire a legal staff to write their ad copy? It was absurd.

Our new ad forced them into a corner and exposed the silliness of their position. Could we expect the "peaceful" jihadis who were so offended by the prior ad to lovingly accept this one? The revised ad pointed to the absurdity of the government censoring one but being forced to approve the other. They, and the law as interpreted by Judge Gorton through the Ridley decision, were enforcing subjective standards that inevitably led to allowing viewpoints they approved of and denying those with which they disagreed.

We decided to test them yet again and submitted a third ad, again looking like the first two, and reading: "In any war between the civilized man and the savage, support the civilized man. Support Israel. Defeat violent jihad." We wanted to see exactly where the MBTA decides to say we can go this far and no farther, and then expose their subjectivity and politically motivated rulings.

This one, too, was denied. Judge Gorton rejected our motion for relief from the transit authority's ban on our ads on the basis that "such blatant games-manship and deliberate confrontations" didn't warrant granting relief.

Indeed. But whose gamesmanship was it? Who was toying with our most basic and fundamental freedom? It was not us, Judge Gorton. We were not playing games. We were, and are, dead serious about the First Amendment. We were fighting for that most basic element of the world's first moral government based on individual rights. These tinpot bureaucrats dictating what could and could not be said according to their prejudices mirrored the most closed societies.

And yet, perhaps it was all for the best. These rulings were based on bad precedent. We knew going in that overcoming the Ridley decision would be an enormous hurdle. Ridley needs to be overturned. That battle needs to be fought, and we are the ones who will do it.

The enemies of freedom invoked the freedom of speech to kill freedom of speech. Free speech is for them and them alone. It spoke to the heart of matter and the reason why we fight. Those who enforce free speech restrictions expose who and what they really are.

These enemies of freedom mean to destroy the founding principles of this nation.

You won't like what comes after the Constitution—not if the jackboots have their way.

The Anti-sharia Ad Campaign

The war in the information battle-space kept heating up.

In an effort to stop the protection of constitutional liberties, in February 2012 the Islamic Circle of North America kicked off a national sharia disinformation campaign in Kansas City. They picked Kansas City because the Missouri state legislature at that time had reintroduced "Anti-sharia Legislation" into the Missouri house.

They were running billboards and radio ads in an attempt to deceive and mislead the American people about sharia. A billboard reading "Sharia: Got Questions? Get Answers!" and referring people to a phone number and a cynically addressed website, *www.defendingreligiousfreedom.org*, were the kickoff of a national propaganda campaign to con the American people. The premise of the campaign was an insult to every freedom-loving non-Muslim and Muslim of conscience. The idea was that opposition to the oppressive, racist, and misogynist sharia was supposedly an infringement on the First Amendment protection of religious freedom.

ICNA is a Muslim Brotherhood group, according to a captured internal document of the Brotherhood, which also states that the Brotherhood's mission in the US is "eliminating and destroying Western civilization from within and sabotaging its miserable house."[16]

Muslim Brotherhood groups in America were and are trying to norm sharia, mainstream sharia. The Muslim Brotherhood group ICNA was lying to Americans about sharia and advancing a false narrative about the most extreme and radical ideology on the face of the earth.

We were on the forefront of this fight. Our billboards in Kansas City countering the ICNA billboards went up and we crafted radio ads that broke at the same time. They read: "Sharia: Got Fatwa? Get Help!" with a phone number and a website referral—to *www.defendingreligiousfreedom.us.*

The very simple and clear-cut legislation that the Missouri state legislature was considering should have been the proverbial no-brainer. The fact that it was being met by so much resistance, both overt and covert, indicated how very needed it was.

How could anyone oppose a law that sought to prevent foreign laws from undermining fundamental constitutional liberties? Our 30-second radio ads said:

> Subversive groups will tell you that sharia is just private religious law. They're lying. Sharia is a political system that contravenes American freedoms in numerous ways. Sharia asserts authority over non-Muslims. It mandates discrimination, harassment, and second-class status for both non-Muslims and women. It denies free speech, which we're seeing in America increasingly under the guise of 'hate speech laws.' How can anyone support sharia when it undermines our fundamental constitutional liberties? Look for our billboards on I-7.

On March 2, 2012, *The Washington Post* ran a piece written by Omar Sacirbey for the *Religion News Service*: "Muslims launch campaign to 'understand' sharia." It began: "Against a backdrop of heartland fears that US

Muslims seek to impose Islamic law on American courts, a leading Muslim group will launch a campaign on Monday (March 5) to dispel what it called misconceptions about sharia."[17]

The article said that ICNA was sponsoring the "roughly $3 million dollar campaign" that "will feature billboards in at least 15 US cities, 'sharia seminars' on 20 college campuses, and town hall-style forums and interfaith events in 25 cities."[18]

This sinister, deceptive *taqiyya* (religious deception, sanctioned in Islam) campaign had 3 million dollars, and we were having trouble scraping together two nickels for our campaign countering it with the truth. If we had three million dollars, everyone in America would have known the truth about sharia.

The *New York Times* Surrenders to Savagery

In March 2012, the *New York Times* ran a full-page ad headed, "It's Time to Quit the Catholic Church." I decided to try an experiment and submitted an ad soon afterward headed, "It's Time to Quit Islam." We used the same language as the anti-Catholic ad. The only difference was that ours was true, and what we described about the mistreatment of women and non-Muslims under Islamic law was true. The anti-Catholic ad, by contrast, was written by fallacious feminazis. Nonetheless, in a craven capitulation to sharia blasphemy laws, the *Times* rejected my ad.

Bob Christie, senior vice president of corporate communications for the *New York Times*, called to advise me that they would have accepted my ad but, considering the situation on the ground in Afghanistan, now would not be a good time, as they did not want to enflame an already hot situation. He said they would be reconsidering it for publication in "a few months." So I said to Mr. Christie, "Isn't this the very point of the ad? If you feared the Catholics were going to attack the *New York Times* building, would you have run that ad?" Christie said, "I'm not here to discuss the anti-Catholic ad."

"But I am, it's the exact same ad," I said.

"No, it's not," he shot back.

"I can't believe you're bowing to this Islamic barbarity and thuggery. I can't believe this is the narrative. You're not accepting my ad. You're rejecting my ad. You can't even say it."

Christie then sent me a follow-up letter, claiming that, "We delay publication in light of recent events in Afghanistan, including the Koran burning and the alleged killings of Afghani [sic] civilians by a member of the US military. It is our belief that fallout from running this ad now could put US troops and/or civilians in the region in danger."[19]

It was most disingenuous for the *Times* to refuse to run our counter-jihad ad based on their concern for US troops in Afghanistan. Liars. Who had done more to jeopardize our troops and American citizens than the pro-jihadist *New York Times*? Was the *Times* concerned that they were putting our troops' lives in danger when they ran front page articles on Abu Ghraib every day for a month? Starting on May 1, 2004, the *Times* had a front page article on Abu Ghraib every day for 32 days.

Despite the obvious hypocrisy of the *Times*, the mainstream media fell into line. It took a couple of days to get their arms around how to frame the *Times'* self-enforcement of sharia, but the *Huffington Post* and the left lemmings soon began to follow the *Times'* line, claiming that running my ad would endanger lives.

Really? What nerve. What was lower than using our brave men and women to cover for the *Times's* cowardice and anti-freedom editorial policies? That was so … left.

Meanwhile, the uber-left, George Soros-funded *ThinkProgress* was in a tizzy. In their piece, they never mentioned the anti-Catholic ad or the *Times'* inconsistency. But they could not have missed them, as those were the central aspects of the story. *So they knew.* This proved that *ThinkProgress* was intentionally misleading its readership. Their story made it sound as if I just wanted to run an anti-Islam ad out of racist, Islamophobic, anti-Muslim bigotry.

Even Fox's take on the story was skewed. They called me an anti-Islam activist. I am a counter-jihadist. Why doesn't the media distinguish between the two? Their lack of distinction implies the two are interchangeable. How Islamophobic! Fox also refused to run a graphic of either ad, as "both were offensive." More abridgment of free speech in adherence to sharia. They did not address the motive, fear, or sharia behind the *Times's* craven hypocrisy. Instead, they focused on the inconsistency of the *Times* accepting one ad and rejecting another, without clearly explaining why or giving the reasons for the inconsistency, which accords with Fox's increasing tendency not to address this subject matter at all.

Megyn Kelly referred to our ad as anti-Islamic. It was not. The ad was a rebuttal. Also, it was worth noting that Trace Gallagher, a *Fox News* anchor, ran the *Times*'s pathetic excuse unchallenged. In my interview with Fox, which they severely edited, I questioned the dishonesty of the *Times*'s position. Why didn't Fox mention any of that? Why did Fox give the *Times* a free pass, while jumping to repeat the Islamic supremacists' "anti-Islam" label of me?

This, too, was Islamic law in America. The *Times*'s refusal to run our ad, and the media falling into line with the *Times*, is adherence to the blasphemy laws under sharia. They had no reservations about submitting to the bloody demands of sharia. This was surrender to savagery.

Contrary to Bob Christie's claims, the *Times* never ran my ad. But it did run yet another full-page, anti-Catholic ad in 2014, once again demonstrating its double standard and hypocrisy.[20]

The Islamic Apartheid Ad Campaign

In March 2013, we submitted to the New York City MTA a series of ads highlighting the grim reality of Islamic apartheid. There were four different variants. All of them were headed, "This Is Islamic Apartheid." They all declared, "Stop US Aid to Islamic States." One depicted the road to Mecca in Saudi Arabia, with a highway sign saying, "Makkah [that is, Mecca]—Muslims Only" and "Jeddah—Obligatory for non muslims [sic]." The second depicted gays being executed in the Islamic Republic of Iran, with the legend "Gay Under Islamic Law (Sharia)." The third showed a woman being caned in Indonesia, with the caption, "In many Islamic countries, rape victims are tortured or killed unless they agree to marry their rapist." The fourth stated, "Close to one million Jews have been killed or exiled from Muslim lands since 1948."

The ads were my response to repulsive, anti-Semitic ads from American Muslims for Palestine that began running in New York City that same month, saying "End Apartheid Now! Stop US Aid to Israel." My ads focused on the real apartheid, Islamic apartheid—the institutionalized oppression of women, gays, and non-Muslims under Islamic law.

Human rights scholar Anne Bayefsky notes that, "There were once an estimated 900,000 Jews," in the Muslim world, "but today there are less than a few thousand. They were given a choice: die, convert or flee."[21]

106

That's apartheid. The slaughter of gays across the Muslim world— *that's* apartheid. The persecution of Christians across the Muslim world—*that's* apartheid. Muslims are freer in Israel than in any Muslim country.

Gays for Sharia

Our AFDI ads highlighting the Muslim oppression of gays under sharia rolled out on buses in San Francisco in April 2013. The ads simply quoted statements of various Muslim leaders, including Muslim Brotherhood Sheikh Yusuf al-Qaradawi and Iran's former President Mahmoud Ahmadinejad saying that, according to Islam, homosexuals should be put to death.

The ads were swiftly condemned by the San Francisco Board of Supervisors (that is, its city council) and the Human Rights Commission. They obviously support the brutal oppression of gays under sharia, or why would they oppose these ads? The Board of Supervisors passed a resolution condemning my ads as "Islamophobic." Hamas-tied CAIR crowed in a statement, "The resolution is the first of its kind in the nation, sending a clear message that San Francisco's elected leaders stand against hate and Islamophobia."[22]

"The first of its kind." Imagine that. You would think that the ultra-progressive San Francisco Board of Supervisors would pass a resolution against Muslim gangs targeting gays and shooting them in the face with a "rifle-style" BB gun while videotaping the attacks, as happened in San Francisco in March 2010.[23] There was a concerted effort within the San Francisco police department to bury this story, and it is only because one officer leaked the report to the media that anything was ever reported. The Muslims chose their victims, "because they appeared to be gay."[24] Perhaps the Board of Supervisors could have passed a resolution against San Francisco law enforcement for covering up a string of Muslim anti-gay violence incidents.[25]

You would think that the "first of its kind" resolution from the San Francisco Board of Supervisors might condemn honor violence, clitoridectomies, religious apartheid, and gender apartheid. No, the San Francisco Board of Supervisors passed a resolution, a "first of its kind" against our ads, against my work. Did they condemn the actual quotes used by high profile Muslims against gays? Worse than that, when pressed by blogger Pete Ingemi if they would refuse to condemn the anti-Muslim statements of Islamic world figures, they refused.

Theresa Sparks, the transgender head of the San Francisco Human Rights Commission, also issued a statement condemning our ads. Sparks was something of a spark for our new AFDI campaign because of her ridiculous statement that, "It's actually easier to get insurance for sexual transition procedures in Iran than in America."[26]

Perhaps that is because gay men are forced to have transgender operations in Iran. Forced. Not all gay men want to become women and have their manhood cut off. But Sparks thought this was a fabulous policy. Such delusion is without peer. In Iran, gays are forced to choose between sex change operations and death.

For someone so clear about being true to herself and being who she is, Sparks is either blind or cowardly. The persecution, subjugation, and oppression of gays *is* based on religiously-motivated hatred—it's sharia. Not every Muslim subscribes to it, of course. But the ideology behind it is very much the problem. Sparks claims, on the contrary, that it's cultural. What culture is that? Islamic culture. Sparks is sharpening the blade of her own executioners.

Sparks joined a chorus of media trolls and *Huffington Post* "human rights attorneys" such as Engy Abdelkader who claimed our ads, "suggest that all Muslims hate gays." That was a red herring. The ads suggested no such thing. The oppression and persecution of gays is epidemic in the Muslim world, and Sparks and Abdelkader were sanitizing this horror.

And many in the gay community suffer here in the United States.

How many attacks do we not hear about so as not to offend the sensibilities of the Muslim community? These attacks were increasing across the country where there were large Muslim communities, not to mention the gay-bashing in sharia zones in the UK, France and across Europe. Shame on Sparks and Abdelkader.

Meanwhile, over at *Salon*, Chris Stedman, the Assistant Humanist Chaplain and the Values in Action Coordinator for the Humanist Community at Harvard, published a vicious piece attacking me for calling attention to the persecution of gays under Islamic law.[27] This came just days after the San Francisco Board of Supervisors' unanimous resolution condemning my ads standing up for gays. Stedman and Sparks could have formed a new organization: Gays for Sharia.

Stedman was a chaplain. Now that's a mouthpiece, a chaplain who smears and defames. What will Harvard think of next? In Stedman's subheadline, he called me a "Crusader," despite the fact that I am... Jewish. That gives you an indication of the quality of Stedman's inflammatory smear.

More indications of how Stedman played fast and loose with the facts came when he described the Ground Zero mosque as the Islamic Community Center in lower Manhattan, claiming it was neither at Ground Zero nor a mosque. Uh, Chris, it was indeed going to be a mosque, and it was to be built on the site of a building that was destroyed in the 9/11 attacks—that is, at Ground Zero.[28] But the left never lets the facts get in the way of a good lie. Stedman also trotted out that venerable leftist, opportunistic, and very well-compensated fundraising machine, the Southern Poverty Law Center, that smears every proud patriot as a threat. And he said that I had spent millions. Not. Even. Close. If I had that kind of money, my ads would have been *everywhere.*

In justifying Muslim oppression of gays under sharia, Stedman pulled out the old "religion-based bigotry" card but failed to mention that Christians and Jews were not slaughtering gays under canon law or Jewish law.

It was wild to me that this nasty little man was turning himself inside out to defend an ideology that hangs gays in public, tears their faces off with razor blades in Gaza, and throws them off tall buildings, as ISIS does. And he claimed I have no support among gays.

He could have talked to Michael Lucas, the famous gay adult entertainment magnate. "I just returned from Tunisia (and I travelled half the Muslim world)," Michael wrote me when the ads began running in San Francisco, "and I think gay Muslims, or I should rather say gay Arabs, would agree with your ads because they know first hand the persecution they undergo on a daily basis. It is a shame that, instead of fighting for the rights of LGBT people in Muslim countries, 'political gays' are fighting against you. You are doing a fantastic job uniting people against evil and waking Americans up. Gays should join your movement."

Another gay activist, Artie Galvin, wrote on Facebook, "I stand with Pam Geller 100%. She is not a hate monger and she is a supporter of the LBGT movement. I am gay and know a lot of other gays who back her up. There is not one thing that she has said that is inaccurate or untrue. She doesn't hate Muslims but rather the ideology of hatred and violence that is so much a part of Islam."

Pat York of my organization Stop Islamization of America (SIOA)'s LGBT division said, "The American LGBT community is just as woefully uninformed about the harsh, deadly, current realities of Islam as anyone else. It is for this reason that an LGBT division of SIOA was recently created. The American LGBT community is allowing itself to be deceived and used for political reasons. As a community we do not need the stigma of being allied with a group that is dedicated to 'destroying Western civilization from within,'" as the Muslim Brotherhood has stated in a captured internal document.

Cynthia Yockey, who blogged under the moniker "Conservative Lesbian," wrote, "Pamela Geller is a true friend of the LGBT community. She has the courage to tell the truth about the menace of Islam. I admire her and respect her work."

And gay activist Mark Koenig wrote in an email to me:

> I am a gay man living in Atlanta, GA, and I have an honest and sincere answer for Mr. Stedman: Not only do I categorically support Ms. Geller, I consider her to be a freedom-fighter of the highest order. She has endured years of slander and even death threats from supporters of the evil ideology that is Islam, simply for telling the truth about it. Mr. Stedman is evidently ignorant of the unconditional condemnation and death-sentence prescribed for homosexuals in the Islamic holy texts. This is more than just an aberrant interpretation or a small group of 'extremists' who take these writings literally and act upon them. Homosexuals are routinely executed in Islamic countries simply for BEING homosexual. In fact, Israel is the ONLY nation in the Middle East where gay people can be open about their sexuality without fearing for their lives.[29]

Yet the useful idiot Stedman, as if he recognized the power of the truth and therefore sought to silence it, even urged the fundraising site Indiegogo to take down our AFDI fundraiser.

The visceral response of the San Francisco Board of Supervisors, the Human Rights Commission, Theresa Sparks, and the uber-left media in San Francisco, as well as Chris Stedman, to our "Gays for Sharia" ad campaign was obscene proof of how desperately needed this awareness campaign was.

They called my ads hateful when I merely quoted political, spiritual, and cultural leaders in the Muslim community.

History will not be kind to these useful idiots. They will be ridiculed and despised by future generations yearning and fighting for freedom.

The FBI "Faces of Global Terrorism" Ad

In July 2013 in Seattle, the FBI ran a terrorism awareness campaign featuring bus ads depicting photos of sixteen of the world's Most Wanted Terrorists. This was a publicity campaign sponsored by the Joint Terrorism Task Force for the US Department of State's Rewards for Justice (RFJ) program. The RFJ program offers up to $25 million for information that helps stop terrorism.

However, Muslim groups and the politicians in their pockets actually succeeded in having the ad campaign removed. I determined that AFDI was going to have to do the FBI's job for them and we resolved to put the ads back up.

The RFJ program had been quite successful. Through it, the State Department's Bureau of Diplomatic Security paid over $125 million to more than 80 people who offered genuine information that led to jihadis being jailed and that prevented acts of jihadist terror. This program was instrumental in leading to the arrest of jihadist Ramzi Yousef, who went to prison for his role in the 1993 World Trade Center jihad bombing. This program saves lives.

It was hard to believe that this program bothered anyone, but it did. Jeff Siddiqui, founder of American Muslims of Puget Sound, claimed that Seattle-area Muslims called him saying the Most Wanted Terrorists ad campaign made them "concerned for their safety."[30] He said the ad would be just as bad if the government had posted an ad on buses with the faces of people from a single ethnic group and the caption "the face of murderers in the United States."

Muslim groups wailed and *dhimmi* Congressman Jim McDermott (D-WA) did their bidding. He wrote to the FBI demanding they pull the campaign, which he claimed was, "offensive to Muslims and ethnic minorities" and encouraged, "racial and religious profiling."[31]

McDermott claimed that the FBI's Most Wanted Terrorists list included people of other races and "associations with other religions and causes," but "their faces are missing from this campaign."[32] He said the ad would, "likely only serve to exacerbate the disturbing trend against Middle Eastern, South Asian, and Muslim Americans."

What trend? In reality, FBI statistics showed that Jews were significantly more likely to be targets of hate crimes than Muslims.[33] And the ad was not unfair. Of the FBI's 32 Most Wanted Terrorists only two are not Muslims.

So if he wanted the FBI to leave Muslims off the Most Wanted Terrorists ad, he'd first have to convince Muslims to stop committing terror attacks in the name of Islam. Instead, McDermott and Siddiqui succeeded in getting the FBI to remove the ads.

That's right: the FBI caved to sharia demand to not offend Muslims. The FBI was putting Americans at risk by submitting to the outrageous demands of Islamic supremacists. It was not the fault of the FBI that the world's most dangerous terrorists were jihadists. That was, and is, the reality. You cannot avoid the consequences when you avoid reality. Capturing these mass murderers was significantly more important than propping up the fictional narrative of victimhood and nonsensical hurt feelings. People were being slaughtered every day in jihad attacks.

It was obvious the ads had to go back up. We took it upon ourselves to alert the public to the nature and magnitude of the terror threat and submitted the same ad, with minor variations in the color scheme and design to avoid copyright issues, to Seattle Transit.

In August 2013, we received their response. *They refused it.* They refused what was essentially the same ad that the FBI had run the previous month. It was a spectacular submission to terror. Seattle's King County was refusing our ad because they considered it disparaging to Muslims. The ad was a poster for the worst terrorists on the FBI's most wanted list. Their refusal was devastating, and provided further proof of all that I had been warning about all these many years.

We filed suit. We retained David Yerushalmi again to represent us, and he quickly filed a Freedom of Information Act request asking for all communications between the FBI and Seattle Transit related to the creation and termination of the ad. We weren't going to take this capitulation to Islamic supremacism lying down.

We lost the first round and filed an appeal. Seattle found a technical error in our version of the ad. We corrected it and re-submitted. The struggle is ongoing. This case is still in the courts.

AFDI's Honor Killing Ad Campaign

Some were determined not only not to fight against us, but to aid the enemy.

In November 2013, Edmonton Transit in Canada decided that helping Muslim girls was "racist:" it caved in to Islamic supremacist demands and took down our AFDI bus ads offering help to Muslim girls living in fear of honor killing.

The enemedia in Canada called our ads "dishonorable," "controversial" and, above all, "racist."[34] It was "dishonorable" and "controversial" and "racist" to save lives? Under sharia it was, but no free person in Canada should have stood for sharia ruling on their soil. Nonetheless, in Edmonton, Sikh Councillor Amarjeet Sohi, who should have known better than to carry water for the Islamic supremacists who oppressed his people for centuries, ordered officials to take down the signs, immediately.

Yet vicious blood libels against Israel were just fine, and were running on transit systems across Canada at the time of this ruling.

Apparently Muslims complained about our ads. Why?

Was this how the Canadian Muslim community was responding to the desperate circumstances of Muslim girls living in devout Muslim homes? By denying, obfuscating and dissembling? The Muslim community was protecting the Islamic honor code, while smearing and libeling the truth-tellers who were coming to the aid of these girls as "racists."

Honor killing is a grim reality that is largely ignored, and girls are suffering as a result. Muslim fathers kill their daughters for real or imagined sexual indiscretions that have supposedly dishonored the family. Nothing is done, because political correctness prevents us from speaking about the problem honestly. Muslims commit 91 percent of honor killings worldwide, and Islamic law stipulates no penalty for a parent who kills his child.[35]

The fact that Islamic supremacist groups are so threatened by these ads showed how desperately they were needed. Clearly we struck a nerve: these Muslim groups didn't want people speaking out against honor killing, and so we had to speak out louder than ever.

Remember: what happens in Canada will soon enough happen in the US. Canada is just farther down the same road we are on, the road of appeasement and capitulation to Islamic supremacists.

AFDI Equal Rights for Jews Campaign

"The Palestinian Authority is calling for a Jew-free state. Equal rights for Jews."

Our ads proclaiming this went up on buses in Denver in December 2013. And they were a sight for the sore eyes tired of the propaganda and Jew-hatred of anti-Semites and Islamic supremacists.

I ran these ads to counter the vicious blood libel ads that were running in Denver at the time, luridly accusing the state of Israel of ethnic cleansing: "Want peace? Stop ethnic cleansing in Palestine." These vile ads went up on Denver-area buses while the Jewish National Fund was holding its national conference there.

The Denver Post wrote of these ads:

> But we also understand why some people are upset. It's because the accusation is false.
>
> This is not a close call. You may criticize Israeli policy toward the Palestinians and peacemaking, or toward the Arabs within Israel (although they enjoy political rights that are the envy of most residents of the Middle East), but you cannot accuse Israel of ethnic cleansing and expect to be taken seriously by those familiar with the facts.[36]

AFDI's Share the Land Campaign

We also countered the lies in Seattle that same month, when the Jew-haters were at it again. The relentless Seattle Mideast Awareness Campaign (SeaMAC) launched another vicious Goebbels-style blood libel against the Jews in Seattle. Their ad read: "Share the land. Palestinian refugees have the right to return. Equal rights for Palestinians."

We could not let that go unanswered. Our ad read: "Share the land. The Palestinian Authority kills any Muslim who sells land to a Jew. Equal rights for Jews."

This was absolutely true. *The Jerusalem Post* reported in 2002: "The Palestinian Authority (PA) Mufti, Ikremah Sabri, issued a fatwa (religious decree), banning the sale of Arab and Muslim property to Jews. Anyone who violated the order was to be killed. At least seven land dealers were killed that year. Six years later, the head of the PA's General Intelligence Service in the West Bank, General Tawfik Tirawi, admitted his men were responsible for the murders."[36]

Yet when I submitted that ad to Seattle Transit in December 2013, I was refused. Again. And again, I sued. Yes, this was Seattle, whose transit authority we had already sued for its refusal to run our FBI Global Faces of Terrorism ad.

The "Moderate Muslims" Ad Campaign

I was determined to shed as much light as possible on the truths that the US government and the mainstream media seemed determined to obfuscate.

A new series of six AFDI ads began running on 100 New York City buses in September 2014. One key new ad pointed up the uselessness of the distinction between "moderate" and "extremist" Muslims, depicting two photos of Abdel-Majed Abdel Bary, a London-based Muslim who pursued a career as a rap artist until he turned to jihad and went to the Islamic State. The first photo showed Abdel Bary as a rapper; the second depicted an Islamic State jihadi just before he beheaded American journalist James Foley. The killer in the second photo had his face masked, but at the time I developed this ad, British intelligence was investigating Abdel Bary for the murder of Foley.[37] The ad bore the legend, "Yesterday's moderate is today's headline."

I developed this ad because the United States and other Western nations had paid insufficient attention to the fact that Muslim communities in the West had not made any concerted effort to expel supporters of jihad terror from their midst, and had done nothing at all to teach against the jihadist understanding of Islam, even though they ostensibly rejected it. This had the effect that we saw illustrated by the trajectory of Abdel-Majed Abdel Bary: people taken as "moderate" turned out to be "extremist."

Another ad in this series emphasized the sameness of the beliefs and goals of various jihad groups—and one of their chief US enablers: "Hamas is ISIS. Hamas is al-Qaeda. Hamas is Boko Haram. Hamas is CAIR in America. Jihad is jihad." (Israeli Prime Minister Benjamin Netanyahu said much the same thing around this time.) CAIR has had several of its officials convicted of jihad terror activity, and has opposed every counter-terror measure ever proposed or enacted. It also has been shown to have abundant links to Hamas. This is not the "moderate" group of media myth.

The third ad quoted Netanyahu stating another unpopular truth: "Hamas is using civilians as human shields. We use missiles to protect our people. They use their people to protect their missiles." The fourth ad pointed out that "Christians are becoming extinct everywhere in the Middle East except Israel" and called for an end to US aid to Islamic countries in light of the ongoing and increasing Muslim persecution of Christians.

The New York *Daily News* was outraged. When it found out about this campaign, it ran a story with the screaming headline, "Shocking anti-Islam ad campaign coming to MTA buses, subway stations."[38]

Shocking? Shocking was beheading journalists with six-inch knives. Shocking was kidnapping hundreds of non-Muslim girls, gang-raping them and selling them at slave markets. Shocking was one million Christians being ethnically cleansed or slaughtered from Syria. Shocking was thousands of American, European, Australian, Canadian Muslims flocking to Syria and Iraq to fight for the Islamic State.

Shocking was the media's deceitful and corrupt coverage of jihad. Imagine, in the wake of the beheading of a journalist, a major newspaper was calling my ads "anti-Islam" and me a "notorious flamethrower."[39] These people were beyond help.

The ads conveyed a stark reality and a brute fact: Islamic terrorist groups like al-Qaeda, the Islamic State, the Taliban, Hamas, Hezbollah, al-Shabaab, Ansar al-Sharia, the Egyptian Islamic Jihad, the Muslim Brotherhood, Lashkar-e-Taiba, and many more, have access and influence among the "moderate" Muslim communities around the globe for both recruiting purposes and financial support. Indeed, Western Muslims-turned-jihadists are far more likely to come from the community of "ordinary practitioners of Islam" than from any other community.

Jihadists were beheading journalists and journalists were out for my head.

In the spring of 2015, American Muslims for Palestine was at it again. But so were we. AMP was yet again libeling Israel and calling for it to be thrown to the jihadi wolves. And I was once again countering them every step of the way.

The new AMP ad pictured Israeli Prime Minister Benjamin Netanyahu holding a sign, and it quoted Netanyahu, "America is a thing you can move very easily," and adds: "Stop the disrespect—End US Aid to Israel."

AMP was invoking the ugly anti-Semitic stereotypes in which Jew-haters have long trafficked. This was part of a systematic campaign by many different Islamic and leftist groups to dehumanize and demonize the Jewish State. This vicious propaganda was running unchallenged even by pro-Israel groups that ought to have been at the forefront of this battle.

To counter the AMP ads, we revived our renowned ads reading, "In any war between the civilized man and the savage, support the civilized man," with the new tagline, "Increase aid to Israel. Stop funding jihad."

We also rolled out a new ad reading: "'Oh Allah, vanquish the Jews and their supporters. Oh Allah, vanquish the Americans and their supporters. Oh Allah, count their numbers, and kill them all, down to the very last one.'—Palestinian Legislative Council Speaker Sheikh Ahmad Bahr. Stop the disrespect—End US Aid to the Palestinian Authority and Gaza."

And another: "'The Palestinian people does not exist. The creation of a Palestinian state is only a means for continuing our struggle against the state of Israel.'—PLO executive committee member Zahir Muhsein. Stop the disrespect—End US Aid to the Palestinian Authority and Gaza."

We were determined to make sure that those ads would both roll out in every city where the AMP ad ran.

The AMP's agenda was frankly insidious. The organization was run by Dr. Hatem Bazian, a University of California at Berkeley professor who equated the Boston jihad bombings with "Islamophobia."

Increasingly, I saw that the more I spoke the truth, the uglier the enemy's response became, which, of course, made me smile. New York City transit authorities demanded that I provide substantiation for the quotes in my new ads. This was nothing new. Every time I submitted an ad, I had to provide evidence of everything I was asserting. I highly doubt that AMP was held to the same standard. Were they ever asked to prove that Netanyahu really said what they quoted him saying in their ad? Were they asked to provide the context? I doubt it.

More than ever, we had to educate the American people. And we were getting it done. AFDI was fighting the propaganda putsch of the AMP and other leftist and Islamic supremacist groups by going on the offense and taking the message to the people. We were bringing the truth about Israel, the global jihad against free people, and Islamic supremacism directly to the people. We forced a media discussion of the grim realities of jihad and sharia that they usually swept under the rug.

Now more than ever, when voices and work such as ours are increasingly silenced, we have to be bolder and go on the offense.

AFDI's "Islamophobia?" Ad Campaign

I rolled out a new campaign in November 2014 that was designed to show the absurdity of the mainstream media focus on "Islamophobia" amid growing jihad violence worldwide.

The charge of "Islamophobia" was and is used to intimidate people into thinking there was something wrong with opposing jihad violence.

Our ads were designed to increased awareness of the nature and magnitude of the jihad threat, and put an end to the denial and willful ignorance about that threat, so that we can adopt effective counter-terror measures based on that realistic appraisal.

The Muslim groups that complain most loudly about "Islamophobia," like Hamas-tied CAIR, have opposed every counter-terror program that has ever been proposed or implemented.

The ad listed some of the recent victims of jihad. "Islamophobia? 'When you meet the unbelievers, strike the necks' (Koran 47:4). Is it ISLAMOPHOBIC to oppose these beheadings? RIP Colleen Hufford, Lee Rigby, Palmira Silva, James Foley, Alan Henning, David Haines, Daniel Pearl, Nick Berg, Steve Sotloff, Herve Gourdel, and the millions slaughtered in the cause of Jihad."

That was all. The message was that it is not Islamophobia to oppose jihad terror. Those victims, and preventing others from joining them, should have been our focus, not the fictional "backlash against Muslims" upon which the media always focused.

We hoped to raise awareness about the need for Muslims in the US not just to denounce ISIS, but to teach young Muslims why this understanding of Islam was wrong and had to be rejected.

Predictably, the media mounted a campaign against the ads, quoting Hamas-tied CAIR and never giving the ads a fair and evenhanded presentation. Meanwhile, hundreds of ordinary people wrote to me thanking me for putting these ads up and getting the truth out that the media was determined to obscure and obfuscate.

The BDS Jewish Leaders Ad Campaign

AFDI also endeavored in November 2014 to out the Jews who fund the anti-Israel Boycott, Divest, Sanction (BDS) movement.

The scandal of it could not be overstated: Jewish leaders and philanthropists, including UJA-Federation President Alisa Doctoroff; Karen R. Adler, President of the Jewish Communal Fund and JCRC Board member; David Hochberg; Carole and Saul Zabar; Sally Gottesman, Edith Everett and others were prominent donors to the New Israel Fund, an organization that funded BDS and other anti-Israel initiatives.[40]

Alisa Doctoroff hoisting cocktails with the NIF in her lavish apartment was no different from the uniformed Nazis who were invited to and attended Jewish communal gatherings, nor from the hope expressed by Dr. Heinrich Stahl, the Berlin Jewish community leader, for a better Nazi understanding of the Jewish situation.

Preceding Kristallnacht, the Nazis held several days calling for Germans to boycott Jewish-owned businesses. This was the direct antecedent to the BDS movement.

Murray Koppelman, an 80-year-old American Jewish philanthropist, visited Iran. NIF CEO Daniel Sokatch said that Koppelman was "a pillar of the American Jewish community." When Koppelman came back, he declared his intention to support the New Israel Fund in a major way. That's right: he observed the oppression of Iranian women and decided to fight Israeli "intolerance."[41]

As Iranians were determined to build a nuclear bomb—and oppose America—a Jewish American became a major New Israel Fund donor, pledging to match every new donor up to $500,000 in support of the New Israel Fund.

Meanwhile, Doctoroff used her position at UJA to promote the New Israel Fund's agenda. We were determined to shame these philanthropists who funded BDS groups—particularly the New Israel Fund.[42] Doctoroff had also gushed about "Palestinian" so-called "non-violent activism."[43] She insisted that getting Muslims jobs was the answer to supposed injustices in Israel. A 2009 *JTA* article reported that Doctoroff said that, "She was inspired by the progress being made by those involved with the initiatives the fund is helping support. 'You see people who have been energized, been utilized, that their value is being fulfilled,' she said. 'They are participating in making Israel a better place, whether they are Arab or Jewish. Their examples show us there are things that one can do.'"[44]

Then there was the far-left *Jewish Daily Forward*, which named Michael Sarid the chief development officer at the Forward Association, its parent company.[45] Sarid had posted on Facebook urging Muslims in Israel to apply for permits to fight to build all over Israel, saying, "I support NIF, so that organizations like ACRI can bring lawsuits to enforce civil rights."[46]

Civil rights for Muslims—as Jews were being killed daily.

Birthright Israel announced in November 2014 that it would no longer work with New Israel Fund. Why? Because they were viciously and inveterately anti-Israel.[47] All Jewish organizations, including The Forward, UJA-Federation and Jewish Communal Fund, should have followed suit. The New Israel Fund and Alisa Doctoroff were supporting moral evil.[48]

Yet weeks after her support for BDS was first exposed, Doctoroff had still not responded to countless emails, calls, or requests for comment from UJA-Federation donors.[49] This was true despite the fact that there were significant forces in the UJA calling for her resignation because of her support for the New Israel Fund.

Those who supported the New Israel Fund did not represent Jewish interests. Period. We demanded that any American Jew who supported the New Israel Fund withdraw such funding. The New Israel Fund should have been ostracized by the Jewish community and all supporters of Israel.

But it wasn't. And so AFDI began planning a new nationwide ad campaign to expose Jewish groups and leaders who were funding Boycott, Divestment, and Sanctions (BDS) campaigns. Our AFDI ad campaign was intended to bring public awareness to their activities and ultimately move them to stop harming the Jewish State of Israel.

The initial five ads targeted some of the principal Jewish organizations and philanthropists that were aiding the enemies of Israel, noting that they funded "New Israel Fund's (BDS) Boycott, Divestment and Sanction. Stop the Jewish Destruction of Israel." The individual ads named as BDS funders the UJA, Alisa Doctoroff, Carole and Saul Zabar, the Bronfman Foundation, and Edith Everett.[50]

The NIF was so radical an organization that its own lawyer, Michael Sfard, testified as an expert witness for the Palestine Liberation Organization.[51] Sfard provided paid testimony for the PLO. And he was an attorney for a number of organizations that were funded by the New Israel Fund.

We intended to shame these philanthropists who fund BDS groups—particularly the New Israel Fund, and to demand that any American Jew who supported the New Israel Fund withdraw such funding. These leaders are 21st-century kapos, but worse. These silver spoon dilettantes didn't have a gun to their heads; it was voluntary, and they meant to take us all down. They talked about plurality and diversity of thought, but they didn't welcome me or Caroline Glick or any other fiercely proud Jews. They were leftists aligned with the jihad force.

Now our ad campaign was necessary to move the ball—and to compel the targeted donors once and for all to stop funding the enemies of Israel. This campaign was urgently needed: the perfidy of these Jewish leaders had gone on long enough. In the age of Obama, we no longer had the luxury of indulging them. As Obama continued to turn the US against her principal Middle Eastern ally, we needed a strong, united front of Jews and supporters of Israel who demand that the US continue to be as faithful a friend to the only democracy in that region as she had been to us.

But it was not to be. So desperate were the New York political elites to keep these ads from running, that they changed the rules about what kind of advertising they would accept on subways and buses—just to prevent our ads from running.

A century of free speech in New York's most public square—the streets, the buses, the subways—came to a screeching halt on April 29, 2015 when the MTA voted to ban all issue and political advertising. The other topic of discussion, by the way, was the billions in debt the MTA was. The five public speakers, including me, all spoke in defense of free speech, opposing the ban. Every board member who spoke in the executive session, with the exception of MTA Board member Charles Moerdler, spoke in defense of free speech.

But the vote for the ban passed—a craven sore loser move in light of our AFDI victory in court just the week before, compelling the MTA to stop blocking our free speech and allow our MyJihad ads to run. Enemies of freedom were rejoicing across the world.

The meeting kicked off with discussion about the MTA's billion-dollar debt. Still, this irresponsible and totalitarian vote against political ad revenue was voted in. What was interesting, but not surprising, was Moerdler, who led the jihad against free speech. Here's what was not surprising: that the discussion was not about the MyJihad ads. Moerdler, in a vicious and disgusting tirade, instead attacked our anti-BDS ads that exposed wealthy Jewish donors who supported Boycott, Divestment and Sanctions initiatives against Israel. Moerdler railed against our ads exposing wealthy donors' support of the New Israel Fund, which supported BDS organizations, shrieking about *lashon hara* (speaking negatively about another person).

Actually, truth was not *lashon hara*, but calling me an egomaniac and a zealot, as Moerdler did, was. Calling our ads "filth," Moerdler failed to acknowledge the damage and destruction of BDS to the Jewish State. Even an Israeli court ruled that funding BDS was terrorism. But Mr. Moerdler and his country club buddies were OK with that.

This was a classic case of the powerful trumping the rights of the common man so as to protect their little club. The political and media elites only allowed the public discourse to fall within a certain political spectrum. My ads drove them crazy because they fell outside of that spectrum; I was vaulting over their controls and bringing truths to the public that they didn't want known. They had to move to shut me down.

Clearly, the April 2015 hearing was a fait accompli. When the vote came in, despite the overwhelming support for free speech, Moerdler's grin was perfectly evil. I could only imagine the pats on the back over brandy and cigars that would come later.

This was a stunning assault upon our First Amendment rights. Even Board members expressed real concern about the ban. We weren't the only ones who saw the problem with this: Christopher Dunn, associate legal director for the New York Civil Liberties Union, said: "It is unconscionable that you are thinking about barring all political ads from the transit system."[52]

New York City is the capital of the free world. The world looks to us. What message did the MTA send? It was a dark day for freedom.

Muhammad Ad Campaign

A good many readers of my website wrote to me in the spring of 2015, concerned about a deceptive ad that the Islamic Circle of North America (ICNA) was running in a number of American cities. ICNA is an Islamic organization that has been probed by the FBI for ties to terrorism. They were running a deceptive Muhammad propaganda campaign claiming that Muhammad advocated peace and women's rights. They have also run a pro-sharia for America ad campaign.[53]

ICNA's billboards in Atlanta claimed that "Muhammad—peace be upon him—believed in peace, social justice, women's rights," along with a phone number to find out more about Islam.[54] They were planning on having 100 of these billboards around the country by the end of 2015, while hosting conferences in various cities around the country about sharia and Muhammad.

We countered ICNA's lies with the truth about Muhammad. Our ad read, "Muhammad believed in war, denial of rights to women, denial of rights to non-Muslims, deceit of unbelievers," and directed people to an AFDI website, *TruthAboutMuhammad.org*. At that site, we laid out abundant evidence for what we said about Muhammad—evidence taken from core Islamic texts.

We submitted our ads to go up in Atlanta in the same areas as the ICNA *kitman* billboards. But Clear Channel rejected our ad, saying it wasn't very nice. So we submitted a different ad, using Muhammad's own quotes. That way Clear Channel could not say we were editorializing or opining. Our new ad quoted Muhammad saying, "I have been made victorious through terror"; "I have seen that the majority of the dwellers of Hell-fire were you (women)"; and "I have been commanded to fight against people."

Clear Channel rejected that ad, too.

ICNA is dedicated to "establishing a place for Islam in America"—which means a place for jihad and a place for sharia.[55] ICNA, like Hamas-tied CAIR, is a terror front group whose "Muslim advocacy" front masks their true Islamic supremacist agenda. Despite the carefully constructed myth surrounding Muslim Brotherhood groups in America, advanced by a hostile and pro-jihadist media, the truth about these subversives is out there.

ICNA works closely with radical Islamic organizations and invites radical speakers to its conferences. It was named in the Muslim Brotherhood document—entitled "An Explanatory Memorandum on the General Strategic Goal for the Group in North America"—as one of the Brotherhood's 29 likeminded "organizations of our friends" that shared the common goal of destroying America and turning it into a Muslim nation.[56]

These "friends" were identified by the Brotherhood as groups that could help teach Muslims "that their work in America is a kind of grand Jihad in eliminating and destroying the Western civilization from within and 'sabotaging' its miserable house by their hands ... so that ... Allah's religion [Islam] is made victorious over all other religions."[57]

The Muslim Brotherhood group ICNA was lying to Americans about Muhammad, Islam, and sharia in order to advance a false narrative about the most extreme and radical ideology on the face of the earth. Period. They didn't want Americans to know the truth that the gendercide of honor killings, the clitoridectomies, the stonings, and the 1,400 years of cultural annihilations and enslavements are all sharia-mandated and inspired by Muhammad's example.

When Clear Channel rejected our ad, I had a discussion with Jack Jessen of Clear Channel, who said that he could not run our ad. I asked Jessen why, and he said that it had a "negative connotation to it."

I told him that I was using direct quotes from Muhammad. But he said it was "very negative-based" and that he "considered it an attack" on ICNA. I pointed out that I hadn't even mentioned ICNA and that the ICNA ad wasn't honest. I explained that the ICNA is a terror-tied group and explained their background.

I said that we didn't oppose his running it, because it's a free country. But if he was going to run that kind of propaganda, he had to allow a counterpoint. He had to allow the truth. At least our ads featured quotes, *direct quotes from Muhammad.*

Jessen admitted that he "didn't know enough about the details of it," but he just knew that's the way he perceived it.

I reiterated that I was not attacking ICNA in the ad—I even offered to change the layout, the colors, which were similar to those in ICNA's ad. I explained that he was running something that was completely and utterly false because he perceived it as good. But it was not good. I explained that he was helping to disarm the American people in a very grave threat.

I told Jessen that I was willing to work with him. I changed the ad once, but for him to say absolutely no was just so wrong. It was unconscionable.

He suggested I talk to another company in Atlanta. I asked if he knew of a company in Atlanta that would run it. He said that he did not.

So I responded that it was Clear Channel that ran the ICNA ad. How did he reconcile that?

He could not answer. I gave him the primary sources of the quotes. So whom was I attacking? Muhammad said it.

He said that he didn't recognize the names of the sources of my quotes. "I have been made victorious through terror," "I have seen that the majority of the dwellers of Hell-fire were you (women)," and "War is deceit" all came from Sahih Bukhari, the source of Muhammad's words and deeds that Muslims consider most reliable.[58]

In contrast, Jessen admitted that he used Wikipedia to vet our ad.

He admitted that he was in "a difficult position."

I said, "You're an advertising company that is obviously taking issue-related ads. So if this ad doesn't go up, you know that Clear Channel will come under attack for not taking this ad, because they are showing a preference."

He said that he would talk to his people in corporate and get back to me. He never did.

The Muhammad Cartoon Ads

Soon after the jihad attack on my free speech event in Garland, Texas, in May 2015, because the freedom of speech was under violent assault, AFDI announced a new ad campaign to defend freedom of speech and stand up to violent intimidation.

Because the media and the cultural and political elites continued to self-enforce sharia without the consent of the American people by refusing to show any depictions of Muhammad or showing what it was in Texas that had jihadists opening fire, we planned to run an ad featuring the winning cartoon by former Muslim Bosch Fawstin from our Muhammad Art Exhibit and Cartoon Contest in Garland, Texas.

We wanted to let the American people *see* what the cowardly press was censoring in accordance with the blasphemy laws under sharia.

The ad campaign was submitted to the Washington, D.C.'s transit authority to run on buses and train dioramas in the Foggy Bottom, Capitol South, Bethesda, L'Enfant Plaza, and Shady Grove stations.

Drawing Muhammad is not illegal under American law, but only under Islamic law. Violence that arises over the cartoons is solely the responsibility of the Islamic jihadists who perpetrate it. Either America will stand now against attempts to suppress the freedom of speech by violence, or will submit and give the violent the signal that we can be silenced by threats and murder.

We cannot submit to the assassin's veto.

It was the jihadis, not I, who made the cartoons a flash point. If we surrender on that point and stop drawing Muhammad, we've established a precedent of surrendering to violent sharia enforcement, and once established, we will be made to reinforce it again and again. Islamist government is a unique threat to free speech and liberty.

There was nothing about this cartoon that incited violence. It was within the established American tradition of satire. If America surrendered on this point, the freedom of speech is a relic of history.

Many people on both the left and the rght were saying that we should do nothing to provoke Islam. The immediate answer would seem to be that we should do nothing to provoke violent jihadis, that the prudent thing to do would be to avoid doing things that anger them. But if we did that, they would not stop coming at us. In September 2014, an Islamic State spokesman boasted: "We will conquer your Rome, break your crosses, and enslave your women, by the permission of Allah, the Exalted. This is His promise to us; He is glorified and He does not fail in His promise. If we do not reach that time, then our children and grandchildren will reach it, and they will sell your sons as slaves at the slave market."[59]

In light of that, what is the point of asking whether or not we should provoke them? They're already provoked. A more useful question was whether it was really productive and helpful to signal to them that we would acquiesce to their threats of violence and change our behavior accordingly, or whether we would instead signal to them that their violent threats were not going to frighten us into submission.

In June 2015, 100 billboards depicting the Muhammad cartoon went up around St. Louis. They also went up in and around the northern tri-county area of Marion, Baxter and Boone counties in Arkansas. But in what could only be called an end-run around the First Amendment, the Washington Metropolitan Area Transit Authority (WMATA) banned "political ads" after AFDI submitted our free speech campaign.

As one of my readers pointed out, no contemporary medium of communication may pass the test of being merely commercial and non-political. The *New York Times* runs an editorial page every day—not to mention the slant of their "straight news"—and therefore, if they can advertise, so can the *Village Voice*, the *Socialist Militant*, and *Dabiq* (ISIS' four-color magazine), for that matter.

The WMATA threw in public safety for good measure, as if these craven quislings knew what was conducive to the public good. Color me skeptical. They said the buses would be a target for jihadis. Yet if we've learned anything since 9/11, it is that America is the target. The West is the target for Islamic terrorism. The whole country is on heightened alert for an Islamic State attack on July 4th. Abridging our freedoms so as not to offend savages is surrender and un-American. It results in more demands, more surrender, more capitulation to sharia law (which is what WMATA did).

Running and hiding is no strategy in a war. Operation Fetal Position is a recipe for disaster.

Lamar Advertising Runs Anti-Israel Billboards, Refuses AFDI Pro-Freedom Billboards

As sharia adherence became increasingly the norm, outrages to free speech were increasingly commonplace. The *Observer* reported in February 2016 that "approximately five miles south of Chicago's O'Hare International Airport, alongside the Interstate 294, stands a large anti-Israel billboard."[60] This ad was running on billboards owned by the national billboard company, Lamar Advertising—which repeatedly turned down my AFDI pro-freedom ads.

The billboard that we had hoped to counter was a vicious attack sponsored by the notorious anti-Israel group known as the Seattle Mideast Awareness Campaign (SeaMAC), and screaming, "Boycott Israel Until Palestinians Have Equal Rights." Muslims serve in the Israeli Knesset and have more rights in Israel than they do in Muslim countries. After complaints poured in about this ad, Lamar took them down, but only under pressure. The whole episode revealed how the public square is increasingly available only to a far-left perspective; other points of view are shut out.

When initially challenged about the ads, Lamar outrageously took cover in the freedom of speech, saying: "We do not accept or reject copy based upon agreement or disagreement with the views presented."[61] Really? For nine months before that statement was issued, AFDI had submitted various ads to 15 cities. All were rejected, yet every ad was fact-based.

Our Muhammad ad that we submitted in July 2014, for example, consisted of three Muhammad quotes. And while private and government agencies had no problem running blatantly dishonest ads about Muhammad, such as the false and deceptive ads about Muhammad that Lamar was running from the Muslim Brotherhood group the Islamic Circle of North America (ICNA), they rejected his direct quotes. That was sharia.

Our ad quoted Muhammad saying: "I have been made victorious through terror;" "I have seen that the majority of the dwellers of Hell-fire were you (women);" and "I have been commanded to fight against people"—all authenticated quotes from approved Muslim sources. Lamar asked us to provide them with the sources of all the quotations; we did so.

Then they rejected the ad "pursuant to their advertising policies." They gave no further explanation. Where was Lamar's commitment to the freedom of speech then? "We think SeaMAC has a right to present their views and would also support the right of those who disagree with SeaMAC." But apparently Lamar did not believe that AFDI had any such right.

Lamar was so solicitous of SeaMAC that when it took its billboards down, it said in a statement: "We have tried to contact SeaMAC to discuss these issues but have not received a reply to our telephone and email messages. Therefore we have decided to remove the SeaMAC copy as soon as possible."[62] Lamar was anxious not to offend the vicious Jew-haters; but did not deign even to explain why they were rejecting our truthful and much-needed ads.

This is the war on truth. George Orwell said: "The further a society drifts from truth the more it will hate those who speak it." Lamar loved SeaMAC and its lies. It hated AFDI and the truth. It was just another indication of how far our society was drifting from its moorings.

British Taxi Ads

In the summer of 2016, when the Muslim mayor of London, Sadiq Khan, banned advertisements on buses and subways of bikini-clad women, I decided that London needed a dose of the truth.[63] I bought space on 100 London taxis to run ads featuring quotes from the Muslim prophet Muhammad: "I have been made victorious through terror," "I was shown hell-fire and that the majority of its dwellers were women," and more. The ads also directed people to an AFDI website, *TruthAboutMuhammad.org*.

We were running these ads on taxis because the sharia-compliant London transit authority refused to run them on buses, even though at the time we

The Ground Zero mosque protest, September 11, 2010 in lower Manhattan. The crowd of tens of thousands stretched as far as the eye could see.

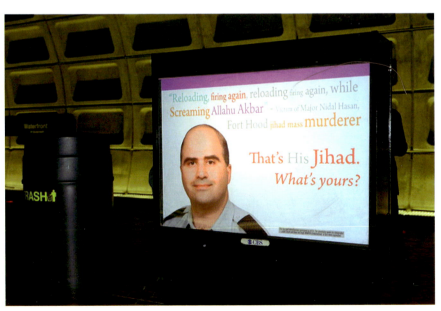

. The AFDI #MyJihad ads, lampooning CAIR's whitewashed #MyJihad ad campaign with the actual words of high-profile jihadis.

CAIR LEADERS CONVICTED OF JIHAD TERROR–RELATED CRIMES

GHASSAN ELASHI, MOUSA ABU MARZOOK, RANDALL ROYER, BASSEM KHAFAGI, RABIH HADDAD

THE COUNCIL ON AMERICAN-ISLAMIC RELATIONS, CAIR, CLAIMS TO BE A CIVIL RIGHTS GROUP. IN FACT, IT'S HAMAS IN THE U.S.

"CAIR has ties to terrorism and intimate links with HAMAS."
- Sen. Charles Schumer

C**A**IR
H
A
M
A
S

TruthAboutCAIR.com   AFDI.us

"This is a paid advertisement sponsored by the American Freedom Defense Initiative. The advertising space is a designated public forum and does not imply WMATA's endorsement of any views expressed."

The AFDI Truth About CAIR campaign, blowing the lid off the media's love affair with this unsavory self-proclaimed civil rights organization.

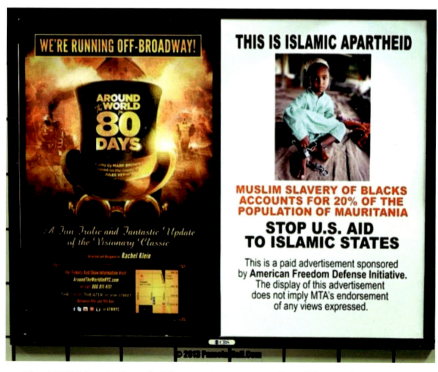

The AFDI Islamic Apartheid campaign, turning the tables on the anti-Israel blood libel apartheid ad campaigns.

The Sunday magazine cover of the UK's Independent, *calling me "The Most Dangerous Woman in America" for opposing the most brutal ideology on the face of the earth.*

Members of the SWAT team who were responsible for taking out the jihadis at the Muhammad Art Exhibit and Cartoon Contest, Garland, Texas, May 3, 2015.

AFDI hits Times Square with a billboard advertising our documentary film,
Can't We Talk About This? The Islamic Jihad Against Free Speech.

Addressing the crowd at our Rally of Remembrance for the Victims of Jihad, near
the site of the largest terrorist attack ever on American soil, on September 11, 2011.

The AFDI Islamic Jew-hatred ad on a San Francisco city bus.

Triumphant after a long legal battle with the New York City MTA, in which we won the right to run our "Civilized Man" ads in response to a vicious anti-Israel subway campaign.

The AFDI Islamorealism ad on a train platform in Westchester, New York.

The ADFI Truth About the Qur'an campaign on subway clocks in New York City.

My lawyer, David Yerushalmi of the American Freedom Law Center, and I after making our winning arguments against the New York City MTA, with the ad we won the right to run.

Bosch Fawstin's winning cartoon in the AFDI Muhammad Art Exhibit and Cartoon Contest.

Floyd Resnick, my longtime chief of security, to whom this book is dedicated, at my side post-Garland for an AP interview.

Bismillah Ar Rahman Ar Raheem

"The New Era"

To our brothers and sisters fighting for the Sake of Allah, we make dua for you and ask Allah to guide your bullets, terrify your enemies, and establish you in the Land. As our noble brother in the Phillipines said in his bayah, "This is the Golden Era, everyone who believes... is running for Shaheed".

The attack by the Islamic State in America is only the beginning of our efforts to establish a wiliyah in the heart of our enemy. Our aim was the khanzeer Pamela Geller and to show her that we don't care what land she hides in or what sky shields her; we will send all our Lions to achieve her slaughter. This will heal the hearts of our brothers and disperse the ones behind her. To those who protect her: this will be your only warning of housing this woman and her circus show. Everyone who houses her events, gives her a platform to spill her filth are legitimate targets. We have been watching closely who was present at this event and the shooter of our brothers. We knew that the target was protected. Our intention was to show how easy we give our lives for the Sake of Allah.

We have 71 trained soldiers in 15 different states ready at our word to attack any target we desire. Out of the 71 trained soldiers 23 have signed up for missions like Sunday, We are increasing in number bithnillah. Of the 15 states, 5 we will name... Virginia, Maryland, Illinois, California, and Michigan. The disbelievers who shot our brothers think that you killed someone untrained, nay, they gave you their bodies in plain view because we were watching.

The next six months will be interesting, To our Amir Al Mu'mineen make dua for us and continue your reign, May Allah enoble your face.

May Allah send His peace and blessings upon our Prophet Muhummad and all those who follow until the last Day.

Abu Ibrahim Al Ameriki

The ISIS Fatwa, a call to target Pamela, "The New Era" by Abu Ibrahim Ameriki

Robert Spencer and me.

submitted these ads, they were running an "Allah is Greater" Islamic prayer ad campaign.

I was told by John Kehoe, a representative of Media Agency in London, that the London buses would not accept my ads, despite the fact that the buses were running ads proclaiming the greatness of Allah. It was Media Agency that suggested I run the ads on taxis instead. I agreed.

I had signed contracts and paid in full on May 13, 2016. On that day, we released an announcement: "AFDI—Taxi Supersides Contract Between Media Agency Group and Pamela Geller is Signed and Filed!" On June 27, 2016 I wrote to John: "John, Please confirm that the ads are up and running today." The following day, I received an email from Gabrielle Conneely of Transport Media, saying: "All taxis are now posted and on the road." But here's the thing: the ads never ran.

Transport Media lied. They said that hundreds of our ads were running on London taxis. When I asked for proof of placement—environmental shots of taxis bearing the ads on London streets—they stopped answering my emails.

If the ads had been running, there would have been an uproar in the *dhimmi* British media. *The Guardian* would have been furious that we dared to insult Muhammad by quoting his exact words.

Also, don't you think that if the ads had been running, every Muslim cabbie in London (i.e., every cabbie in London) would have been on strike and up in arms (some literally) and refusing to drive, or peeling off the ads, etc?

But there was nothing. Not one word.

The ads never ran. These perfidious Albionites wanted to lie to you and take your money. They never ran the ads.

Can you imagine what would have happened if they had tried to pull this on jihad or sharia groups?

On June 28, I wrote the following to Kehoe and Conneely, as well as to my attorneys in Britain:

> Please immediately supply environmental (street) photos of these taxis featuring our ads running around London. Despite your assurances that they are running, we have received no reports from our numerous contacts in the city of any sightings of these taxis. There has been no discussion of them, either pro or con, in social media or in the British press. Given the highly controversial nature

of the ads in light of the British political scene today, it is virtually inconceivable that these ads would run without either a murmur of dissent or one single affirmation of support.

We can only conclude that your assertions that they are running are not accurate, and unless we receive atmospheric photos forthwith, we will be undertaking discussions with our British attorneys (cc'd here) about possible legal action.

And so in August 2016, we filed suit, through my British law firm, Taylor Rose. We were fighting for freedom there harder than most Brits.

These ads should have run, and the British police should have been poised to defend the freedom of speech. This was yet another example of the crushing imposition of Islamic law in Britain—from my being banned from entering the country for the crime of opposing jihad, while the most vicious Islamic preachers who incite to violence and murder were routinely allowed in, and now to Sadiq Khan's transit authority stealing tens of thousands of dollars from those of us who are fighting for our most basic freedoms.

San Francisco Wages War Against Free Speech

In April 2017, in a unanimous vote, the uber-left San Francisco autocratic government shut down free speech on transit systems after AFDI submitted our latest ad campaign to the San Francisco Municipal Transportation Authority to run on buses across the city.[64]

Their action was once again emblematic of the left: Silence your opponents, as all totalitarians do.

Here is where the euphemistically named "Free Speech Movement" has taken us: not to free speech at all, but to oppression and tyranny. This was yet another outrageous violation of our First Amendment rights. Freedom of speech is the foundation of a free society. Without it, a tyrant can wreak havoc unopposed, while his opponents are silenced.

Inoffensive speech needs no protection. The First Amendment was developed precisely to protect speech that was offensive to some in order to prevent those who had power from claiming they were offended by speech opposing them and silencing the powerless.

Our latest ad merely called for support of President Donald Trump's immigration ban, and it ran the names of refugees into the United States who had been convicted of Islamic terror-related crimes. We intended to run it in sanctuary cities across America where the freedom of speech had not yet been banned. Sadly, the list of cities where it has been banned was ever-increasing. New York; Washington, D.C.; Boston; Miami and Chicago have all banned "political" and "cause-related" advertising.

Predictably, every news report on the San Francisco transit free-speech ban blamed *me*. Every news report ran photos of my ads only. No establishment media news report mentioned that my ads were a response to vicious Islamic Jew-hating ads. None of the news reports showed the ugly, vicious ads that prompted me to run ad campaigns on San Francisco buses in the first place. One group that has run anti-Israel ads is The American Muslims for Palestine, which ran an ad nationwide calling for "an end to Israeli apartheid and to unconditional American aid for Israel."

Once again, this repulsive, anti-Semitic campaign was nothing less than a Goebbels-style demonization of the Jews. I could not and did not let it go unanswered. The anti-Israel ads that have run all over the country used exactly the technique that Hitler's minions used. If you read the writings of Goebbels, the Nazi narrative was that they were the victims. They were the put-upon ones. That's how they sold annihilation. It's not surprising that Islamic supremacists would appropriate the propaganda methods of the Third Reich, as they partnered with Hitler and shared the same goal.

It's funny, but the very first time I saw one of these vicious, anti-Semitic ads in the New York subway system, before I had ever even imagined running an ad, I thought, how is that legal? How can they allow that Naziesque propaganda on the platform and trains of the New York subway system? It irked me, and it propelled me onto this road.

These anti-Semitic ads were a blood libel.

The SFMTA, WMATA, NYCTA or the transit systems in Chicago, Miami, Denver et al had no problem with them. But they banned political ads after I submitted ads. Our ads of truth made these quisling cretins curl and convulse in service to barbarians.

But there was a silver lining to this ban: the savages couldn't run their lies and their libel anymore. Their tactics in denying me my freedom of speech backfired against their own allies. Good.

The Back the Ban Campaign

In April 2017, I developed an ad calling on Americans to support President Trump's travel ban and listing the names of jihadis who had come from countries included in the ban. The names came from a list supplied by the Trump administration from Justice Department information. Besides the names, the ad read: "Trump is right! Back the ban. Names of US refugees convicted of Islamic terror."

San Francisco, the left-wing mecca of radical liberalism, moved towards shutting down free speech on their transit systems after we submitted this campaign to the San Francisco Municipal Transportation Authority to run on buses across the city.

This action was emblematic of the left: silence your opponents, like all totalitarians do. Here is where the euphemistically named "free speech movement" has taken us—oppression and tyranny. This was yet another outrageous violation of our First Amendment rights.

These bans are a ban on the truth, in accordance with sharia. They say they're just bans on "hate speech," but that's the euphemistic narrative. It was like putting a pretty white bow on a steaming pile of dung.

Circumventing the Ban

We are witnessing nothing less than the shredding of our most important and foundational constitutional right—and it's ongoing.

A federal judge in October 2015 ordered New York City's Metropolitan Transportation Authority to run a series of dishonest advertisements promoting Islamic agitprop in the subway.

Remember, the NYC MTA lost when AFDI sued them for refusing to run our ads that were designed to increase public awareness of the jihad threat. In response to our victory, and determined that nothing go up in their system that would offend delicate Muslim sensibilities, the MTA banned *all* political and issue-related ads and refused to run our ads.

Well, even though our ads were designed to raise awareness of the jihad threat, and the ban was designed solely to prevent our ads from running, the Muslims in New York City who produced the propaganda film *The Muslims Are Coming!* weren't having any of that. This was because, under the new ban, they were prohibited from running their ads as well. And so they sued to get around the ban and get their propaganda up on NYC's MTA systems, claiming that their ad, and the movie it was advertising, weren't political.

Make no mistake. *The Muslims Are Coming!* ad was political. This "movie" was nothing but agitprop for Islam under the guise of—you guessed it— making lame jokes about "Islamophobia." If that was comic, no one was laughing.

Nonetheless, the Muslims sued. And they won (of course), which showed how utterly corrupt the system was. A federal judge ordered the MTA to allow these dissemblers to run a series of advertisements promoting their film in the subway.

And no, *The Muslims Are Coming!* was not a film about the current invasion of Europe. It's political propaganda, a long diatribe about "Islamophobia," despite the obvious advantages of their status as Muslims in America today.

The Muslims Are Coming! poster campaign was a response to AFDI ads. So their ads could run, but ours couldn't? This was exactly why the First Amendment was enshrined in our Constitution—because who would decide what's good and what's forbidden? Sharia-compliant judges?

Where did these fascist fat cats think they were, banning speech that reflected the point of view they opposed? Did they think they were in Nazi Germany? The reckless and authoritarian Charles Moerdler, leader of the MTA board that implemented the ban, invoked Nazi Germany to enact the same restrictions on free speech that led to Nazi Germany's murderous reign.

Public service ads were allowed, and our ads were the embodiment of the public service ad. What could be more serviceable than saving your life?

And meanwhile, the New York and national media's narrative on this read like Al Jazeera. While the mainstream media routinely smeared our ads and us as "anti-Muslim," the media rushed to praise the purveyors of the "Islamophobia" myth, which was designed to intimidate people into thinking there is something wrong with opposing jihad terror.[65]

Jonathan Stempel wrote fawningly in *Reuters* that "ads for *The Muslims Are Coming!* contained what filmmakers Negin Farsad and Dean Obeidallah considered tongue-in-cheek statements such as 'The Ugly Truth About Muslims: Muslims have great frittata recipes' and 'Those Terrorists Are All Nutjobs,' with 'nutjobs' replacing the crossed off 'Muslim' to be 'more accurate.'"[66]

I was glad they won. *The Muslims Are Coming* opened a door for us. In

2016 and 2017, we worked on a groundbreaking new film on the Islamic war against the freedom of speech. In conjunction with Bad Mother Pictures, AFDI developed *Can't We Talk About This? The Islamic Jihad Against Free Speech*, a shocking new film and followup video series detailing the concerted effort by international organizations to compel the US and other Western countries to curtail the freedom of speech and criminalize criticism of Islam.

Featuring exclusive new interviews with Ayaan Hirsi Ali, Geert Wilders, Mark Steyn, Douglas Murray, Ezra Levant, Lars Vilks, Garland Muhammad cartoon contest winner Bosch Fawstin, and many other heroes of freedom, this movie will be the first ever to expose the war on free speech. It is certain to shock the American public and awaken many. These interviews reveal events at Garland and its aftermath that have never before been made public, and demonstrate how far advanced the war on free speech really is.

In this series, we're setting the record straight about our Garland free speech event, at which we were not only targeted by Islamic jihadis but apparently by the FBI as well. But we're doing much more as well: we're telling the whole, as-yet-untold truth about the war on free speech.

Hollywood will never tell this story. The media will never tell this story. Our public schools and universities will never teach our children what happened. The truth must be told.

Can't We Talk About This? was a followup to AFDI's acclaimed 2011 documentary, *The Ground Zero Mosque: The Second Wave of the 9/11 Attacks*. This much-needed new film gives viewers the inside story of what happened in Garland and why, and lays out the full and appalling details of the all-out assault on the freedom of speech that is taking place today—and why this may be the most crucial battleground today in the war for the survival of the United States of America as a free republic.

The web series also features seldom-seen news footage and revealing details not only of the Garland event and the jihad killers who wanted to wage jihad there, but also of the many other battlegrounds in the war for free speech that led up to the Garland attack, including the death fatwa issued in 1989 by the Islamic Republic of Iran against Salman Rushdie for his supposed blasphemy in *The Satanic Verses*; the assassination of Theo Van Gogh by a Muslim on an Amsterdam street in November 2004 for his alleged blasphemy; the Dutch newspaper *Jyllands Posten's* cartoons of Muhammad, published in September 2005, which touched off international riots and killings by Muslims—and most disturbing of all, calls in the West for restrictions on the freedom of speech; the Organization of Islamic Cooperation's years-long struggle at the UN to compel the West to criminalize "incitement to religious hatred" (a euphemism for criticism of Islam); and the US under Obama signing on to UNCHR Resolution 16/18, which calls on member states to work to restrict incitement to religious hatred.

Can't We Talk About This? covers lesser-known skirmishes in the war against free speech as well, such as Seattle cartoonist Molly Norris' "Everybody Draw Muhammad Day" in 2010, after which Norris was forced to go into hiding and change her identity after threats. And it traces what immediately led up to the Garland event—most notably, the January 2015 massacre of Muhammad cartoonists at the offices of the *Charlie Hebdo* satirical magazine in Paris and the subsequent "Stand with the Prophet" event in Garland, at which Muslim groups gathered in the wake of that massacre not to defend free speech, but to complain about "Islamophobia," while AFDI members and supporters protested outside.

We set out the media firestorm that followed the Garland event, as well as the attempts to kill me, and explain why the event's detractors were all missing the point: the freedom of speech doesn't apply only if you like the message; it applies to everyone. And if it is gone, so is a free society.

Can't We Talk About This? tells the whole horrifying story of how advanced the Islamic war on free speech is, and how close leftist and Islamic authoritarians are to final victory and the death of the freedom of speech and free society.

And it allowed us to circumvent the MTA ban. We bought billboards in Times Square and bus ads featuring our ads for the movie. One depicted Theo Van Gogh lying dead on an Amsterdam street, killed by an Islamic jihadi for exposing the plight of women under sharia. It reads "'Can't We Talk About This?' Filmmaker's last words as he was beheaded for insulting Islam." Another bore the same caption, with a layout that was a tribute to ads for Hitchcock's *Vertigo*.

There was a great deal of back-and-forth with the MTA. I didn't even deal with them directly, in case my name alone would bring a refusal. But the ads are running. We will never stop doing everything we can to get the truth to the American people.

– Eight –
CAIR vs. The Truth

AFDI Koran Ads

The Hamas-tied Council on American-Islamic Relations (CAIR) has deceived the media, cultural, and political elites in America for years, to the great peril of the American people. But we were fighting back.

Late in 2012, CAIR unveiled an ad campaign citing the Koran to counter our anti-jihad ads that were at that time running on Washington, D.C. Metro platforms. The ad read: "Show forgiveness, speak for justice and avoid the ignorant." (Koran 7:199).

This verse was actually abrogated. Islamic scholar Ibn Warraq explains:

> Now we see how useful and convenient the doctrine of abrogation is in bailing scholars out of difficulties. Of course, it does pose a problem for apologists of Islam, since all the passages preaching tolerance are found in the Meccan, i.e., early suras, and all the passages recommending killing, decapitating, and maiming are Median, i.e., later: "tolerance" has been abrogated by "intolerance." For example, the famous verse at Sura 9.5, "Slay the idolaters wherever you find them," is said to have canceled 124 verses that dictate tolerance and patience.[1]

Even though CAIR's presentation in this was thoroughly dishonest, citing the Koran was a brilliant idea. So brilliant, in fact, that I decided that would be AFDI's next advertising-education initiative. The objective of this campaign was to educate millions about the ideology behind the tens of thousands of deadly Islamic attacks since 9/11, the brutal oppression and subjugation of non-Muslims, secular Muslims and women, and the 1,400 years of jihadi wars, land appropriations, cultural annihilations, and enslavements.

After much consideration (there were so many vile texts to choose from) and terrific input from *Atlas Shrugs* readers who tweeted, commented, emailed, and posted at Facebook, I chose this verse to initiate the campaign: "Soon shall We cast terror into the hearts of the unbelievers" (Koran 3:151).

What a wonderful way to educate Americans about what actually was in that book. And so I rolled them out in January 2013 on the New York subways. We purchased all the clocks, over 220 of them, in all the New York City subway stations. We bought clocks systemwide—the MTA's term was "clock domination." The ads depicted the Twin Towers burning, with that same verse: "Soon shall We cast terror into the hearts of the unbelievers" (Koran 3:151).

This was our biggest ad buy ever, made possible by the overwhelming support of the American people, in response to our prior ads.

I loved this buy for so many reasons. Metaphorically, it was so powerful. The clock was ticking, from a civilizational point of view. Bombs, at least in movies, tick and are set off by clocks. The placement mirrored the urgency of our message. Also, these ads were much harder to deface. Islamic supremacist thugs and leftist goons often destroyed our other ads within an hour of their being put up. But in the New York subway system, the clocks hang from the ceiling, so the fascists couldn't get to the ads.

The MyJihad Ad Campaign

We kept on taking the battle to CAIR. Early in 2013, a war raged in the information battle-space over the meaning of the word "jihad," as violent jihad raged in Nigeria, Bangladesh, Ethiopia, Israel, Europe, India, and elsewhere. How Orwellian.

Slaughter? What slaughter? Nothing to see here, folks.

The cause of the controversy was the unintentionally comical, but deceitfully dangerous, CAIR #MyJihad ad campaign. CAIR ran a series of ads claiming that jihad equated everything from your daily exercise routine to making friends, in a total whitewash of the Islamic doctrine that sanctions murder and subjugation of unbelievers. Hamas-CAIR used women and children as human shields, taking a page from its mother organization, Hamas.

I formulated a series of ads featuring Islamic authorities and Islamic jihadis explaining jihad as warfare and violence. The fact that some Muslims don't associate jihad with violence does not cancel out the fact that so many do.

True to form, big media stooges ran fallacious "news" stories promoting Hamas-CAIR's campaign. The *New York Times* put its special spin on the dueling jihad campaigns, promoting Hamas-CAIR's bizarro fiction campaign versus the real jihad ad campaign AFDI sponsored. It wasn't just the *Times*. The outrageously compromised NPR also went to work, using our taxpayer dollars to advance the propaganda of jihadists—along with NBC, *Fox News*, and other big media outlets.

It was a large-scale attempt to disarm the American people. You can put a happy child's face on mass murder, but it's still mass murder. Our campaign made the point that minimizing jihad was minimizing mass murder and cultural annihilation. But NPR's Monique Parsons went overboard in her fervor to please CAIR.

She hit the ground running in her first sentence about "an advertising battle going on over the *Arabic* term jihad." It wasn't that "Arabic" was wrong, but it was misleading. Jihad is a religious mandate, and it's an Islamic term. Arabic is the language of Islam.

Parsons said our ads presented "jihadists as violent." Uh, no, they *are* violent. They are killing non-Muslims and more secular Muslims at mind-numbing speed. Counter-jihad blogs cover the mass slaughter, subjugation, oppression, and misogyny every day from Nigeria to Thailand, Ethiopia to Bangladesh, Egypt to Zanzibar, Mali, Malaysia, Iran, and countless other places.

Parsons went on to make the NPR segment about the dual meaning of jihad. Tell that to the hundreds of millions of victims of jihadi wars, land appropriations, cultural annihilations, and enslavements. She happily went along with CAIR's ruse of featuring women and children in their ads whitewashing jihad, in an eerie echo of Hamas' use of women and children as human shields for their jihadis. The tragic irony here was that countless women and children were victims of the jihadist war on innocent civilians. The horror.

Again we saw the poisonous fruit of the left's primitive motives. They work only off emotion and not reason. Parsons *felt* and thus acted, despite the body count. Parsons never mentioned CAIR's unindicted co-conspirator status in the largest Hamas-funding trial in our nation's history, or that the US government named CAIR a Muslim Brotherhood proxy in that same criminal court case.

CAIR has a long record of duplicity and deception. Although it has received millions of dollars in donations from foreign Islamic entities, it has not registered in the US as a foreign agent as required by the Foreign Agents Registration Act (FARA), despite spreading Islamic supremacist propaganda here.

Although it presents itself as a civil rights group, and is a registered non-profit organization (as well as the most influential Muslim group in the US, with active chapters in New York, San Francisco, Los Angeles, Chicago, Tampa, and many other cities), CAIR actually has numerous links to Islamic supremacist and jihad groups. CAIR founders Omar Ahmad and Niwad Awad (who still serves as CAIR's executive director) were reportedly present at a Hamas planning meeting in Philadelphia in 1993, allegedly conspiring to raise funds for Hamas and to promote jihad in the Middle East. CAIR has steadfastly refused to denounce Hamas and Hizballah as terrorist groups.

In 1998 Omar Ahmad, CAIR's co-founder and longtime Board Chairman, said: "Islam isn't in America to be equal to any other faith, but to become dominant. The Koran should be the highest authority in America, and Islam the only accepted religion on Earth." After he received unwelcome publicity as a result of this statement, Ahmad denied saying it, several years after the fact. However, the original reporter, Lisa Gardiner of the *Fremont Argus,* stands by her story.[2]

CAIR's spokesman Ibrahim Hooper once said in a quote attributed to a 1993 interview with the *Minneapolis Star-Tribune*: "I wouldn't want to create the impression that I wouldn't like the government of the United States to be Islamic sometime in the future."[3]

Several former CAIR leaders have been convicted of terror charges. Ghassan Elashi, founder of CAIR's Texas chapter, in 2009 received a 65-year prison sentence for funneling over $12 million from the Islamic charity known as the Holy Land Foundation (HLF) to the jihad terrorist group Hamas, which is responsible for murdering hundreds of Israeli civilians. Mousa Abu Marzook, a former CAIR official, was in 1995 designated by the US government in 1995 as a "terrorist and Hamas leader." He now is a Hamas leader in Cairo.

Randall Todd "Ismail" Royer, CAIR's former civil rights coordinator, in 2004 began serving a 20-year prison sentence for aiding al-Qaeda and the Taliban against American troops in Afghanistan and recruiting for Lashkar e-Taiba, the jihadist group responsible for the 2008 Mumbai jihad massacres. He was released in 2017 and went back to his old job of deceiving the unbelievers.

Bassem Khafagi, CAIR's former community relations director, was arrested for involvement with the Islamic Assembly of North America, which was linked to al-Qaeda. After pleading guilty to visa and bank fraud charges, Khafagi was deported. Rabih Haddad, a former CAIR fundraiser, was deported for his work with the Global Relief Foundation (which he co-founded), a terror-financing organization.

In 2008, the US government filed a memorandum in opposition to a request from two of CAIR's fellow unindicted co-conspirators, the Islamic Society of North America and the North American Islamic Trust, that their "unindicted co-conspirator" designation be removed. (It wasn't.) The memorandum is a useful and illuminating summary of what some of the most prominent Islamic groups in the US have been involved with.

The government memorandum explains how, shortly after Hamas was founded in 1987 as an outgrowth of the Muslim Brotherhood, the International Muslim Brotherhood ordered Muslim Brotherhood chapters throughout the world to create Palestine Committees, whose job it was to support Hamas with "media, money and men." To accomplish this, the Muslim Brotherhood in the US created the US Palestine Committee, which CAIR later joined. The memorandum explains that "the mandate of these organizations, per the International Muslim Brotherhood, was to support Hamas, and the HLF's particular role was to raise money to support Hamas's organizations inside the Palestinian territories."[4]

But in Parsons's way of thinking (I should say *feeling*), this was clearly unrelated to a news story on jihad. Got that?

It was astonishing. And it went on and on. Beth Parker, reporter for *Fox 5* in Washington, D.C., did a news segment on our counter-jihad ads in Washington and didn't contact me or anyone on our side for comment. No, the only opinion Parker got was from CAIR, although Parker never mentioned the bizarre and bogus CAIR jihad campaign running in Washington, which was the impetus for our campaign. How could she have avoided them?

Our ads were running in the same stations as the CAIR ads. It was why they were there. Was Parker clueless or complicit?

She was an incompetent tool—the quintessential useful idiot. Parker gave CAIR's Islamic supremacist executive director, Ibrahim Hooper, run of the mic to spew his libel and defamation.

Did Parker ask Hooper about remarks he made on his hope, as he said in a 1993 interview with the Minneapolis *Star Tribune*, that the "government of the United States would be Islamic sometime in the future"? Did Parker ask Hooper why CAIR was named a Muslim Brotherhood group in the largest terrorist funding trial in our nation's history? Or why they still are considered unindicted co-conspirators in the Hamas funding trial? Did Parker ask Hooper about CAIR's ties with Islamic extremism and terrorism? If she did, none of this was in her report.

That's what CAIR's jihad campaign was all about: aiding Hamas through the media. And the sick slave mentality of the media was vomit-inducing.

But this was another reason why our ads were so effective. These ads exposed the grotesque bias of a media aligned with the jihad force. This may have gotten reporters in with their leftist peers and compromised editors, but the millions of Americans and freedom lovers abroad thought these tools were idiots. They saw with their own eyes what jihad is all about. *They knew.*

Some, of course, refused to even allow people the possibility to see with their own eyes. The New York City MTA rejected these ads, and so we sued yet again. In March 2015, my ace lawyer David Yerushalmi of the American Freedom Law Center (AFLC) argued before the US District Court for the Southern District of New York on our motion for a preliminary injunction, asking the court to enter an order requiring New York City's MTA to run one of our MyJihad ads on New York City buses. The banned ad read, "'Killing Jews is worship that draws us close to Allah.'—Hamas MTV. That's HisJihad. What's yours?" The quotation came from an actual Hamas music video, but the MTA claimed that in reporting on this, *we* were inciting violence against Jews.

I was at the March 2015 court hearing, and let me tell you, the foes of free speech made some telling and fascinating admissions.

The foremost of these concerned CAIR. Yerushalmi asked Jeff Rosen, the Director of Real Estate for the MTA—that is, the wonk who decided what ads to take and what ads not to take—this question: "The MTA does have a standard that prohibits libel, does it not?" Rosen acknowledged that it did. Yerushalmi then asked Rosen about another one of our ad campaigns, which compared CAIR to Hamas and identifying CAIR leaders who have been convicted of jihad terror-related crimes.

Then came the bombshell. Yerushalmi asked, "Now, after this ad ran CAIR contacted the MTA and asked it to remove it on the basis that it violated the libel standard, correct?"

"On the basis that it was defamatory, yes," Rosen answered. Yerushalmi noted that the records the MTA turned over to the court for this hearing indicated that the MTA declined CAIR's request. Rosen was asked why. "My understanding was that their stated objection was that—was not with respect to the naming of the individuals but with respect to the equating of CAIR and Hamas and we did not understand that—based on review with counsel, we did not understand that to be defamatory," he explained.

Yerushalmi drove the point home. "Even when criticized or when challenged by the organization CAIR itself, the MTA allowed my client to criticize Hamas publicly," he said. "And would you understand as a lawyer that linking an organization such as CAIR to Hamas would be defamation, per se?" he asked Rosen (that is, if our claim had been false, which it wasn't). Yerushalmi then reminded Rosen that the MTA had asked us for documentation of CAIR's ties to Hamas, as well as records about the terror convictions of its officials pictured in the ad.

The bottom line: the MTA refused Hamas-CAIR's demand that it take down an ad exposing its links to Hamas because the MTA knew our ad was accurate. CAIR really does have ties to Hamas.

AFDI Counter-CAIR Campaign

We kept up the pressure on CAIR. The mainstream media in Florida glowingly reported in September 2013 about how Tampa's Hillsborough Area Regional Transit (HART) Board of Directors reversed its earlier refusal of a bus ad from the Florida chapter of CAIR. They generally misrepresented the new "acceptance" by HART, making the HART board look like a bunch of big, hairy Islamophobes for rejecting CAIR's cynical and deceptive #MyJihad ad campaign.

Yet, true to form for the mainstream media, they didn't have a word to say about our AFDI ad campaign that told the truth about CAIR and offered help for girls who feared they might become the victim of an Islamic honor killing. Despite the fact that the Florida media wrote about the new CAIR campaign, literally running CAIR's press release as if it were news, not one Florida paper reported on our ad campaign.

What did they fear? That their readers might learn something true about CAIR and its real motives?

CAIR's campaign advanced "embracing diversity," but there was no such diversity in their real agenda: imposing sharia. There is no diversity under sharia, evidenced by the slaughter of *kuffar* by Muslims in Kenya, Nigeria, and Peshawar that was going on at the same time CAIR's campaign was announced.

Our honor killing ad featured heart-rending photos of girls who had been murdered in honor killings, and offered help to girls who are threatened. It was part of our ongoing campaign to raise awareness and bring a stop to the phenomenon of honor killing. These girls have rights, too. They're human beings and yet they're completely forgotten in our politically correct culture. We were standing for the human rights of these girls.

Again, our CAIR ads were a response to CAIR's own campaign. Samantha L. Bowden, communications and outreach director of CAIR-Tampa, said, "We got to set the record straight of who we are and what we do."

I totally agreed: we did indeed have to set the record straight on who CAIR really was and what they were doing. That's why we were running our ads.

These ads were necessary because CAIR was not really the civil rights organization it claimed to be.

Our AFDI ads in Tampa featured several prominent critics of CAIR, as well as victims of the harassment that has been characteristic of the organization's response to those it perceives as standing in the way of its aims. The ads featured:

1. Muslims who came to CAIR for legal help and were suing CAIR for mis-handling their cases and defrauding them:
    a. "It was devastating. I was taken by someone who was supposed to care and represent my needs."[5]—Bayenah Nur, who went to CAIR for help and is now suing CAIR
    b. "CAIR represented itself as the nation's premier civil rights law firm to defend Muslims. Instead, they defrauded me and then cheated

me afterwards."[6]—Iftikhar Saiyed, a Muslim who went to CAIR for employment discrimination

2. Lawmakers and law enforcement officials who told the truth about CAIR:

   a. CAIR "has ties to terrorism" and "intimate links with Hamas."[7]—Sen. Charles Schumer, D-NY

   b. "CAIR, its leaders, and its activities effectively give aid to international terrorist groups."[8]—Steven Pomerantz, Former FBI chief of counter-terrorism

3. Revealing statements by CAIR's own leaders:

   a. "WHO CARES?"[9]—CAIR's National Communications Director Ibrahim Hooper when asked if American Muslims were among the Kenya mall jihad mass murderers

   b. "Islam isn't in America to be equal to any other faith, but to become dominant," and "The Quran, the Muslim book of scripture, should be the highest authority in America, and Islam the only accepted religion on Earth."[10]—CAIR's cofounder and longtime Board Chairman Omar Ahmad

4. A victim of CAIR's opposition to counterterror efforts:

   "[CAIR operatives] lie about my life most of the time and try to destroy my character, my capability, and my trust in the community."[11]—Abdirizak Bihi, Somali Muslim anti-terror leader in Minnesota who tried to stop recruitment in his state by al-Shabaab, the murderous jihad terror group behind the Kenya mall massacre, and was attacked by CAIR for doing so.

Did CAIR condemn the slaughter of non-Muslims under sharia? Had they addressed the oppression and subjugation of non-Muslims under sharia? Were they creating programs within Muslim communities to denounce jihad? What had CAIR done about the 80 percent of US mosques that taught and preached jihad? Nothing. Just the opposite: They deceived and dissembled in the cause of jihad.

But we countered with the truth.

This campaign was part of our ongoing efforts to defend the freedom of speech—as opposed to Islamic prohibitions of "blasphemy" and "slander," which were used effectively to quash honest discussion of jihad and Islamic supremacism. We were standing also for the freedom of conscience—as opposed to the Islamic death penalty for apostasy. And we stood for the equality of rights of all people before the law—as opposed to sharia's institutionalized discrimination against women and non-Muslims.

It was a fight everyone should have been fighting.

The "Truth About CAIR" Campaign

We took it to New York. In May 2014, AFDI placed "Truth About CAIR" posters on key New York City subway platforms, including Times Square, City Hall, Brooklyn Bridge, Third Avenue, 44th Street, and ten other stations.

These posters told the truth about this Islamic supremacist hate group. They showed photos of "CAIR Leaders Convicted of Jihad Terror-Related Crimes:" Ghassan Elashi, Mousa Abu Marzook, Randall Royer, Bassem Khafagi, and Rabih Haddad. Our poster also read: "The Council on American-Islamic Relations, CAIR, claims to be a civil rights group. In fact, it's Hamas in the US" And it again quoted Democratic Senator Schumer, "CAIR has ties to terrorism and intimate links to Hamas."

Because of its multiple ties to terror, CAIR should be shunned by all decent people. Instead, this unsavory gang of thugs was stronger than ever. Morgan Stanley and the local ABC affiliate sponsored CAIR's annual banquet in Chicago the year my "Truth About CAIR" ads ran. And the general silence regarding their terror-linked background has enabled them to infiltrate the highest levels of the political and cultural spheres.

As CAIR's influence grew in the media and government, this ad campaign was necessary to raise awareness among the public, to protect people from being taken in by this unsavory and unscrupulous group.

But these posters were not up a full day when Islamic supremacists, thugs, and Jew-haters were out in full destruction mode, defacing them with pro-"Palestinian" slogans. Truth to sharia adherents is like a cross to Dracula. Brutal.

But I printed up a stack of these posters, knowing how the vandals operated. The defaced posters were quickly replaced and I made an even bigger "Truth About CAIR" buy in other US cities.

The Islamic Jew-hatred Ad

I tangled with CAIR even when my ads weren't directly about them. In May 2014, I ran ads on buses in Washington, D.C. highlighting the Koranic roots of Jew-hatred and the Mufti of Jerusalem's World War II collaboration with Hitler and the Nazis.

The mainstream media in both the US and Europe quickly worked itself into a frenzy. Their worst nightmare was coming true: the truth was getting out.

We put these ads up in response to vicious Jew-hating ads that American Muslims for Palestine, or AMP, unleashed on Washington Metro buses in April 2014. Our ad featured a photo of the Grand Mufti of Jerusalem, Hajj Amin al-Husseini, meeting with Adolf Hitler, and read, "Islamic Jew-Hatred: It's In the Quran. Two-thirds of all US aid goes to Islamic countries. Stop racism. End all aid to Islamic countries. *IslamicJewHatred.com.*"

The ad did so many things. First, it exposed the long-kept secret of the collusion between the Nazis and the Muslim world. Second, it exposed the vicious anti-Semitic material in Islamic texts and teachings. Third, it informed people that two-thirds of all US foreign aid goes to Muslim countries.

Every aspect of this message was important. People today know little to nothing about how the Mufti, the most influential figure in the Islamic world at the time, collaborated with Hitler because of their shared anti-Semitism. The same Islamic anti-Semitism that informed the worldview of the Mufti, incites the "Palestinian" jihad against Israel today and Jew-hatred around the world.

The Mufti organized a Muslim SS division and was responsible personally for the deaths of hundreds of Jewish women and children in Europe, when he wrote to Hitler demanding they not be deported to Palestine. For those two things alone, he should have been executed. He was arrested in southern Germany in May 1945, but escaped while awaiting trial. Yasir Arafat, the modern godfather of terror, was the Mufti's nephew.

It was really a historic moment. These truths were finally being told. Therefore it was no surprise that the jihad-aligned media was in a frenzy to shift attention away from the ads' message.

ABC's Washington outlet quoted a bus passenger saying the ads were "racist." They didn't quote, of course, anyone in support of the ad. The uber-left Israeli newspaper, *Haaretz,* called the ads "anti-Muslim." The ads are "anti-Muslim?" Really? Are all Muslims virulent Jew-haters? Apparently *Haaretz* seemed to think so. That's what the headline implied. Funny how ads that were factual and true were called such names.

For much of the enemedia, the ad was all about... Hitler. Even for them, that was a stretch. It was amazing the lengths the mainstream media would go to avoid mentioning Islam, jihad, and what was actually in the Koran. In an article in, all of places, the *Times of Israel,* they didn't even run the ad, just a big photo of Hitler. In an interview they asked me where I found anti-Semitism in the Koran. I sent them twenty-four verses. They did not run one of them.

It was interesting how the media never looked into what was said in the ad—that Islamic Jew-hatred was in the Koran or that two-thirds of all US aid went to Islamic countries. No. They just obsessed over my unmitigated gall to repeat it. It's my *saying it* that was the problem. The truth was the problem. That was and still remains why we find ourselves incapable of dealing with the gravest threat this nation faces. The problem is that we can't talk about the problem. The American people are being disarmed and defeated by our own elites. These ads challenged that.

The international media went into a frenzy over this ad. Many "news" outlets called it an ad featuring Hitler, as if it were a Nazi ad. The international outcry was immense. The *Washington Post*'s fact-checker contacted me, asking me for documentation of the assertions in my ad—which I supplied to him. I also asked him why he didn't fact-check the numerous anti-Israel ads that ran in Washington and all over the country. He did not respond to my question or acknowledge the evidence I had sent him.

Hamas-tied CAIR, meanwhile, handed out free Korans in response to our ad. They never miss an opportunity for *dawah.*

CAIR's Executive Director, Nihad Awad, fumed. "This is a propaganda campaign designed to incite hatred against American Muslims, and this campaign has been based on false information, taking things out of context from the Koran."[12] Always "out of context." So many Muslims take the Koran "out of context" in the same way, and Awad never said a thing about that.

My goal was accomplished: to leapfrog over a media that was not even-handed, that was advancing the jihadis' propaganda against the Jewish State. And it was working. People were talking. That was a good thing even if the sharia-compliant media was hostile. The truth is a powerful thing, and so many people were unaware of Islamic history and the role of the Muslim world during the Holocaust. But when the ads ran, people finally were talking about the Mufti of Jerusalem and his support for Hitler.

Perhaps they would begin to understand and explore Islamic history and the terrible toll exacted by ignorance of that bloody history. Once understood, the Islamic/Israeli conflict makes complete sense, the Hamas charter (citing Allah and predicting that Islam would destroy Israel) and the jihad against the Jews makes complete sense.

Hamas-tied CAIR ultimately made a further response to the ad campaign with a deceptive and dishonest propaganda campaign of its own.

The CAIR ad featured a smiling trio—a Jew, a Christian and a Muslim—and a Koran verse: "Verily! Those who have attained to faith, as well as those who follow the Jewish faith, and the Christians ... all who believe in God and the Last Day and do righteous deeds—shall have their reward with their Sustainer, and no fear need they have, and neither shall they grieve" (2:62).

What CAIR didn't tell you, however, was this verse only applied, according to Islamic authorities, to Jews and Christians who converted to Islam, as confirmed by Koran 3:85: "Whoever seeks a religion other than Islam, it will never be accepted of him, and in the hereafter he will be one of the losers."

The Jews and Christians ("People of the Book") who do not become Muslims are vile: "Verily, those who disbelieve from among the People of the Book and the idolaters, will be in the Fire of Hell, abiding therein. They are the worst of creatures" (Koran 98:6).

An early Islamic authority and cousin of Muhammad, Ibn Abbas, says this verse was abrogated by Koran 3:85: "Whoever seeks a religion other than Islam, it will never be accepted of him, and in the hereafter he will be one of the losers."

CAIR knew all this and was trying to deceive gullible non-Muslims.

Oblivious to all this, Cathy Grossman of *Religion News Service* asked what I thought of CAIR's new ad campaign that hid behind "faith" groups that were systematically persecuted and oppressed under Islamic law. "The CAIR ad presents interfaith support for the Koran as a text that advocates peace and tolerance. Is this accurate in your view?" she asked me.

I responded:

Obviously Islamic jihadists the world over don't think that is accurate. CAIR never explains why, if the Quran advocates peace and tolerance, there are armed Islamic terror groups all over the globe that point to the Quran to explain and justify their actions, and yet apparently misunderstand its teachings. CAIR never explains why there are so very many misunderstanders of Islam. CAIR never explains why several of its own officials have been convicted for terror-related crimes—why did CAIR hire people who misunderstood the Quran? Don't they do any screening? CAIR never explains why its cofounder and executive director, Nihad Awad, has declared his support for the jihad terror group Hamas, which frequently runs calls for genocide of the Jews on its TV station. Why would Awad endorse a group that obviously doesn't know that the Quran teaches peace and tolerance?

Grossman went on to ask, "CAIR officials say they are buying the ads specifically to respond to your group's May advertising. The CAIR press release calls your organization a hate group and you 'a member of the anti-Muslim inner circle' who has been 'repudiated by interfaith leaders.' What do you think of that characterization?"

"It is a calumny invented by people who are determined to discredit all foes of jihad terror," I responded, "so that jihad terror can advance unopposed and unimpeded."[13]

Very little of this, of course, showed up in Grossman's article.[14] She got a great deal wrong—claiming, for example, that the Koran ads CAIR ran a few months ago were in response to our Koran ads, when actually it was the other way around.

Grossman described CAIR as "a Muslim civil liberties group," omitting the jihad-terror convictions of various of its leaders and the organization's Hamas ties. But Grossman printed every smear of our human rights group as a hate group. Anyone who opposes jihad persecution and slaughter is a hater. She even added that, "Rabbi Charles M. Feinberg, Congregation Adas Israel, said that because of Geller's 'vicious' ads, Muslims are 'being yelled at and disrespected.'"

Shame on "Rabbi" Charles M. Feinberg. What a betrayal of his people. What had he done to combat the vicious Islamic texts that are responsible for the unimaginable death toll of Islamic Jew-hatred over the past 1,400 years? What had this tool said or done about the vicious jihad against the Jews and the Jewish State? One could only imagine what these Islamic supremacists were saying about this kapo when he leaves the room.

Lies, deception, victimhood posturing—all in a day's work for the enemedia in service of jihad.

Evan Sernoffsky of the *San Francisco Chronicle* gleefully reported in January 2015, in an article titled "Anti-Islam San Francisco Muni ads defaced … with messages of love," that "a clever street art activist in San Francisco transformed anti-Islam banners on the back and sides of Muni buses into action-packed messages of love. The controversial ads, which equate Islam with Nazism, were plastered over with pictures of Kamala Khan, Marvel's first Muslim character, as well as new taglines railing against the posters' hateful message."

That's right: The *San Francisco Chronicle* called these acts of vandalism "love." The fallout of a decaying city. San Francisco, Haight-Ashbury—and all that jazz—carrying water for the most anti-gay, anti-woman, anti-Jewish, anti-freedom ideology on the face of the earth. You couldn't make this stuff up.

The supremacist criminals who did it called themselves "Street Cred." They should have been prosecuted to the fullest extent of the law. We filed a police report, but of course, nothing was done. And a reader of my website wrote a brilliant series of letters to the *Chronicle*, pointing out to Evan Sernoffsky that he was encouraging the commission of a felony.

Sernoffsky and those who committed the felony vandalism should have been arrested and prosecuted. In America, we are still a nation of laws, despite the best efforts of those like Sernoffsky, who wanted us to become a nation of thugs.

But it wasn't just Sernoffsky. Numerous people in the media and academia were lauding the defacing of our ads. Were we to understand that the media and academia were encouraging vandalism of speech they didn't like? It certainly seemed so. So it would stand to reason that if you didn't like the creed apartheid, Islamic Jew-hatred, gender apartheid and other hate speech in the Koran, the media seemed to be suggesting that you should vandalize mosques.

Coming so soon after the *Charlie Hebdo* jihad massacre, where 12 people at a satirical magazine in Paris were murdered over Muhammad cartoons in

January 2015, this cheering of anti-free speech vandalism is gruesome. In the wake of the *Charlie Hebdo* attack, the President of the United States should have gone before the world and said that it is now incumbent upon every freedom-loving person, news organization, and media outlet to run those cartoons of Muhammad. Instead, Barack Obama said nothing to erase the bitter memory of the fact that, two years ago, amid other Islamic attacks on free expression, he said, "The future must not belong to those who slander the prophet of Islam."

And so vandalism of ads that are critical of Islamic Jew-hatred was chic. Our ads were defaced with images of the Marvel Comics Muslima "super-hero," Kamala Khan. What was most ironic about this Muslima "superhero" was that she wasn't fighting female genital mutilation, honor violence under Islam, honor killings, misogyny, gender apartheid, creed apartheid, or the sub-class status for women under sharia. No, she was fighting truth. She was attacking free speech. She was enforcing the brutal and extreme sharia.

Now that was funny—and telling—that this was what a Muslima super-hero would end up really fighting.

Meanwhile, the Muslima convert "artist" who created this comic book joke of a character tweeted: "Some amazing person has been painting over the anti-Muslim bus ads in SF with Ms. Marvel graffiti. Spread love."

A cartoonist was carrying water for the ideology that killed cartoonists. A Muslima superhero that was designed to promote a positive image of Muslims being used against the freedom of speech. The *Charlie Hebdo* slaughter was the September 11 attack on free speech and free men. G. Willow Wilson and her Kamala Khan had enlisted on the wrong side. Kamala Khan had become a symbol of the war against the freedom of speech.

But in the case of my ads, in a certain sense, I applauded the vandalism, too. Because it accomplished just the opposite of what these leftist fascists wanted. First, the publicity got our message out to a much wider audience. Second, we negotiated with the San Francisco Municipal Transportation Agency (SFMTA), for recompense and additional free ad space.

Thank you, haters of truth!

These makeovers were so well done and numerous that clearly this vandal-ism was an organized operation, and likely with an insider's cooperation to get at the buses for the time it took to deface our ads without detection. This was suspicious in the extreme.

It took the SFMTA nine months—*nine months*—to run these ads. It initially refused, and it was not until we filed a lawsuit that the ads were allowed to run. And it allowed this?

But we kept fighting back in the courts, and winning. In March 2015, AFDI, scored another major victory for truth and freedom in another city where we had to fight to get these ads posted: Philadelphia. The court ruled that our ads highlighting Islamic Jew-hatred and the Nazi-Islamic alliance, which had been previously denied, could not be prohibited. The judge ruled they had to run.

It was a significant victory, but even then the enemies of freedom didn't give up. The Philly transit authority declared they would no long accept political ads. This new form of censorship came to be known as the Geller Ban.

After our court victory, we prepared to run our first ad campaign in Philadelphia, and apparently our last: the *Philadelphia Inquirer* reported that SEPTA, the Philadelphia-area transit authority, would not appeal a federal court ruling saying that they had to run our ads—instead, they were going to change their rules to prevent all such ads from running in the future. Imagine expending that much time, money and resources solely to suppress the freedom of speech.

"New advertising standards," said the *Inquirer*, "will be created to prohibit all political, public-issue, and noncommercial ads. By consistently refusing all such ads, SEPTA officials say they will satisfy... concerns that selective prohibitions violated constitutional free-speech protections."[15]

Philadelphia's decision was neither the first nor the last time that city authorities changed the rules in response to an AFDI free speech victory.

Time and time again, various city officials and dictatorial bureaucrats censored or banned outright our ads of truth and freedom, while allowing the most fallacious and libelous anti-Jewish, pro-jihad message to run. The mainstream media piled on, as in the *Philadelphia Inquirer* story about this rule change, which called our ads "virulently anti-Muslim," without ever bothering to discover whether or not Islamic Jew-hatred really was in the Koran, or to consider whether it was really wise of the US government to give aid to countries that encouraged that hatred.

This was essentially soft sharia enforcement: the prohibition of any criticism of Islam and of anything offensive to Islam and Muslim sensibilities. It was completely contrary to both the letter and the spirit of the First

Amendment, and so time and time again, we sued and we won. And time and time again, instead of looking after the taxpayer coffers and protecting and defending our freedoms, the fat dictocrats in charge of city transportation agencies and other authoritarian bureaucrats squandered tax monies on their legal fees (and ours), while working to abridge our freedoms.

Miami was the first city to change its rules, after Hamas-tied CAIR complained about our ads offering help to people who had been threatened by their families for leaving Islam. Then Chicago changed its rules after our campaign telling the truth about jihad ran to counter CAIR's cynical, deceptive campaign sugarcoating the grim reality of jihad. New York later changed its rules as well, again because of my ads.

In Philadelphia, not a single "journalist" in the mainstream media questioned even for a second the end-run around the First Amendment that these transit authorities were making by banning cause-related ads. I did three interviews about our free speech victory in Philadelphia: for WPVI-TV, *NJ.com*, and *the Inquirer*, and not one of them in their coverage of the case mentioned me or quoted a single thing I said.

The Lockstep Monster. Only one point of view was allowed.

Bob Stewart of the *Inquirer* was later apologetic, writing me after his story ran: "Unfortunately they halved my space for the story so it's a squeeze job. I'm sure you know the deal."[16]

I responded: "Actually, Bob, I don't know the deal. It is telling that not one of the publications that called me for comment used anything I said. Not one. Free press, indeed. It would be comical if the stakes weren't so bloody high."[17]

And they were. While America slept, these rule changes were rendering the First Amendment a dead letter. The stakes couldn't have been higher.

– Nine –
Jewicidals

When I was a kid I could never get my arms around how the Holocaust happened. Now, as I see Jews align with their worst enemies, I wonder how it doesn't happen more often. I love how I bring out the most cowardly and craven among liberal Jewish and Christian "leadership." How eager these knaves are to do the bidding of annihilationists and Jew-haters.

The *Denver Post* reported in December 2012 that "Colorado Muslim, Christian and Jewish leaders stood together in Denver's main mosque Monday and launched a 'Love Thy Neighbor' campaign—starting with ads on RTD buses. They said the ad they unveiled—at a time on the calendar devoted to love and understanding—is meant to respond to recent national tragedies and to replace anti-Muslim ads placed on buses last month."[1] The ads they were referring to by the manipulative and pejorative term "anti-Muslim" were, of course, my pro-freedom anti-jihad ads.

How silly. All decent and rational human beings love love. These self-righteous nudniks were standing with those who oppressed and subjugated their brothers and sisters. Why weren't these voices of love speaking out against the vile Islamic Jew-hatred that inspires the war against the tiny Jewish State? Why weren't these voices of love speaking out against the systematic extermination of Christians in Muslim lands? Why weren't these voices of love condemning the slaughter of Buddhists in Thailand? Hindus in Pakistan?

No, instead they provided cover for the most brutal and extreme ideology on the face of the Earth, and further obfuscated the most lethal threat the free world faces.

"Love Thy Neighbor." Gotta love it. There is no golden rule in Islam, clowns. This moral equivocation completely ignored the facts on the ground. Jews and Christians simply were not murdering people and justifying the murders by quoting their Scriptures. The violence in the Bible is descriptive, while the Koran's violence is prescriptive. The fantasy these quislings advanced was at odds with reality and the rivers of bloodshed in the cause of Islam. Never do we see Jews slaughtering in the name of HaShem or Christians in the name of Jesus Christ.

Not only that, but the Koran verse quoted in their ad ("And you should forgive and overlook. Do you not like God to forgive you?" (24:22)) was not a general recommendation of forgiveness. According to the revered and renowned Koranic scholar Ibn Kathir this verse, "was revealed concerning As-Siddiq, may Allah be pleased with him, when he swore that he would not help Mistah bin Uthathah after he said what he said about Aishah."

Mistah had accused Aishah of adultery, and Muhammad was anxious to protect his favorite nine-year-old wife. Abu Bakr as-Siddiq, Aisha's father, had said, "by Allah, I will never give anything (in charity) to Mistah, after what he has said about Aisha." But then Muhammad gave the "revelation" of Koran 24:22. Hearing it, Abu Bakr said, "Yes, by Allah, I like that Allah should forgive me." He then resumed giving Mistah the aid he used to give him.[2]

So did Koran 24:22 mean that Muslims should be forgiving and kind toward non-Muslims? No. "Muhammad is the Messenger of Allah, and those who are with him are severe against disbelievers, and merciful among themselves" (Koran 48:29).

You'll never see these Jewish and Christian clerics quoting that. And they weren't the only compromised clerics. In September 2012, I appeared on "Up Close" with Diana Williams, WABC-TV's public affairs show. I debated the Rev. Jim Wallis, founder and editor of *Sojourners*, who was launching his own ad campaign on the subways to hit back at ours.

It was a pity Wallis didn't get his group together to stand up when Christians, Hindus, and so many others were facing vicious persecution in Muslim countries. Where was *Sojourners* when Christians were victimized by jihad? Wallis, like the Denver group, was standing up for those who oppress and kill Christians. Wallis said that people might get hurt because of my ad. He assumed if Muslims became violent, it was the fault of non-Muslims, and non-Muslims were the ones who had to change their behavior to keep the Muslims peaceful.

The enemedia also made much of the fact that the far-left "Rabbis for Human Rights" group also took out ads ostensibly countering my pro-Israel, pro-freedom ads in New York and Washington. These rabbis claimed my ads were "hateful." Yet my ads spoke to the defense of freedom and individual rights for all.

There was nothing hateful about them. September 11 was hate. The March 11, 2004 train bombings in Madrid was hate. The July 7, 2005 train and bus attacks in London was hate. The 2009 Fort Hood jihadi shooting was hate. The attempted Christmas underwear bomber aboard a flight from Amsterdam to Detroit was hate. The Fort Dix Six terror plot in New Jersey was hate. And this was before the unspeakable attacks that would follow in this country at the Boston Marathon bombing, at an office party in San Bernadino, and at Pulse nightclub in Orlando. Pushing back against such hate is not hate.

I doubted the rabbis knew anything about the jihad doctrine that relentlessly seeks to violently impose Islamic law and pursues jihad against non-Muslims. I doubted they knew about the Islamic anti-Semitism deeply ingrained in the Koran and Sunnah, identifying Jews as the worst enemies of Muslims (Koran 5:82) and under Allah's curse (Koran 9:30).

When did they speak out against *that* hate, under which Jews suffer daily? When did they call upon Muslim leaders to reform the Koran and expunge its virulently anti-Semitic texts, which were routinely quoted on Palestinian Authority TV as justifying endless warfare against the State of Israel and Jews everywhere? What topsy-turvy moral compass did they employ to come to the conclusion that the "hater" was not the imams who routinely preached violence and anti-Semitism in mosques and on TV in Judea, Samaria, and Gaza, but me when I called attention to the barbaric cruelty of the jihad against Israel?

These foolish and deluded pro-jihad clerics will answer to a higher authority.

Jewish Day Schools

In December 2015, anti-Jewish attacks were spiking to record levels across the US, Europe, and the world (spurred largely by Islamic Jew-hatred). A "moderate" Muslim country, Algeria, had its army marching in drill chanting, "turn your guns towards the Jews in order to kill them, slaughter them and skin them."[3] On October 9, 2015 in a mosque in Rafah in the Gaza Strip, Sheikh Muhammad Sallah "Abu Rajab" exclaimed from the pulpit, "my brother in the West Bank: Stab!... Oh men of the West Bank, next time, attack in a group of three, four, or five. Attack them in groups. Cut them into body parts."[4] In another Friday sermon at a Gaza mosque on October 23, 2015, another Muslim cleric, Abu Hamza Ashur, brandished an explosives belt and screamed, "Oh people of the West Bank, kill them!"[5]

Amidst all this and more, I learned how Jewish day schools were preparing Jewish youth for what was coming. They devoted entire classes to attacking me.

Leftists are terrified of the truths I tell. They go to any length to make sure people don't hear what I am saying and then agree with me. But this time it backfired. I received this email from a student who had attended a Jewish high school:

> I am an 19-year-old college student. I just wanted to express my support and let you know that a few years ago my high school, Solomon Schechter Westchester, invited a speaker from Truah specifically to bash you for 45 straight minutes. Jill Jacobs said you were a bigoted racist who gives Jews a bad name. My classmates, upon seeing your bus signs and being told they were directed at Islam as a whole, not only jihadists, said they were embarrassed to be a part of your religion.
>
> I tried to walk out but was not allowed. I also had no idea who you were, and upon further research that night, I realized that I agreed with most of what you preached. I saw that you were far from anti-Muslim, only looking to stop the radicalization that the left is too afraid to recognize. I asked the administration if I could invite you in to speak, and they said no on the grounds that you preach "hate speech" and that the school doesn't tolerate that. That was the day I decided to graduate and never return to that cesspool of liberal indoctrination ever again.
>
> Anyway, in light of Hillary's recent comments on Trump I wanted to email you to express my deep concern regarding the direction in which this country is moving.
>
> Hillary said: "He is becoming ISIS's best recruiter. They are going to people showing videos of Donald Trump insulting Islam and Muslims in order to recruit more radical jihadists."

The obvious problem with her statement is the lie she told in the beginning. It's ironic how the left preaches that Islam is the "religion of peace," yet Hillary also insists that they can be so easily converted to terrorists by a simple video (sounds familiar).

Yet that is not the part that worries me. She lies all the time.

I have seen you say it for the past two years, but only now did I really start to believe that there are powerful people in this country who are dangerously close to implementing sharia. It states: "It is a criminal offense in Islam to speak ill of the faith, its Prophet Muhammad, and its holy Scriptures (Koran and Hadith)." Correct me if I'm wrong, but isn't this exactly what Hillary is trying to implement? She indicts Trump for speaking ill of Islam and essentially blames him for the expansion of ISIS.

Am I missing something, or are we not allowed to insult Islam in this country anymore? Not only is she naive enough to assert that Trump's comments are expanding ISIS, but in a way, she is blaming him and every other American who speaks out against the "religion of peace" for instigating this hatred. Instead of addressing the problems with radical Islam, she actually has the nerve to blame Americans practicing their right to free speech for the rise in terror. As if WE need to stop insulting Islam or THEY will commit acts of terror. As if WE should avoid addressing the problems in modern-day Islam because it might upset them, and God forbid we do that.

I supported your cartoon contest. Not because of any personal feelings towards Muhammad (although I do believe he is far from the "perfect man"), but because we need to stop pandering to Jihadists who want to intimidate us into silence. It is our right to make fun of him, just like everyone makes fun of Jesus, just like everyone makes fun of Jews. And it is not only un-American to try and silence those who do, subsequently blaming them for Jihadist terror, it is borderline compliance with Sharia.

Trump has never spoken ill of Muslims in general, much like yourself, only the radical ones. Yet the left, who is so keen on not lumping groups of people together (i.e blacks, Mexicans, etc.), essentially lumps all Muslims in with the Jihadists when they accuse you and Mr. Trump of being bigots and islamophobic. I want you to know that I and many others know the truth: that you are neither bigoted nor racist, that you have dedicated your life's work to stop Jihad and keep Americans safe. There are many of us, as you can see, who recognize your message and agree with your sentiments.

I'm sure you know all of this already, but I just wanted to reach out as a supporter to let you know that I recognize the threat of Islamic terror and I support your work in bringing light to the serious threat we face.

Instead of deconstructing and exposing the lie behind marketing the "Palestinian" myth, Jewish educators and lay leaders have aimed their poisonous barbs toward the proud Jews who are fighting for our people. Think about it. This is a pattern, like the Jewish charities who invited Nazi officers to their event dinners before they were deported and gassed.

The "Palestinian" myth is the "Palestinian" nationality itself. On March 31, 1977, the Dutch newspaper *Trouw* interviewed Zahir Muhsein of the Palestine Liberation Organization. Muhsein said:

> The Palestinian people does not exist. The creation of a Palestinian state is only a means for continuing our struggle against the state of Israel for our Arab unity. In reality today there is no difference between Jordanians, Palestinians, Syrians and Lebanese. Only for political and tactical reasons do we speak today about the existence of a Palestinian people, since Arab national interests demand that we posit the existence of a distinct "Palestinian people" to oppose Zionism.[6]

These Jewish educators are promoting this century's annihilationists before they, too, get their heads lopped off. The sanction of the victim. It's what John Galt meant when he said, "Then I saw what was wrong with the world, I saw what destroyed men and nations, and where the battle for life had to be fought. I saw that the enemy was an inverted morality—and that my sanction was its only power. I saw that evil was impotent—that evil was the irrational, the blind, the anti-real—and that the only weapon of its triumph was the willingness of the good to serve it. Just as the parasites around me were proclaiming their helpless dependence on my mind."[7]

Jewish day schools should be preparing children for what's coming. They should be arming them with knowledge. They should be informing them about Islamic Jew-hatred—the jet-fuel of the holy war against the Jews.

Instead, they take aim against those trying to defend them from what's coming.

Jewish Leftists Blacklist Me from *Times of Israel*

It was ironic and pathetic, but clearly illustrative of how damaged and sick Jewish leftists are, that a publication entitled the *Times of Israel* denied, not once but twice, my application to write a blog. They invited anyone and everyone, but denied me. Instead, they ran a defaming smear against me written by Fiyaz Mughal, the hate-filled, lying propagandist in the UK who supported the ban on my entry into the country.

Mughal has a notorious reputation in the counter-terror community. Remember, his TellMama group lost its government funding in the UK. back in 2013 for lying about anti-Muslim hate crimes.[8] Mughal is, in his way, just as destructive as the Muslim fighters who drop bombs to conquer infidels and impose sharia. Mughal drops bombs in the information battle-space disarming and deceiving the kuffar.

In his *Times of Israel* column, he whined:

> Geller seems to believe that I was instrumental in influencing a banning order being attached to her which is ludicrous since a number of organisations objected to her entry into the UK in 2013, where she was to give a speech shortly after the brutal terrorist murder of Lee Rigby. No doubt that speech would have contained toxic references to Islam and Muslims being a threat to Western society which is the general drift of her narrative. Whatever you may think of this position, and I hope that it would raise alarm bells, Geller plays the "freedom" vs. "Islamic tyranny" line like an orchestra in full swing. However, a deeper look at her past comments show more to her than meets the eye.[9]

Truth is now ludicrous. I didn't just allege that Mughal was involved; his involvement was clear from the documents released under the duty of candor when we challenged the ban. The documents were redacted to conceal who was behind the ban, but their black marker missed one reference, revealing that one of the groups complaining about us was Faith Matters. Faith Matters was founded by none other than Fiyaz Mughal.

Mughal added:

> Take for example, her belief that the Srebrenica massacre in 1995 was a hoax. In fact, she made these claims repeatedly. More bizarrely, she claims that Serbia was not a threat to its neighbours and that the Clinton attack on Serbia in 1999 was "in order to pave the way for an Islamic state in the heart of Europe—Kosovo."[10]

It did.

> Just to add insult to grave injury, in this article she stated: "The facts stand. Seven to eight thousand slaughtered (in Srebrenica) is not even remotely possible. 3,000 Muslim troops were redeployed without their families being told, (there are Muslim confirmations of this). No one 'saw' a single atrocity. And 38,000 out of 40,000 survived the 'genocide.'"
>
> By adding the quotes to "genocide" it was pretty clear that she was disputing that Srebrenica was a genocide and she was effectively a genocide denier. This in contrast with the fact that our previous Prime Minister, the Rt. Hon David Cameron MP had financially supported Srebrenica memorial day as a national event in the UK, precisely to mark the genocide."[11]

The continuing Islamic myth behind what happened in the town of Srebrenica all began with a big lie.[12] During the Bosnian War, both sides committed ugly atrocities—it was war, that's what happens. Little of the terror the Bosnians wrought on the Serbs is ever referenced. And yes, in that war, I sided with the Serbs. But to call a couple of hundred or even a couple thousand of deaths a genocide is a lie. The Muslim world refuses to call the Armenian holocaust a "genocide," and there were millions of victims. Many Muslim world leaders deny the Jewish holocaust was a genocide, despite the extermination of over half the global Jewish population.

Mughal's faux outrage was laughable. I've never heard him decry the ongoing genocide of millions of Christians in the Middle East in jihad wars. Mughal also excoriated me for saying in 2009, "Much like the Jewish councils of World War II Germany that helped assist in what would become the extermination of the Jews, we are witnessing Jewish groups like the CST aiding and abetting Islamic jihad and Islamic anti-Semitism."[13] They are.

Mughal added:

> In fact, more recently in 2016, Geller decided to once again attack one of the most respected hate crime organisation[s?] in the United Kingdom—the Community Security Trust. She stated: "This poll which shows a vicious Jew hatred among Muslims in the UK. This despite the subservience and craven cowardice of UK Jewish leadership. Jewish 'leadership' in the UK (including the Community Security Trust quoted here) supported my ban in the UK. My opposition to jihad and sharia, and my unwavering support of Israel led to my ban and these cretins supported it. Despite their grovelling, look at the poll results."[14]

Mughal patted the CST on the head like the good little doggie they were. They were weak and cowed, having long abandoned their true role of standing in defense of the Jewish people. These organizations are a pox on our house, standing by while Jew-hatred explodes. CST sides with the haters, throwing brave Jews who oppose anti-Semitism under the bus, much the way they did during our ban. Not only did they stay silent—they signed off on the ban.

Mughal also said:

> You see, it is not the fact that Geller ardently supports Israel that led to her ban and nor should it ever be the case. A simple and cursory look and review of her comments clearly show, without even referencing her anti-Muslim bigotry, that she was "not conducive to the public good" in the UK as the then Home Secretary deemed her to be. If anything, genocide deniers and those calling people

"House Jews" and supportive of far right media sources should stay where they are—in her case in the United States.[15]

"Far right," the leftist/Islamic dysphemism for pro-freedom voices. In reality, the fact that I was banned for being pro-Israel is quite clear from a document we received in our duty of candor request.

Mughal is, as has often been noted, nothing more than a mendacious grievance-mongering *taqiyya* artist.

AFDI Rally to Support Israel and Persecuted Minorities Under Islamic Law

August 18, 2014 was a historic day. For the first time, defenders of Israel and representatives of minorities persecuted by Islamic jihadists from around the world gathered together to stand for life and for freedom. Finally, the truth.

Thousands of people gathered in Union Square in Manhattan for our AFDI rally, and onlookers couldn't have missed the difference between our rally for life and the pro-Palestinian rallies for death. Our's was a true celebration with singing, dancing, and joy in living—a stark contrast to the genocidal Jew-hatred at the rallies for supporters of jihad.

We stood in Union Square, all the potential victims of jihad, in the coalition that needs to come together worldwide to defend freedom. We stood for life against death, for truth against lies, and for good against evil.

Our speakers provided harrowing insight into the full breadth and depth of the havoc and destruction that Islamic jihadists have unleashed upon the world. New York Assemblyman Dov Hikind gave a stirring appeal for Israel in its struggle against the jihad. He was followed by the eloquent Ethiopian Jewish spokesman Mordechai Tasman, and then an IDF soldier who spoke of his own experiences.

What was unprecedented about our rally was that these strong defenders of Israel were joined by others, including spokesman Haider Elias of the Yazidi, a Kurdish religious minority.

The singing and dancing was striking, exhilarating. This was most truly a celebration of life. We love life; they love death. This is our power. This is why we will win.

Predictably, the mainstream media ignored this groundbreaking event.

CBS New York interviewed me, but their piece on the rally didn't use a single word I said, and characterized the rally as solely pro-Israel, without any mention of our stand for persecuted Christians, Yazidis, Hindus, and others. Instead, CBS's report sympathetically focused on how many "Palestinians" were killed in Israel's defensive response to their most recent round of jihad attacks against the Jewish State. It was typical and egregious. There were speakers from all over the world, representing minorities at the front lines of Islamic persecution, including the Yazidis, and the media carried not a word. That wasn't newsworthy?

– Ten –
Garland, Texas: ISIS Attacks the Homeland

In January 2015, I organized a rally against an anti-free speech Islamic conference in Garland, Texas and the leftists were in lockstep, goosestep with the Islamic supremacists. Once again we got the foes of freedom riled.

Leaders of the Muslim community in America held their "Stand with the Prophet" conference in Garland in support of Muhammad and the restriction of "Islamophobic" speech. One week before people were murdered by jihadis at the *Charlie Hebdo* offices in Paris. The massacre was punishment for satire and even examination of Islam and Muhammad that the magazine published.

The event featured John Esposito, head of the Saudi-funded Alwaleed bin Talal Center for Muslim-Christian Understanding at Georgetown and Siraj Wahhaj, an unindicted co-conspirator in the 1993 World Trade Center bombing and close friend of the mastermind of that bombing, the "Blind Sheikh" Omar Abdel Rahman. Saturday's "Stand with the Prophet" event sought to combat "Islamophobes in America"—including me.

This was in line with Islamic supremacist groups' longstanding objective of defaming, smearing, and marginalizing anyone who opposes the jihad agenda. They said they wanted to defend Muhammad—which meant to silence those who noticed such defenders of Muhammad days ago murdered twelve people in Paris, adding to a global body count in the tens of thousands since 9/11.

Nevertheless, the Garland, Texas superintendent of schools allowed this anti-American group to hold this conference agitating for an abridgment of the First Amendment—despite the fresh horror that befell the staff of *Charlie*

Hebdo for violating the draconian sharia blasphemy laws mandating death for criticism of Islam. The Islamic law restricting free speech has no place in the American public sphere. It is anathema to the principles upon which this great nation was established.

The United States and other Western nations have paid insufficient attention to the fact that Muslim communities in the West have not made any concerted effort to expel supporters of jihad terror from their midst, and have done nothing at all to teach against the jihadist understanding of Islam, even though they ostensibly reject it. That showed the hypocrisy of this "Stand with the Prophet" event.

At our rally outside this sharia event in Garland thousands of freedom-loving Americans took a stand. Block after block, row after row, Texan after Texan, American after American, we said no to the restrictions against free speech as mandated under Islamic law.

The rally was an enormous success. Thousands of Americans joined us to oppose the most radical and extreme ideology on the face of the earth. They demonstrated their indomitable commitment to freedom. We will never give in, never submit, and never be subjugated.

The media coverage of our rally was vicious, ugly, and dishonest. It was extraordinary in the wake of the Paris jihad attack, where journalists were mercilessly slaughtered in cold blood, that journalists were covering and advancing the most extreme and brutal ideology on the face of the earth. The Paris jihadists screamed in the streets (while making a Nazi salute, by the way), "we have avenged the prophet."[1]

This conference was the same kind of initiative: It was called "Stand with the Prophet." And what did the media call it? A "peace conference." The local station WFAA ran a story with the headline, "Muslims group gathers for peace, faces threats, protest."[2] And the news story featured only smiling young women wearing hijabs.

This coverage and the "Stand with the Prophet" conference were both part of the same anti-free speech initiative. The Islamic supremacists are out for blood, determined to criminalize criticism of Islam (and opposition to jihad terror) under the guise of fighting against "Islamophobia" and "hate speech." The media cover for them.

Our rally stood for the freedom of speech against all attempts, violent and stealthy, to impose Islamic blasphemy laws on Americans and stifle criticism of Muhammad and Islam. As Muhammad's followers killed more and more people, we needed critics of him more than ever—and free people needed to stand up against these underhanded attempts to stifle all criticism of Islam, including honest investigations of how jihadists use Islamic texts and teachings to justify Jew-hatred, violence, supremacism, and oppression.

The foes of free speech never give up. And neither should its defenders.

The Muhammad Art Exhibit and Cartoon Contest

I wasn't about to give into violent intimidation. On May 3, 2015 I held the Muhammad Art Exhibit and Cartoon Contest in Garland, Texas, in the Curtis Culwell Center, where the "Stand with the Prophet" conference had been held.

It was a beautiful event. Geert Wilders was the keynote speaker and we presented contest winner Bosch Fawstin with a check for $12,500 for his winning cartoon, which depicted Muhammad saying, "You can't draw me!" and the artist responding, "That's why I draw you." That perfectly summed up what the event was all about: standing up against jihadist bullying and defending the freedom of speech. At the event, we featured historical images of Muhammad, many drawn by Muslims, alongside contemporary images of the Islamic prophet.

Everything went off without a hitch—until a member of my security team came in and told us there had been a shooting outside. Two Islamic jihadists from Phoenix, armed with rifles and explosives, drove up to the Curtis Culwell Center in Garland and attempted to gain entry to our event just as it ended. I was hurried to a safe room, while the audience was led to an auditorium in another part of the Curtis Culwell Center as police searched the area.

The jihadis wounded the security guard Bruce Joiner. He was shot in the left calf by one of the savages. Thank G-d, he has fully recovered. Both jihadis were then killed by members of the security team I had hired. Bruce Joiner was wounded in a battle that is part of a longstanding war: the war against the freedom of speech. Joiner is a hero in that battle.

We had been aware of the risk, spent thousands of dollars on security, and it paid off. The jihadis at our free speech event were not able to achieve their objective of replicating the massacre at the offices of the *Charlie Hebdo*. They were not able to kill anyone. We provided enormous security, in concert with the superb Garland police department. The men who took the aspiring killers down may have saved hundreds of lives.

Make no mistake: if it weren't for the free speech conference, these jihadis would have struck somewhere else—a place where there was less security.

So why were some people blaming me? They said, "Well, she provoked them! She got what she deserved!" The attacks against me were astonishing. Laura Ingraham was one of many on the right who attacked me. Ingraham is a devout Roman Catholic. I understand that Roman Catholics don't like their religion mocked. But Roman Catholics don't kill when their religion is mocked—and so no one talks about the importance of avoiding "provoking" them and how we must "respect" them. Roman Catholics have learned that. Mormons and others have learned that—look at the play *The Book of Mormon* on Broadway, which won twelve Tony Awards. The Mormon Church's official response wasn't a call for murder. Instead they released a rather measured and polite statement.[3]

Why must Ingraham condescend to Muslims and think they cannot learn tolerance? On the right, Ingraham was hardly alone in condemning me (although Ingraham has a history of flip-flopping of this issue—she supported the Ground Zero mosque before she didn't). Bill O'Reilly, Martha McCallum, Greta Van Susteren, the list is long. But by then I was not surprised, because there has for years now been an element of the right that is cowed, defensive, apologetic, submissive, and weak.

This incident has been a defining moment. Some I thought were true proved false, and some I thought were false proved true. Rich Lowry, Bret Stephens, and Dennis Prager surprised me with their support. David French and Ian Tuttle were wonderful.

Critics, on the other hand, said I was insulting an entire religion, a view held by our moderate allies such as Egypt and Qatar. They were wrong to assume we must submit to sharia in order to placate moderates, rather than saying that moderates need to accept the freedom of speech.

Even New York Republican Peter King blamed me for the assassination attempt on my life at my free speech event in Garland. The jihadis are endangering lives, not me. He is saying we should curtail our activities in the face of violent intimidation. If that's the best congressman we have on this issue, we're sunk. That is the road to surrender and slavery. I will never take it.

There has always been a subjugated, weak element of the conservative movement. That faction doesn't like me any more now than it ever did.

Garland was the first ISIS attack on American soil. Needless to say, every major newspaper and magazine attacked me in the wake of it. I was taken aback when *Time* magazine asked me to pen an explanation for why I did what I did. I was, of course, only too happy to oblige.

If it is hate to stand up for free speech, we are in big trouble.

The media and the cultural and political elites continue to self-enforce sharia without the consent of the American people.

This is ultimately not about me; it is about whether America will stand for freedom or surrender.

In December 2016, while hitting President-elect Trump and supposedly defending the freedom of speech, Megyn Kelly on NPR referred to "Pam [sic] Geller, who there's no question is a hateful person, who held this Draw Muhammad contest down in Texas."

Kelly said this in the context of defending the freedom of speech: "Now she's a provocateur and she's not a fan of anyone who's Muslim from the sound of what she says, but this is America and she has the right to say those things. And she has the right to have a contest like that."[4]

But in smearing me as "hateful," Kelly demonstrated that she didn't really know what was at stake when Islamic jihadis attacked our free speech event in Garland. Why was I hateful for standing for the First Amendment? Was she copying the tactics of Islamic propagandists, smearing as "hateful" those of us who refused to submit to the most brutal and extreme ideology on the face of the earth?

And I was a "provocateur"? Why? The Garland attack was part of a long-standing jihad war against the freedom of speech. Those who say I provoked the jihadis don't remember, or care to remember, that as jihadis were killing the twelve Muhammad cartoonists in Paris, their accomplice was murdering four Jews in a nearby kosher supermarket. Were the Jews "hateful"? Did they "provoke" the jihadis?

I held the event in the same venue where Muslim leaders held a conference in support of sharia, in support of the ideology behind the *Charlie Hebdo* jihad massacre. Was that provocative? Should we submit to the devout Muslims who use violence to impose the speech laws under the sharia?

Drawing Muhammad offends Islamic jihadists? So does being Jewish, as many anti-Semitic attacks have proven, or being gay. Or being a free woman. How much accommodation of any kind should we give to murderous savagery? To kowtow to violent intimidation will only encourage more of it.

Megyn Kelly should know that.

What did Megyn Kelly know about my work as a whole? What did she do to help Rifqa Bary, the Ohio teenager who was threatened with death by her father for converting from Islam to Christianity? What had Megyn Kelly done for the other Muslim girls who wanted to live a free life, and whom I helped to safety?

Megyn Kelly never had me on her show while she was on Fox. She covered the jihad attack against our free speech event in Texas for over a week but did not have me on. How does she know what I think, or why I did what I did? She made her "stand" for free speech regarding the Garland jihad attack while excoriating me. The thing about Kelly is that she assumed my mantle and championed my work while attacking and smearing me; that is the hallmark of a true second-hander.

Meanwhile, the scalawags, scoundrels, and misanthropes to whom she gave a platform on her show were reprehensible. Kelly had oppressors and terror-tied operatives on her show, including representatives of CAIR. The January 2016 lovefest between Kelly and Michael Moore on her Fox show pulled the curtain back. It was jarring. Even the *Washington Post* called it "a televised love-in."[5] When she moved to NBC, Fox added value by subtracting her.

This is a war.

Now, after the *Charlie Hebdo* attack, and after the Garland attack, what are we going to do? Are we going to surrender to these monsters?

The attack in Garland showed that everything my colleagues and I have been warning about regarding the threat of jihad, and the ways in which it threatens our liberties, is true. Islamic law constitutes a unique threat to freedom of speech, the foundation of a free society that, without it, tyranny can wreak havoc unopposed.

Putting up with being offended is essential in a pluralistic society in which people differ on basic truths. If a group will not stand for being offended without resorting to violence, that group will rule unopposed, while everyone else lives in fear.

If they cannot be criticized in the United States, we are in effect accepting Islamic law as overriding the First Amendment. This would establish Muslims as a protected class and prevent honest discussion of how Islamic jihadists use the texts and teachings of Islam to justify violence.

Some say that "hate speech" should be censored. But what constitutes "hate speech" is a subjective judgment that is unavoidably influenced by the political perspective of the one doing the judging. Allowing this sort of censorship would mean nothing less than civilizational suicide. Many in the media and academic elite assign no blame to an ideology that calls for death to blasphemers—i.e., those who criticize or offend Islam. Instead, they target and blame those who expose this fanaticism. If the cultural elites directed their barbs and attacks at the extremist doctrine of jihad, the world would be a vastly safer place.

As I continue to say, you can try to avoid reality, but you cannot avoid the consequences of avoiding reality. The cartoon-inspired shootings in Garland, Paris, Copenhagen, and elsewhere, targeting defenders of free speech—and the raging jihad across the Middle East, Africa, and Europe—were the disastrous consequences of avoiding reality.

I encourage all Americans to watch the videos of the Garland event and see what Islamic supremacists wish to silence: basic, elemental free speech arguments.

But we are unbowed. Even when the venue was in lockdown and hundreds of attendees were ushered down into the auditorium, the crowd was singing the Star Spangled Banner and God Bless America. In the face of fear, they were staunchly and uniquely American.

To learn who rules over you, simply find out whom you cannot criticize. I believe if the international media had run the Danish cartoons back in 2005, none of this would have happened. The jihadis wouldn't have been able to kill everyone. But by self-censoring, the media gave the jihadis the power they have today.

We must take back our freedom.

The FBI and the Garland Jihad Attack

In March 2017, *60 Minutes* ran a segment on the art exhibit and jihad attack that followed in Garland.

60 Minutes revealed that an undercover FBI agent was in a car directly behind the jihadis, Elton Simpson and Nadir Soofi, when they started shooting.

Seconds before security guard Bruce Joiner and police officer Greg Stevens were attacked, the agent took a cell phone photo of them. There was no SWAT team or FBI counter-terror force in place. Nothing.

An FBI agent was in constant contact with the jihadis leading up to and during the attack. The Justice Department noted in its press release on the indictment of Erick Jamal Hendricks, another Muslim who plotted the Garland jihad attack, that he was in regular touch with an "undercover FBI employee" (UCE):

> On April 23, 2015, Hendricks allegedly used social media to contact Elton Simpson, who, along with Nadir Hamid Soofi, was inspired by ISIL and launched the attack on the "First Annual Muhammad Art Exhibit and Contest" in Garland. Simpson and Soofi opened fire, wounding a security guard, before Garland police returned fire and killed both Simpson and Soofi. According to the complaint, Hendricks also connected UCE-1 with Simpson via social media; communicated with UCE-1 about the contest in Garland; and directed UCE-1 to go to the contest. Hendricks allegedly said: "If you see that pig (meaning the organizer of the contest) make your 'voice' heard against her." According to the complaint, he also asked UCE-1 a series of questions related to security at the event, including: "How big is the gathering?" "How many ppl?" "How many police/agents?" "Do you see feds there?" "Do you see snipers?" and "How many media?" Shortly thereafter, Simpson and Soofi committed the attack on the cartoon drawing contest.[6]

CBS failed to mention that. We twice filed an inquiry with the appropriate FBI internal affairs division. We were summarily ignored.

CBS did not talk to us or ask us if the FBI warned us—which they did not. Nor did CBS mention that Geert Wilders, the leader of the Netherlands' second largest political party, was there and was targeted for assassination as well. Imagine if they had been successful. Dutch freedom fighter Geert Wilders was the keynote speaker; he has been living with armed guards for years for supposedly "insulting Islam." My colleague Robert Spencer has received numerous death threats from Muslims. Cartoon contest winner Bosch Fawstin drew Muhammad.

Did Obama's pro-Islam FBI want us all dead?

What other conclusion can be reached? CBS blamed the FBI spying on Simpson, which made him go rogue, and Soofi's business failing for his going jihad. Never the correct and obvious explanation: Islam.

But the big story was the FBI.

CBS's segment worked from the incitement, entrapment angle—which was absurd. These same jihadis, we learned, were plotting an attack at the Super Bowl and planning to travel to Syria to join ISIS, and we're supposed to believe they were entrapped? What could anyone say to you or me that would make you a mass murderer? Nothing.

While I do believe that undercover FBI agents have to play along with the jihadis they're dealing with, because in order to be in an informant you have to have credibility, it's a whole other thing if you're encouraging and cheering on the proposed murder of Americans who are standing in defense of the freedom of speech, and then not doing anything about it. Why did the FBI only have one agent there? And not a team waiting for them to shoot back?

We never got answers. In the wake of Garland, the media attacks on us were the overwhelming and overarching story. But outside of that, one of the stories that bubbled to the surface was that the FBI knew about the attack before it happened, but did not alert law enforcement or my security apparatus. When I first heard that the FBI had prior notice of the attack, I thought that it was very short-term notice. It was assumed by many people that the FBI had some sketchy prior knowledge but nothing particularly specific.

Now we learned they were in on the planning of the jihad attack, and did nothing about it. The FBI only got around to alerting Garland police about Simpson's jihad plans three hours before our event. It was Garland police, not the FBI, that coordinated all the super security efforts with our own security team.

One of the FBI agents told Simpson to "tear up Texas," and an accomplice of Simpson was even communicating with the undercover agent at the time of the attack. The *Daily Beast* reported that this accomplice, "asked the undercover officer about the Draw Muhammad event's security, size, and police presence, during the event, according to an affidavit filed in court. The affidavit does not specify what the undercover responded to questions about size and security."[7] Why not? Why weren't the agent's answers released?

They knew about the attack, yet they didn't have a team there in case the jihadis started shooting? It's hard to escape the conclusion that the Obama FBI wanted me and the other speakers at the event dead.

What was Obama trying to do? Teach Americans a lesson? Enforce the edict that he enunciated in the wake of the Benghazi jihad slaughter, that "The future must not belong to those who slander the prophet of Islam"?

If people had died at our Garland event, the murders would have had a blood-chilling effect on the freedom of speech in America. That, in my view, appears to have been what the Obama administration wanted—and certainly that's what the enemedia wanted in the wake of our event, as it gleefully and relentlessly blamed us for violating sharia blasphemy laws and getting shot at.

In July 2017, even the Garland police refused to release documents on the FBI agent who colluded with the Garland jihadis. We expect this from an obviously broken FBI, but the Garland police?

The Fatwa

Soon after the Garland jihad attack, ISIS issued its fatwa:

> The attack by the Islamic State in America is only the beginning of our efforts to establish a *wiliyah* [an error for wilayah, administrative district] in the heart of our enemy. Our aim was the *khanzeer* [pig] Pamela Geller and to show her that we don't care what land she hides in or what sky shields her; we will send all our Lions to achieve her slaughter. This will heal the hearts of our brothers and disperse the ones behind her. To those who protect her: this will be your only warning of housing this woman and her circus show. Everyone who houses her events, gives her a platform to spill her filth are legitimate targets. We have been watching closely who was present at this event and the shooter of our brothers. We knew that the target was protected. Our intention was to show how easy we give our lives for the Sake of Allah.[8]

This was just the beginning. After the ISIS fatwa, I got so many death threats it became a daily occurrence. Jihadis gave out what they thought was my home address on Twitter, calling for me to be murdered. Police camped at the entrance to my building. Once I found a live shell right outside my door; I don't think the police left it there.

One typical email I received from a Muslim at that time read: "You deserve to be raped in every hole by hordes of Muslims, slapping and choking you, spitting in your mouth and pissing in ya face."[9]

Another Muslim wrote on my Facebook page: "If there is a freedom of speech to insult Islam, then there is a freedom of killing those who insulted Islam."[10]

Another Muslim posted pictures of me next to photos of bloody dismembered bodies, and wrote: "Bitch and the infidel and the insect to hear if they do not cancel your page on Facebook that insulted Muslims try to follow you where .saqom I will withdraw the bones of your body the greatness of his bone and do I cut Naked body parts and burned in front of Aailtk.accaffr Aasalibih Stdfie I swear to you the price of your life. The bomb around your home and be in the grave."[11]

Facebook didn't take down *his* page, of course, but I've had mine censored many times.

I debated British jihadi Anjem Choudary on *Hannity*. We discussed the fatwa issued against me by ISIS. When I pointed out to Choudary that the ISIS alert referred to me as "*khanzeer*" (pig—the same term Muhammad used before he beheaded thousands of Jews), he said *khanzeer* [pig] was a term too good for me.[12]

Andrew Bostom pointed out, "But not once has *Hannity*... informed the *Fox News* viewing audience that this ugly, Jew-hating reference derives from a specific verse in the Koran, sura (chapter) 5, verse 60 (Koran 5:60)."[13]

The Boston Plot

I heard about the jihadist plot to behead me when CNN called me for comment, citing anonymous law enforcement sources. I neither confirmed nor denied. I knew nothing.

When the plot came to light, Boston Police Commissioner William Evans confirmed that a knife-wielding jihadi fatally shot by terror investigators had "discussed beheading a well-known conservative blogger before changing his target to police officers."[14]

USA Today reported that "Evans confirmed on the *Today* show that the person Rahim had targeted was New York-based blogger Pamela Geller, an outspoken anti-Muslim activist."[15]

When it came to light in June 2015 that Boston jihadis Usaama Rahim, Dawud Sharif Abdul Khaliq (David Wright), and Nicholas Rovinski were plotting to behead me, the mainstream media went into full panic mode, trying to deny the plot against me and downplay its significance.[16]

The media wanted to make it all about Pamela Geller—"controversial," "provocative," "inciteful"—as if they thought that if they got rid of me, they would be rid of the problem.

The media has been avoiding reality since 9/11, and now we are suffering the consequence. There is a problem in Islam with or without Pamela Geller. By virtue of this jihadist murder plot against me, I became the proxy for every freedom-loving American who refuses to submit to violent intimidation.

I am the Islamic State's target because I am, unlike most of the mainstream media, refusing to bow down to them and submit to their dictates. They want to make an example out of me in order to frighten the rest of the US into silence and submission—that is, to frighten those who have not already submitted.

I am often asked, "Aren't you afraid?" Of course, but it is far scarier to do nothing.

This is not about me. They mean to kill everyone who doesn't do their bidding and abide by them voluntarily.

This is a showdown for American freedom. Will we stand against this savagery, or bow down to them and silence ourselves?

Rahim ultimately grew impatient with the prospect of traveling to New York to kill me, and decided to attack a police officer in Boston. He was killed. But this won't end with me or with the police whom Rahim and Abdul Khaliq ultimately decided to target, because the Islamic State and other jihadis have vowed nothing less than to destroy America. They have detailed manuals plotting full-scale insurrection and blood in the streets here. The attempt to kill me was was another step toward forcing the US into subjugation.

The one thing that was consistently ignored that came out of Garland was that ISIS was not just coming, it was here. And we are thwarting attacks on a now weekly, sometime daily, basis.

Will the media realize what's at stake, and that their heads are next, or continue to target me because they hate my message of freedom? Even after the Boston plot was uncovered, they continued to target me. Nor has law enforcement shown any particular interest.

Reuters ran the headline, "Activist says Boston beheading plot targeted her; police express doubt."[17]

That was just a blatant lie. These people were depraved. Considering the horror, the planned savagery against an American citizen for supporting free speech, *Reuters* had nothing to say about the jihadists, the mosque, the ideology, the gore—instead, they just made stuff up to demonize and smear someone fighting for freedom.

Braying for blood.

What's more, before I ever heard of this plot, the FBI asked me for an urgent meeting, at which they told me that something serious was being planned. But they wouldn't tell me what it was. Now we know.

Meanwhile, people saw me being targeted and thought, "Well, that's her business," or, "She provoked them." They didn't realize that whatever happened to me wouldn't stop with me. More demands would follow. The worst thing we can do is accommodate their demands—that will only prove to them that violence and threats work, leading only to more violence and threats.

Why isn't the media talking about who and what is behind their holy war? The Boston mosque that Rahim attended was a terror mosque—as was the Phoenix mosque attended for ten years by the Garland jihadis Simpson and Soofi.[18] Simpson tried to gain the respect of men in his mosque by quoting Islamic teachings word-for-word. He was featured in a 2012 video fundraiser for the mosque. And two other members of the same mosque, Hassan Abu-Jihaad and Derrick Shareef, are now in prison for jihad terror activity.[19]

Yet the imam to these jihadis claimed he was shocked by Simpson and Soofi's jihad—that they were gentle fellows. Are we supposed to believe that they learned Peaceful Islam at the mosque but were "radicalized on the Internet"?

Again, why aren't the supposedly peaceful teachings of Islam that are supposedly taught at American mosques not able to withstand the jihadis' appeal?

This mosque ought to be investigated. The FBI should be surveilling this mosque, impounding their phone records. Was anyone from the mosque in contact with Muslim groups in Garland? Was there any communication between Phoenix and Garland?

Several surveys have shown that 80% of mosques in the US teach hatred of infidels and the necessity to replace the Constitution with sharia. No one cares.

Meanwhile, the *Boston Globe* reported in September 2016 that

> one of the men charged earlier this year with supporting the terror group ISIS and conspiring to recruit others to a 'martyrdom operations cell' has agreed to plead guilty in federal court in Boston. Nicholas Alexander Rovinski, 25, of Warwick, RI, was charged in June 2015 with conspiracy to support ISIS. He was later indicted on charges of conspiracy to commit acts of terrorism transcending national boundaries, and obstruction of justice, and faces life in prison. He is slated to plead guilty Thursday."[20]

He faced life in prison after pleading guilty to two terror charges, but will probably not be sentenced to life. Mystery surrounds this case; he was supposed to be sentenced in May 2017, but then the sentencing was moved back without explanation to October 26, 2017.[21] The government was working on a plea agreement with Rovinski. There was a significant difference between Rovinski and his fellow jihad conspirator, David Wright: Rovinski came into the plot later in time, and played less of a role. The deal that will likely guide his sentencing will require him to receive a sentence of at least 15 years.

The maximum sentence for aiding ISIS is 20 years. The first count in Rovinski's case involved the initial charge against him: conspiracy to provide material support to ISIS. Prosecutors were unlikely to get a guilty verdict on that one, because while Rahim and Wright were both in touch with ISIS operatives in Syria, Rovinski was not. He reportedly has cerebral palsy and walks with a limp, and is very limited in speech and movement. Wright, not Rovinski, was the ringleader of the plan to behead me. The evidence is overwhelming against Wright.

In conversations that were recorded by law enforcement officials, Rovinski says very little. Rahim decided that he didn't want to wait until July 4th, which was initially the day they had chosen for their jihad attack.[22] He, of course, eventually grew so impatient that he discarded the idea of traveling from Boston to New York to behead me, and suddenly decided to kill a police officer in Boston instead.

In the conversations, Wright exhorts Rahim to stay firm, very much like the Blind Sheikh in the plotting of the 1993 jihad attack against the World Trade Center. Wright is speaking constantly. Rovinski is hardly heard.[23]

I am skeptical, however, of the possibility that he is repentant or has reformed. Rovinski wrote two letters from prison to Wright. He was still calling for beheading and clearly was a convinced and committed jihad terrorist, eager to murder for Allah.

Authorities are hiding the fact that Nicholas Rovinski has left Islam and returned to Catholicism, but I was told this by the prosecutor in the case, Stephanie Siegmann. The prosecutor told me that he has not only renounced Islam, but done so publicly, and has returned to the Catholic Church. If that is true, he will not be part of the privileged Muslim population in prison, and will not receive the perks they receive (better food, more time outside the cell for prayers, etc.). He may also be in danger from Muslim inmates who want to enforce Islam's death penalty for apostasy.

The Rahim/Wright/Rovinski jihad plot was to behead me, but of course, *Boston Globe* reporter Milton J. Valencia never bothered to ask me for comment when he wrote about it. It was typical of an enemedia that is only interested in allowing pro-jihad, pro-sharia voices to be heard.

Bottom line: if it were up to me these people would have been designated enemy combatants. This was not a law enforcement issue. This was war.

Nor were they alone. In August 2016, it was revealed that a Muslim in North Carolina was also involved in the plot against me. He posted this portion of the ISIS fatwa: "Our aim was (Geller) and to show her that we don't care what land she hides in or what sky shields her. We will send all our Lions to achieve her slaughter."[24]

Islamic jihadists want to make an example of me. They want to prove by killing me that they can and will act with impunity in the US, and that Americans must submit to sharia blasphemy laws—or else.

The tremendous cowardice of American media in submitting to their wishes and not showing Muhammad cartoons only encourages those who are calling for my death, as it shows them that they can get what they want by means of violent threats.

This is ultimately not about me; it is about whether America will stand for freedom or surrender.

I don't want to die, but I will not live as a slave.

– Eleven –

Freedom of Speech in the Age of Jihad

When the jihad threat is reported on, it's reported on only in the most twisted way. When jihadis attacked our free speech event in Garland, Texas they were not blamed, I was.

That was not the opening salvo. It was the closing bell. Anytime you step out over the red lines that have been drawn, you're going to lose a toe.

There was no premeditation in anything I did. From the very beginning, my work was just the normal reaction of a free human being. Everything I did was a reaction to something. I didn't one day decide to do bus ads; it all began when I was trying to help a girl who wanted to be free, Rifqa Bary.

That girl is alive today because of "Islamophobes." We are the only reason she is alive. Then it was on my way to the courthouse that I saw a bus ad that invited people to "Come to Islam." So, naturally, a light bulb went off in my head: what about those who are leaving Islam? And so began the Bus Wars. I never imagined that my ads would be controversial. I was just setting the record straight.

If anyone had told me on September 11, 2001 that pursuing the defense of freedom would render me radioactive and toxic, that those who stood in defense of freedom and Americanism would be smeared, defamed, and libeled, their good names and reputations destroyed, I would have had you Baker-Acted. But that is exactly what happened. The ugly and vicious attack on my work illustrates one of the enemy's foremost tactics in its war on Americanism and freedom.

This is not a career, but a calling. No one in his or her right mind would take this work on if not compelled to—if he or she didn't feel that it had to be done.

Most of the people who got into this work after 9/11 ultimately ran for the hills or trimmed back on the truth, incapable of withstanding or unwilling to withstand the withering campaign of personal destruction. It got so bad that my name became synonymous with racist islamophobicantimuslimbigot—yes, one word.

The well-oiled leftist/Islamic machine is enormous, with tentacles everywhere: the media, academia, social media, Wikipedia—it's not an industry, it's a cartel, a monopoly. They have billions, and they spend it. Everywhere.

That means this widely touted idea of an "Islamophobia industry" is patently absurd. In reality, there are little funds for this work, because so many people fear being associated with it. They decry a number they created, claiming $57 million went to groups that oppose jihad and sharia (this is the so-called "Islamophobia industry") over the past 15 years.

Mind you, this amount is dwarfed by the amounts that the purveyors of the "Islamophobia" narrative receive. Those who are making these absurd accusations are superabundantly well-funded: CAIR has received millions from the Saudis. George Soros rains money upon Media Matters, the Center for American Progress, and similar organizations.

The media hype about the "Islamophobia industry" is like an obscenely fat man begrudging a starving man a crust of bread.

But any lover of freedom would have been tarred the same way I was, and many have been. It is because my work, the ad campaigns, lawsuits, conferences, protests, and websites have been so effective that I am painted as such a terrible monster. I am but a proxy in this long war. What has happened to me is what happens, in small and large ways, to every American who stands for freedom.

If things continue the way they are going, Americans will wake up one day and not recognize their own country. Then they will say, *how did I get here?*

Our unprecedented freedom crippled America when jihad came to this country. It wasn't the horror of the largest attack in the homeland in American history. It was the war in the information battle-space. It was the war of ideas. The left's creeping coup on our most important and influential centers of academia, media, literature, music, film—upon our *culture* in general—led us to the present state of the world. The left worked hard at replacing our shared values of individualism and reason with irrationalism. The ideal of the rational man was murdered by the self-made savage—college educated, middle class savages. Americans were relentlessly propagandized until millions no longer believed in the reality of evil.

The Enemedia

In case you've ever wondered why you never got the straight story on Islam directly after 9/11, and still haven't, and why the media seems in the tank for jihad, here's a clue:

The Society of Professional Journalists (SPJ) issued a directive a couple of weeks after 9/11; for sheer propaganda, their "Diversity Guidelines" are hard to beat. In fact, the enemy who attacked our country in an attempt to bring it down may just as well have been writing the narrative.

The "guidelines," adopted at the SPJ's national convention on October 6, 2001, urged journalists to "take steps against racial profiling in their coverage of the war on terrorism and to reaffirm their commitment to use language that is informative and not inflammatory."

How? Among other things:

> Seek out people from a variety of ethnic and religious backgrounds when photographing Americans mourning those lost in New York, Washington and Pennsylvania.
>
> Seek truth through a variety of voices and perspectives that help audiences understand the complexities of the events in Pennsylvania, New York City and Washington, D.C.
>
> Seek out experts on military strategies, public safety, diplomacy, economics and other pertinent topics who run the spectrum of race, class, gender and geography.
>
> Regularly seek out a variety of perspectives for your opinion pieces. Check your coverage against the five Maynard Institute for Journalism Education fault lines of race and ethnicity, class, geography, gender and generation.[1]

Translation: *even if the horror, murder, and bloodshed of jihad are inflammatory, don't tell the people.*

There's more.

To deflect attention away from the Islamic character of jihad, reporters should "portray Muslims, Arabs and Middle Eastern and South Asian Americans in the richness of their diverse experiences."[2]

Portray the beheaders, the homicide bombers, and the infiltrators in the "richness of their diverse experience"? You mean the stonings, amputations, sharia, clitoridectomies, Jew-hatred, Christian-hatred, Hindu-hatred, the brutal conquests of India and Persia, the caliphate? Of course not!

Journalists, the SPJ directed, should "make an extra effort to include olive-complexioned and darker men and women, Sikhs, Muslims and devout religious people of all types in arts, business, society columns and all other news and feature coverage, not just stories about the crisis."[3]

In other words, make an extra effort to depict Muslims not engaged in jihad.

Above all, don't talk about the Islamic aspect of terror attacks, especially right after they happen:

> Avoid using terms such as 'jihad' unless you are certain of their precise meaning and include the context when they are used in quotations. The basic meaning of 'jihad' is to exert oneself for the good of Islam and to better oneself... Avoid using word combinations such as 'Islamic terrorist' or 'Muslim extremist' that are misleading because they link whole religions to criminal activity. Be specific: Alternate choices, depending on context, include 'Al Qaeda terrorists' or, to describe the broad range of groups involved in Islamic politics, 'political Islamists.' Do not use religious characterizations as shorthand when geographic, political, socioeconomic or other distinctions might be more accurate.[4]

Who cares if the jihadis call themselves Muslims and say they're fighting for Islam? Celebrate diversity!

The SPJ continued:

> Do not represent Arab Americans and Muslims as monolithic groups. Avoid conveying the impression that all Arab Americans and Muslims wear traditional clothing. When describing Islam, keep in mind there are large populations of Muslims around the

world, including in Africa, Asia, Canada, Europe, India and the United States. Distinguish between various Muslim states; do not lump them together as in constructions such as "the fury of the Muslim world."

Yet the "Islamic world" does. The *ummah*—a word you often hear in Muslim discourse—is the worldwide community of Muslims, regardless of national origin.

Instead, journalists should focus on largely imaginary backlash. "Cover the victims of harassment, murder and other hate crimes as thoroughly as you cover the victims of overt terrorist attacks."[6] And so the media dutifully covered the bogus tales of "harassment" just days after 3,000 Americans were brutally murdered by Muslims on our own soil. The same thing happened after the Fort Hood massacre.

The SPJ is telling journalists to throw Americans under the bus and kiss the adherents to the Islamic ideology that murdered our people and want to take over this country.

Then, of course, they reach for the cheap moral equivalent. "When writing about terrorism, remember to include white supremacist, radical anti-abortionists and other groups with a history of such activity."[7] There aren't any—except maybe three in an outhouse somewhere in Appalachia. But not to worry: make it up, or pull Timothy McVeigh out of your hat.

Just how long has the Muslim Brotherhood been strategizing the takedown and takeover of the US and the West? Decades. And while we have no coherent strategy for fighting the enemy—hell, we can't even name them—they have a war plan that is so detailed and exact that every *t* is crossed and every *i* dotted. That we are not fighting back effectively is, in large part, because the SPJ is doing its best to make sure no one knows there is a war on. As Osama bin Laden himself said in 1998:

> On that basis, and in compliance with God's order, we issue the following fatwa to all Muslims:
>
> The ruling to kill the Americans and their allies—civilians and military—is an individual duty for every Muslim who can do it in any country in which it is possible to do it, in order to liberate the al-Aqsa Mosque and the holy mosque [Mecca] from their grip, and in

order for their armies to move out of all the lands of Islam, defeated and unable to threaten any Muslim. This is in accordance with the words of Almighty God, "and fight the pagans all together as they fight you all together," and "fight them until there is no more tumult or oppression, and there prevail justice and faith in God."

We—with God's help—call on every Muslim who believes in God and wishes to be rewarded to comply with God's order to kill the Americans and plunder their money wherever and whenever they find it. We also call on Muslim *ulema*, leaders, youths, and soldiers to launch the raid on Satan's US troops and the devil's supporters allying with them, and to displace those who are behind them so that they may learn a lesson.[8]

Wonder what the SPJ thinks about that?

The SPLC's Hit List

In demonizing and marginalizing the rational and principled voices, by ruining them, the left is opening the door for the worst voices. Because at some point, people realize that they are just crying wolf—if they accuse me, a Jewish girl of Eastern European lineage, of being a Nazi, they have made themselves absurd. So by the time they're calling white nationalist leader Richard Spencer a Nazi, even though he really is one, no one takes it seriously anymore. If this movement is hijacked, the left did that. We were never Nazis. That was never who we were. But the left marginalized us and opened the door to skinheads. They don't have to smear, defame and libel real Nazis. Real Nazis do a fine job of it themselves. But they do it to us because we are not Nazis, we're rational and right, not racist or bigoted.

And so the Southern Poverty Law Center (SPLC), in a vicious hit piece on me, labeled me "the anti-Muslim movement's most visible and flamboyant figurehead."[9]

I am not "anti-Muslim," any more than foes of the Nazis were anti-German, but this label was one of the numerous ways I was stigmatized and demonized for my work for freedom. I've never been anti-Muslim, I've always been pro-freedom, and that's where this fight takes you—to the center of the culture war.

As the jihad threat grows, so does the enemies' war on our most effective leaders. The SPLC, traffickers in blood libel and incitement to murder, is a hate group that the left counts on to smear, defame and destroy those who are brave enough to oppose their totalitarian agenda. In October 2016, this Soros-funded opposition research smear machine produced a libelous "report" designed to destroy the most effective anti-jihad voices and mandate that our voices are never heard.

The SPLC report stated:

> These propagandists are far outside of the political mainstream, and their rhetoric has toxic consequences—from poisoning democratic debate to inspiring hate-based violence. The *Columbia Journalism Review* has said as much, pointing out that misinformation and falsehoods in media "may pollute democratic discourse, make it more difficult for citizens to cast informed votes, and limit their ability to participate meaningfully in public debate."[10]

It advised reporters to "use credible sources; don't give credence to the fringe," and sharply criticized "the politicians and pundits who seek personal and ideological gain by starting or spreading false memes."[11]

This was turning the truth on its head. The reality was this: it was the left and these well-funded, Goebbels-inspired hate groups such as the SPLC that, in their own words, "pollute democratic discourse, make it more difficult for citizens to cast informed votes, and limit their ability to participate meaningfully in public debate."[12] They work furiously to silence dissent and impose a totalitarian straitjacket on the public discourse regarding these issues. They only allow voices that toe their propaganda line about Islam being a religion of peace and Muslims as the victims, rather than the perpetrators, of terrorism.

And they call us "extremists," the same word the enemedia euphemistically uses of jihad killers—as if we were equivalent to those who blow themselves up and cut off heads while screaming "Allahu akbar."

All of their profiles of me, of which there have been many over the years, are riddled with falsehoods, inaccuracies, and outright lies. They claim that I insist that Obama is the "love child" of Malcolm X; that is patently untrue. The SPLC also stated that I "have spoken to a neo-fascist group in Germany," when in fact I have never even been to Germany. They quoted statements from me such as this one: "Islam … is an extreme ideology, the most radical and extreme ideology on the face of the earth," as if it were obviously false and offensive, when in reality it is true.[13]

The SPLC made no attempt to prove it was false. It takes for granted the far-left lemmings who swallow its lies will continue to nod their heads and go along, without stopping to think that—as murderous jihad attacks become a near-daily occurrence in Western Europe and soon in the US — maybe I have a point.

The SPLC also said that in 2013, I was "banned from entering the United Kingdom to speak to an EDL rally for fear of stirring 'inter-community violence.'"[14] This violence was going to come from one side only. The British government was afraid that if we were there Muslims would attack and, in order to appease them, they banned us. Our ban was a tacit recognition that there is a jihad threat. It was not a repudiation of that threat.

But the SPLC included this anyway, knowing that their readers would not put two and two together.

As the SPLC is a patent and obvious foe of the freedom of speech, it is no surprise that they would hate our Muhammad Art Exhibit and Cartoon Contest (which they erroneously called "a 'Draw the Prophet' cartoon contest"). They said it was "an obvious provocation aimed at Muslims, who regard graphic depictions of Muhammad as blasphemous—which drew two angry US-born jihadists who were killed when they attacked the event."[15]

So even when jihadis attack and try to kill us, the SPLC is on their side, because what we were doing was "blasphemous." The SPLC actually justifies murder in this case—but you can just imagine what they would be saying if a Jew or a Christian had reacted to blasphemy against his faith by deciding to murder the "blasphemers."

Some of their claims were bitterly ironic. As Obama was busy shipping hundreds of billions of dollars to the *mullahs* in Iran, the SPLC excoriated me for saying that he sought to "appease his Muslim overlords" and "wants jihad to win."[16] Did they not know that Iran would use those billions to fund terrorism? Or did they just not care?

"An ardent defender of Israel, Geller has described the press there as largely 'Jewicidal,'" they said.[17] After recent revelations about how Soros-funded groups paid for favorable coverage of the Iran deal and the Muslim migrant invasion, and the close collaboration between the mainstream media and the

Clinton campaign, the SPLC was still pretending that the enemedia was made up of fair, objective journalists.

Facts are the enemy to these haters and destroyers. Facts, evidence, *reality* are tossed off by the SPLC like some out-of-date, old-fashioned idea. Truth is "hate." Truth is "Islamofauxbic." Anyone who criticizes oppression, subjugation, and supremacism is smeared, defamed, and blacklisted. Posturing as humanitarians, vicious hate groups such as the SPLC are deemed legitimate authorities by cultural and political power players.

In reality, the SPLC is not a group dedicated to the defense of human rights. It is a hard-left attack machine. Vets, patriots, and freedom's defenders are in its crosshairs. Even Ben Carson, a black man and former presidential hopeful, was on their list of racist extremists until they succumbed to pressure—even from leftists—to remove him. They can't win on the facts, so they must silence us.

Hack Attack!

In January 2015, the anti-free speech thugs were at it again. *Atlas Shrugs* was taken down by a massive DDoS attack. It began on a Thursday, and three days later, on Sunday afternoon, was still metastasizing. This attack was unprecedented in its size and scope. Jihadis and their leftist errand boys were so desperate to silence me and my message that they devoted tremendous resources to take down my site.

My site host, Media Temple, said they couldn't cope with the attack. Never in their history had they seen anything like it. The DDoS attack didn't just take down my site. It also took down Media Temple and threatened all of their clients, and even attacked the servers that Media Temple uses at Net Data Center, a service provider that promises "uninterrupted operations." Net Data Center could not handle the massive traffic that the attackers were sending and finally had to pull the plug on *Atlas Shrugs*.

The timing was noteworthy. Our ads calling attention to Islamic Jew-hatred in San Francisco had gotten an immense amount of national and international press. And above all, I had just held a free speech rally to counter the "Stand with the Prophet" anti-free speech conference in Garland, Texas.

At that time, my website reached close to 100,000 readers a day (it grew considerably after that, despite their best efforts). No wonder they wanted so very much to take it down and keep it down. My website stood for the freedom of speech against all attempts, violent and stealthy, to impose Islamic blasphemy laws on Americans and stifle criticism of Muhammad and Islam.

In November 2016, I launched the redesigned website, *The Geller Report* (the new *Atlas Shrugs*)—sleek, fast, gorgeous, and smart. Like the women in our movement. On that same day my Facebook page reached over half a million followers, too!

For months I worked on a redesign of *The Geller Report*. I rebuilt and redesigned *Atlas Shrugs*, to provide more news and information in a more engaging format. The home page and home screen had a new, visual design built around big stories, trending headlines, and the latest news the enemedia censors and scrubs. Stories and photos load faster. Less waiting time! Easier to share! And so much more of the content you count on—truth and transparency.

The new site is also less vulnerable to DDoS attacks. It was important that we have the best technology, the best security, and the best platform after the previous massive DDoS attacks.

Behind it all is your favorite news curator, *moi*!

Suing the Social Media Monsters

For years, every day I received emails from readers and members of my various Facebook groups, asking for help after having been blocked for posting a story or comment that might offend Muslims.

This is America, not Saudi Arabia. Enough.

In July 2016, I filed suit.

The American Freedom Law Center (AFLC) filed a federal lawsuit on behalf of AFDI in the US District Court for the District of Columbia, challenging Section 230 of the Communications Decency Act (CDA) under the First Amendment. In a press release, the AFLC explained that "Section 230 provides immunity from lawsuits to Facebook, Twitter, and YouTube, thereby permitting these social media giants to engage in government-sanctioned censorship and discriminatory business practices free from legal challenge."[18]

The AFLC explained that we were "often subject to censorship and discrimination by Facebook, Twitter, and YouTube" because of our beliefs and views, "which Facebook, Twitter, and YouTube consider expression that is offensive to Muslims. Such discrimination, which is largely religion-based in that these California businesses are favoring adherents of Islam over those who are not, is prohibited in many states, but particularly in California by the state's anti-discrimination law, which is broadly construed to prohibit all forms of discrimination. However, because of the immunity granted by the federal government, Facebook, Twitter, and YouTube are free to engage in their otherwise unlawful, discriminatory practices." [19]

For years I documented the outrageous bias of Facebook's speech policies. Notoriously one-sided, those who oppose jihad terror, support Israel, and stand against the most brutal ideology on the face of the earth are systematically blocked and banned. In June 2016, Facebook took down my page and blocked me after a devout Muslim opened fire on a gay nightclub in Orlando, Florida. Forty-nine people were murdered. It was the most deadly terrorist attack on US soil since 9/11. Facebook said they took down my page because of their rule against "hateful, obscene, or threatening" content.

But it was not hateful, obscene, or threatening to oppose jihad terror such as we saw in Orlando. Truth is not hateful or obscene. What was hateful, obscene, and threatening was Facebook moving to silence everyone who speaks honestly about the motivating ideology behind such attacks. And it is still doing so.

After the Orlando jihad massacre, they went into full damage control mode. Orlando showed jihad for what it was. They're committed to obscuring that knowledge and making sure people remain ignorant and complacent about the nature and magnitude of the threat.

They also banned my own account for thirty days. This has happened before—when I get too close to truths they want to cover up. They're afraid these truths will get out, and that people will start acting to remove the feckless and traitorous leaders who got us into this fix.

And to those of you who say, "Forget Facebook, we'll do without it," I say no. I am sick and tired of the suppression of our speech. We are unable to engage in the public square. And yes, Facebook is the public square. It's where we connect. We have to fight for it. Shouting into the wilderness is not freedom of speech. My Facebook page, combined with my other pages (SIOA, SION, AFDI), reached a million followers. It was a critical connection.

Facebook has immense power over organic media—the sharing of our information and news between friends and associates. I would say too much power. They're trying to change the discourse by restricting our access to information.

Gizmodo reported in May 2016:

> Facebook workers routinely suppressed news stories of interest to conservative readers from the social network's influential "trending" news section, according to a former journalist who worked on the project… Several former Facebook "news curators," as they were known internally, also told *Gizmodo* that they were instructed to artificially "inject" selected stories into the trending news module, even if they weren't popular enough to warrant inclusion—or in some cases weren't trending at all.[20]

"News curators," what a Goebbels-like term.

Those of us who connect on Facebook have known this for years. We see it. We feel it. Which is why it is critical for our Facebook followers to share our stories on their news feeds. It is up to us to educate people.

Facebook's unlawful, discriminatory practices have been mandated at the highest levels. In September 2015, German Chancellor Angela Merkel strong-armed Facebook's Mark Zuckerberg to censor posts critical of the migrant invasion in Europe. CNBC reported that Merkel was "overheard confronting Facebook CEO Mark Zuckerberg over incendiary posts on the social network."[21] What kind of incendiary posts? Pro-jihad terror posts? No. Merkel was angry about posts criticizing her policy of inundating Germany with Muslim migrants.

The CNBC report continued:

> On the sidelines of a United Nations luncheon on Saturday, Merkel was caught on a hot mic pressing Zuckerberg about social media posts about the wave of Syrian refugees entering Germany, the publication [*Bloomberg*] reported. The Facebook CEO was overheard responding that 'we need to do some work' on curtailing anti-immigrant posts about the refugee crisis. 'Are you working on this?' Merkel asked in English, to which Zuckerberg replied in the affirmative.[22]

This was so typical of the elites. They control policy, they control the media, they control the culture—but they can't control the people. And this makes them crazy. If they could, they would program the people's minds directly.

And so they try to change the people by restricting their access to information. My page "Islamic Jew-Hatred: It's In the Quran" was taken down from Facebook because it was "hate speech." Hate speech? Really? The page ran the actual Koranic texts and teachings that called for hatred and incitement of violence against the Jews. Up only two weeks, it had 10,000 followers. So who exactly was responsible for any "hate speech" that may have been present on the page?

When they took down the page, photos such as Pamela Hall's iconic photo of a Muslim holding a sign saying "Death to the Juice" at an anti-Israel rally in New York City disappeared. That photo is news. Facebook policy dictates that truth is hate speech.

I started a new page, "Islamic Antisemitism: It's in the Quran." But that page didn't live long on Facebook either.

Why was Zuckerberg scrubbing evidence of Muslims inciting people to commit acts of hatred and violence? Why did his policies allow for vicious posts and pages against Israel to stand, but exposing the truth behind that Islamic hate is prohibited? That's sharia.

Another time I received a warning on our "Stop Islamization of America" pages because of another actual photo of Muslims daubing a building wall with "Kill the Jews" and "Jihad against Israel." Meanwhile calls to "rape and dice" me appear on Facebook regularly and don't get taken down. I doubt they receive warnings either.

Dexter Van Zile, the Christian Media Analyst for the Committee for Accuracy in Middle East Reporting (CAMERA), wrote in 2014:

> Recently, my correspondents have alerted me to another page on Facebook. The end of the URL includes the phrase "The Truth About Jews" and the page itself promotes Blood Libels against the Jewish people. It's titled "Jewish ritual murder." The page has all the stuff you'd expect on an anti-Semitic Facebook page. It has 248 "Likes" and includes anti-Jewish libels from all over the world. The page includes a disclaimer that is simply bizarre: "Comments that are offensive, obscene, vulgar, irrelevant to this page or classified as

spam will be removed." The entire page is offensive and obscene. And the page, which has been in existence since March 2012, is an exercise in vulgar anti-Semitism.

Yes, people have complained about the page. And yes, Facebook has responded with messages indicating that the page does not violate the company's community standards. Will the page eventually be removed? Probably. But why doesn't Facebook delete this stuff when first apprised of its presence on their website?[23]

Why, indeed?

And there was so much more. *The Blaze* reported that "a legal group accused Facebook of favoring anti-Semites over Jews following an experiment it conducted. It created two Facebook groups with nearly identical content, but with the words 'Jews/Israelis' and 'Arabs/Palestinians' swapped."[24]

Shurat HaDin posted a video entitled "The Big Facebook Experiment," showing Facebook's anti-Israel and pro-Palestinian bias. Their pro-Israel group included a post saying, "Death to all the arabs," while their pro-Palestinian group included a post saying, "Death to all the jews."

Then they reported both groups to Facebook. The pro-Israel group was taken down. The pro-Palestinian group wasn't.

Nitsana Darshan-Leitner of Shurat Hadin commented:

Facebook's management is required to act immediately against the blatant incitement being waged for years against Jews and Israelis in the social network it owns and manages. The in-depth investigation we conducted proves beyond any shadow of a doubt that [Facebook's] claims of equality in the face of its conduct against any individual or group of people are at best erroneous and false in the worst case…

It cannot be that in 2015 a publicly traded commercial company will carry out a racist policy which so blatantly discriminates in favor of any party. The investigation we conducted proves that indeed there is bias in favor of one political party and against Israelis and Jews in particular. Jews and Israelis around the world should be very concerned over the results of the investigation and understand that the most famous social network in the world is working actively in favor of the Palestinians.[25]

Facebook was increasingly doing the bidding of vicious Muslim thugs and supremacists. I received a number of emails weekly from Muslims living in Muslim countries who had left Islam and live in terror and fear of being found out. They pleaded for help and advice.

One group of Arab ex-Muslims, after having their material repeatedly deleted by Facebook, prepared a petition at *Change.org* asking Facebook to stop deleting Arab Atheist and secularist groups.

It was terrible and getting worse. As it continued to seize power and control, the left was venturing onto dangerous ground. We well know the bloody outcome of this trajectory. This has to end now.

In October 2016, the Obama Justice Department responded to our lawsuit, and leftist publications and pundits rubbed their hooves in glee.

In order for us to sue Facebook (which is our intent), we first needed to knock out the federal immunity statute, Section 230 of the CDA, which prevented us from suing Facebook. Our lawsuit was therefore against the federal government. Once we knocked out the immunity, then we could sue Facebook, Twitter, and YouTube.

In response, the Justice Department simply tried to dodge the issue, saying we were suing the wrong entity. Our lawyers issued a full-throated response, but before it appeared, the left began crowing, publishing hit pieces about our case filled with hyperbole and nonsense. The government filed a very predictable motion that, unsurprisingly, raised two issues: our standing to sue and state action. To have standing to sue, one must show an injury in fact that is fairly traceable to the action one is challenging, and that can be redressed by the court. The government conceded in its motion that we showed that.

However, the government argued that the injury was from the social media giants and thus not fairly traceable to them, and therefore the injury was also not redressable by the court. But "fairly traceable" did not require a direct injury from the entity being sued. If the action we are challenging materially increased the probability of injury, we have met that standard. And we clearly have: as everyone knows, the *only* reason why social media can discriminate against us the way they do is because of the immunity granted by the federal government.

The second argument that the Justice Department made in its response to us related in many ways to the first. The DOJ argued there was no constitutional violation because the harm caused (the censorship) was by a private actor (social media). That was generally true, *but* the Supreme Court has declared in *Denver Area Educ. Telcomms. Consortium* that the government is responsible when it enacts laws that change the legal relationship between two groups, including the selective withdrawal from one group of legal protections against private acts, regardless of whether the private acts can be attributed to the government. That was the situation here, precisely.

The challenged congressional statute—which, by definition, is an act of Congress—alters the legal relations between us as plaintiffs on the one hand and Facebook, Twitter, and YouTube on the other, such that these media giants are permitted to censor, with impunity, our speech based on its content and viewpoint. Consequently, state action lies in the enactment of this federal statute, regardless of whether the private acts are attributable to the government. And the resulting injury is "fairly traceable" to the challenged statute and "redressable" by the relief requested. In sum, the government's motion should be denied.

Our response to the government challenge noted:

> Through the use of Facebook, Twitter, or YouTube, anyone person with access to the Internet can become a town crier with a voice that resonates farther than it could from any soapbox, and the same individual can become a pamphleteer. In sum, the Internet, particularly through social media, has become the new marketplace of ideas.
>
> Today, the impact of the Internet as a medium of worldwide human communication cannot be overstated. Social media, particularly including Facebook, Twitter, and YouTube, are exceedingly important for worldwide human communication and thus provide important forums for that communication. Denying a person or organization access to these important social media forums based on the content and viewpoint of the person's or organization's speech on matters of public concern, as in this case, is an effective way of silencing or censoring speech and depriving the person or organization of political influence and business opportunities.
>
> Businesses that provide Internet services in California, such as Facebook, Twitter, and YouTube, are subject to § 51 of the California Civil Code, which prohibits discrimination on the basis of political

affiliation, religious affiliation, or political or religious beliefs, including speech expressing those beliefs. Facebook's, Twitter's, and YouTube's discrimination against Plaintiffs as set forth in the Complaint violates § 51 of the California Civil Code, but for § 230 of the CDA.[26]

By way of Section 230, the government was empowering this type of discrimination and censorship. By its own terms, this statute permitted Facebook, Twitter, and YouTube "to restrict access to or availability of material that [they] consider to be obscene, lewd, lascivious, filthy, excessively violent, harassing, or otherwise objectionable." But this statute did not provide any kind of objective standard for determining which speech is "objectionable."

Consequently, Section 230, according to our response:

- is a content- and viewpoint-based restriction on speech;
- is vague and overbroad and lacks any objective criteria for suppressing speech;
- permits Facebook, Twitter, and YouTube to engage in government-sanctioned discrimination and censorship of free speech;
- permits Facebook, Twitter, and YouTube to engage in government-sanctioned discrimination that would otherwise violate California Civil Code § 51;
- permits Facebook, Twitter, and YouTube to engage in government-sanctioned censorship of speech that would otherwise violate Article I, section 2 of the California Constitution;
- confers broad powers of censorship, in the form of a "heckler's veto," upon Facebook, Twitter, and YouTube officials, who can censor constitutionally protected speech and engage in discriminatory business practices with impunity by virtue of this power conferred by the federal government;
- grants Facebook, Twitter, and YouTube and their officers, agents, and employees unbridled discretion to censor Plaintiffs' speech such that their decisions to limit Plaintiffs' speech are not constrained by objective criteria, but may rest on ambiguous and subjective reasons; and
- permits Facebook, Twitter, and YouTube to restrict Plaintiffs' speech based on its content and viewpoint.

Can we guarantee that the judge will agree with us? No plaintiff can ever do that, and certainly not in the types of cases we bring. If the district court judge dismisses our case, will we pursue this further, including possibly to the Supreme Court? Yes. This issue is too important. With this power of censorship, social media can seriously alter the terms of the public debate, and indeed, is already doing so.

For years I have documented the outrageous bias of Facebook's speech policies.

The left needs to handicap and shut down the opposition, because its positions do not stand up to refutation and cogent analysis. That's why the "liberals" are working hard to shut down free speech. Liberal, indeed. But we will continue to fight them every step of the way.

Late in 2016, the left-wing elites and their running dogs in the enemedia began one of their fictional publicity campaigns that they masquerade as urgent news. Their latest terror was "fake news"—a term that the Trump administration would soon turn against them.

The *New York Times* reported shortly after the 2016 presidential election that Google and Facebook "have faced mounting criticism over how fake news on their sites may have influenced the presidential election's outcome."[27]

That was fake news in itself: "fake news" didn't influence the presidential election's outcome, all-too-real news about the wrong direction in which our nation was headed under Barack Obama did. Nevertheless, the *Times* said that "those companies responded by making it clear that they would not tolerate such misinformation by taking pointed aim at fake news sites' revenue sources."[28]

How would they do that? "Google kicked off the action on Monday afternoon when the Silicon Valley search giant said it would ban websites that peddle fake news from using its online advertising service. Hours later, Facebook, the social network, updated the language in its Facebook Audience Network policy, which already says it will not display ads in sites that show misleading or illegal content, to include fake news sites."

A Facebook spokesman explained: "We have updated the policy to explicitly clarify that this applies to fake news. Our team will continue to closely vet all prospective publishers and monitor existing ones to ensure compliance."[29]

The "fake news" controversy became a huge international story, with the *Los Angeles Times* among those leading the charge with headlines such as "Want to keep fake news out of your newsfeed? College professor creates list of sites to avoid:" "Fake news writers: 'Hillary Clinton, here are your deplorables,'" and "Fake news writers abuse the 1st Amendment and endanger democracy for personal profit."[30]

There is conspiracy theory and there is conspiracy fact, and what we had on our hands at that point was one mother of a left-wing conspiracy. You can't make this stuff up. It's diabolical. In the run-up to the election, I reported on a number of fake conservative news sites created by left-wing operatives in order to discredit the conservatives. If you have a bogus conservative site, it makes a legitimate conservative site look questionable. "News sites" such as the *Baltimore Gazette* and the *National Report* were dropping hoaxes for months to discredit conservatives who might pick up the story.

I always understood that the objective was to taint the conservative news sphere. Sites were created to spread disinformation and shame the right-wingers who jumped on it. This is classic disinformation. It's always games, games, games… from the people who brought you Soros's rent-a-mob—rioting, looting, and destruction in cities— going so far as to risk a few deaths all for the cause.

But what I didn't see coming was their ultimate goal: the shutdown of free speech. The left wants to crush free speech, which has been in their crosshairs for some time now.

The left was always preaching about true democracy, but they seize power as fast and ruthlessly as they can. And they were always harping about "controversial" matters that either don't exist, are fabricated, or are of little import.

If a blogger or news writer gets a story wrong, does that designate him or her, or his or her site, as "fake news"? If that's the case, they'll have to shut down the *New York Times*, the *Los Angeles Times*, the *Boston Globe*, ABC News, NBC News, CBS News, and CNN. They get things wrong *all the time*. Every article written about my colleagues, my work, or myself was fake. Most of what they wrote and didn't write about the Orlando mass slaughter at the gay nightclub was disinformation and deception.

If you issue a correction, does that somehow remove the fake news scarlet letter? It was all a big fat lie—an end-run around the First Amendment, and it was disastrous. It was indeed true that Facebook had too much power, but banning "fake news" sites was hardly the solution. That was Zuckerberg's fix-it? It would have been funny if it hadn't so Hitlerian.

Facebook has too much power, period. Its news curators, mini-Goebbels, are more frightening than Kafka's antagonists.

Facebook should be broken up like Ma Bell was. Facebook doesn't decide what's good and what's forbidden. Left-wing fascists do not and must not decide what news people can and cannot see. But that was exactly what we were seeing on Facebook. Facebook, where I had a million followers, made sharing my posts almost impossible.

And not just Facebook. The independent news site *Zero Hedge* reported in April 2017, "After the *Wall Street Journal* began routing out Nazis on YouTube, in an effort to get ads scrubbed from their videos, a massive over-haul of YouTube's advertising policies began, shortly thereafter. It was incredible, really, as if Google was simply waiting for an excuse."[31]

I experienced this firsthand. It was happening to me on YouTube and Google Adsense and on Facebook. These left-wing behemoths meant to strangle and starve us out, while left-wing smear machines (A.K.A. think tanks) were funded by Soros, and in many cases, the US government.

In late July 2017, my website, the *Geller Report* (previously *Atlas Shrugs*) all but disappeared from Google search. Forty thousand posts and articles, fourteen years of work. Once a source of thousands of referrals a day, Google referrals were whittled down to nothing. Turkey's Anadolu Agency reported in July 2017 that "queries about Islam and Muslims on the world's largest search engine have been updated amid public pressure to tamp down alleged disinformation from hate groups.... Google's first page results for searches of terms such as 'jihad', 'sharia' and 'taqiyya' now return mostly reputable expla-nations of the Islamic concepts. Taqiyya, which describes the circumstances under which a Muslim can conceal their belief in the face of persecution, is the sole term to feature a questionable website on the first page of results."[32]

The article didn't explain how Google decided what results were "repu-table" and which were from "hate groups," but it had come under pressure from Muslim leaders, and was bowing to their demands. Sharia blasphemy laws were being implemented at Google.

The leftist masters of the universe were, without our consent, arbitrarily and capriciously abridging and surrendering our most basic fundamental freedoms. The internet is the last frontier in the war on free speech. We cannot and will not cede the field.

I wonder what Google's fake news algorithm looks like. *Tablet* revealed in July 2017 that Google's algorithms are skewed to be anti-Semitic and pro-jihad. The statement "Many terrorists are radical Islamists" was, according to Google's mechanized formula for finding and eliminating "hate speech," "92 percent likely to be seen as toxic," according to *Tablet*'s Liel Leibovitz. This factual statement, "Three Israelis were murdered last night by a knife-wielding Palestinian terrorist who yelled 'Allah hu Akbar,' too, was 92 percent likely to be seen as toxic."[33]

Leibovitz explained:

> The machines learn from what they read, and when what they read are the *Guardian* and the *Times*, they're going to inherit the inherent biases of these publications as well. Like most people who read the *Paper of Record*, the machine, too, has come to believe that statements about Jews being slaughtered are controversial, that addressing radical Islamism is verboten, and that casual anti-Semitism is utterly forgivable.
>
> The very term itself, toxicity, should've been enough of a give-away: the only groups that talk about toxicity—see: toxic masculinity—are those on the regressive left who creepily apply the metaphors of physical harm to censor speech, not celebrate or promote it. No words are toxic, but the idea that we now have an algorithm replicating, amplifying, and automatizing the bigotry of the anti-Jewish left may very well be.[34]

In late July and early August 2017, many of my videos were removed from YouTube. YouTube was purging videos en masse under the guise of "hate speech" or "controversial religious or supremacist content." They claimed it was to counter terrorism, when in fact it was to silence those who dissented.

Who watches the watchman?

All of Islam is "supremacist." So following that policy would require every video exhorting and preaching for Islam should be banned. But the same week that YouTube was banning my videos, news came out that a group of British jihadis were preaching bloodshed and murder and recruiting for jihad in videos that YouTube left up for over a year.

The stranglehold that leftist social media giants have on the means of communication must be broken—before it's too late. This is America, not Saudi Arabia. Enough.

In the twentieth century, the US government used anti-trust laws to dismantle US corporations with far less money and infinitely far less power. Never in the history of mankind has such absolute power in the information battle-space been in the hands of so few. If the body politic understood this and the ramifications of inaction, they would be terrified. And rightly so.

Our social media pages and events are scrubbed, censored and blacklisted. For years I documented the outrageous bias of Facebook's speech policies. Notoriously one-sided, those who oppose jihad terror, support Israel, and stand against sharia, the most brutal and extreme ideology on the face of the earth, have been systematically blocked and banned.

Truth is not hateful or obscene. What was hateful, obscene and threatening was that Facebook was moving to silence everyone who speaks honestly about the motivating ideology behind such attacks. And it is still doing so.

Shouting into the wilderness is not the freedom of speech. Talking to yourself is not freedom of speech.

The Sherman Antitrust Act ought to be used to break the monopoly Facebook wields over free speech in the social networking sector. Thomas Lifson of the *American Thinker* sees the problem as I do and supports "legislation that requires social media to censor only direct threats, making it illegal to delete content on any other basis. Social media platforms must be viewpoint neutral. That threat is necessary to counter the pressure Facebook obviously faces from Muslim governments like Pakistan's. Losing a billion-plus-strong market like the 57 Muslim countries is obviously undesirable for Facebook, so its management is responding to pressure."[35]

The value of that market would have to be balanced against the value of markets like the United States that could stand up for free speech. By seeming to cave in to the demand that Islam be the only subject that cannot be discussed openly and honestly, anywhere in the world, Facebook is in the process of handing the first global triumph to sharia by enforcing its ban on blasphemy.

PayPal Bans Me

In August 2017, in the wake of the vehicular attack by a neo-Nazi psychopath in Charlottesville, the left moved to crush all dissent, and Paypal banned AFDI. This was happening while hate groups like CAIR and the SPLC were getting millions from left-wing corporate managers. The SPLC received a two million dollar pledge from Apple, and MGM Resorts International will match employees' donations to terror-tied group CAIR.[36]

The left was awash in funding. And they meant to cut off everything from those working in defense of the free and the brave. I received a notice from Ronita Murray in PayPal's Brand Risk Management department that PayPal had suspended my account, permanently.

William Jacobson over at *Legal Insurrection* wrote:

> Being cut off from domain registrars and other aspects of the Internet backbone is something we expect from totalitarian governments. Now that power is in the control of almost-uniformly left-wing corporate managers.[37]

I had an exchange with Just before the ban from PayPal came down, I had an exchange with Lauren Kirchner, a goose-stepping, leftist second-hander masquerading as a journalist from *ProPublica*, an uber-left non-profit, threatening advertisers and payment services that were found on my site. I was not the only target; other counter-jihad sites received this vicious "interview request" as well: former Muslim Ali Sina, *Bare Naked Islam*, and others were also targeted.

Here is part of the interview, which, I might add, Kirchner did not run. Not one word.

We would like to ask you a few questions:

1) Do you disagree with the designation of your website as hate or extremist? Why?

Of course I do. All my work is in defense of the freedom of speech, the freedom of conscience, the equality of rights of all people before the law, and individual rights. The claim that I operate a hate group is a vicious smear and eerily evokes the circumstances that preceded the rise of the Nazis in the 1930s.

2) We identified several tech companies on your website: PayPal, Revcontent, Disqus, and Newsmax. Can you confirm that you receive funds from your relationship with those tech companies? How would the loss of those funds affect your operations, and how would you be able to replace them?

Once you start shutting down people on the claim that they operate "hate groups," you have made the use of such platforms contingent upon holding certain political opinions. Beware, because in doing so you will be setting a dangerous precedent: one day your own opinions could be out of favor, and you will find yourself cut off.

3) Have you been shut down by other tech companies for being an alleged hate or extremist web site? Which companies?
No, because everyone recognizes that the Southern Poverty Law Center's "hate group" designation is outrageously biased, and based on dissent from its hard-left stances. The SPLC makes a practice of lumping in groups with legitimately dissenting views with actual hate groups such as neo-Nazis, the Nation of Islam, etc. This is an attempt to delegitimize and silence all those with views that differ from its own.

4) Many people opposed to sites like yours are currently pressuring tech companies to cease their relationships with them—what is your view of this campaign? Why?

It's a quintessentially fascist initiative. The fascists shut down all dissenting views. You are imitating them.[38]

Anyone the left calls a Nazi is now shunned, ruined—their livelihood murdered. PayPal ultimately relented after a massive outcry from supporters of my work. Thousands of retweets, I don't know how many phone calls and emails. But an hour after I posted news about the suspension, they reversed themselves. Excelsior! Nonetheless, PayPal had made it clear where they stood. I moved all of my accounts off PayPal.

These leftists must be exposed and held accountable.

CNN Ambushes Me

From MSNBC and ABC to CBS and CNN and (increasingly) Fox, the mainstream media speak with one voice: leftist, anti-Trump, and determined to whitewash and deny the connection between Islam and terrorism. Yet even though they control virtually all the news outlets, they're still desperate to silence every dissenting voice, no matter how small its platform. And so in May 2017, CNN tried to ambush me.

A CNN reporter named Simon Ostrovsky contacted me with an invitation to be interviewed for a CNN *Money* program. "It's about ad revenue on YouTube. I saw that you published a post about revenue dropping in YouTube, and you attributed it to Google and Facebook being left-leaning companies that were censoring alternate points of view. Would you be able to tell us how significant the impact has been and if it's ongoing and if you see this as a wider campaign to undermine your message?" he said.

Having a sense of what CNN was after, I responded: "Simon, Yes, the revenue drop has been drastic. Who else will be on? I am not interested in an ambush." He responded with reassurances: "This would be a package, so it would not be a studio discussion with other guests. Just me and you, and I'd like to cover a couple topics including the revenue on YouTube and AdSense and your views on why the changes are taking place and if you agree with the characterization of your content as advertiser un-friendly. Are those areas you are O.K. to talk about?"

I agreed to go, since I was currently in the lawsuit challenging Section 230 of the CDA. They can censor as much as they wish without fear of legal action. We are trying to remove that protection and preserve the freedom of speech. As it is, this protection gives them enormous power. I have well over a million followers who voluntarily chose to receive my content, and Facebook is blocking them from getting it. This dramatically affected the advertising revenue upon which I depend not only for the upkeep of my site, but for my own livelihood; it fell 90 percent in mid-February 2017 and never recovered.

Ostrovsky asked me to bring my laptop to CNN's studios so that I could show him my Google AdSense account and Google Analytics, to show the precipitous drop in referrals from Facebook, Google AdSense, YouTube and related sources. I did. Ostrovsky saw that revenue from Facebook was down from $150 a day at this time six months ago to $30 a day now.

But Ostrovsky had lied in his emails to me. He wasn't really interested in how Facebook and the rest were censoring me at all. He had a thick stack of copies of posts that were 10 years old and older from my website. He was calling out my advertisers, claiming that I was inciting war crimes and that these advertisers were supporting my incitement by placing ads on my website. "Advertisers should know what they're supporting," he said.

He pointed to a 2006 headline in which I had called for bombing Gaza, because of the rockets they were firing at Israeli civilian installations. This was the basis for his claim that I was inciting war crimes.

I explained to him that this post had to be understood in its historical context. At that time, jihadis in Gaza were sending rockets into Israel and hitting Israeli civilian institutions: schools, synagogues, hospitals were all at risk. So I was calling for defense against that. Ostrovsky responded, "Well, that's not in the headline." I said, "Yes, you have to read the story. It's patently dishonest and journalistic malpractice to get me here and ambush me with a vicious, destructive narrative."

Ostrovsky had much more. He pulled out a *Daily Caller* piece in which I had said that Islam is the problem. He said, "Don't you realize that's deeply offensive to many Muslims?" I answered, "Jihad is deeply offensive to many Muslims. We have to be able to talk about the problem, or we will never be able to deal with it properly. You are adhering to sharia. Under sharia, you cannot criticize Islam. There is a death penalty in sharia for blasphemy, apostasy and hypocrisy. You are bringing this to America. I don't live under sharia. I can talk about these matters freely, as we must."

Then Ostrovsky said, "If you said, 'Judaism is the problem,' that would be anti-Semitic." To that I responded, "If Jews were slaughtering people while screaming, 'HaShem akbar,' I would say that Judaism is the problem. If Christians were killing in the name of Christ, I would say Christianity is the problem. But they aren't, and it isn't."

"Fox is a major corporation," Ostrovsky said. "Don't you think they should know what they're supporting?" I said, "They know they want to reach 150,000 people. They aren't supporting everything that's on my page. Do you think CNN advertisers are supporting its scrubbing of all mention of jihad from the reporting of jihad attacks? The Manchester attacker was screaming Islamic prayers on the street in the weeks before the attack—was that on CNN? Do CNN advertisers approve of this being swept under the rug at CNN?"

I told him that CNN's advertisers should not be paying his salary to destroy people with lies and defamation. He asked me what lies CNN had told. We could have been there for days as I answered that question, but I gave him just one example: CNN's headline after President Trump's speech in Saudi Arabia: "Trump silent on human rights." Now all of a sudden CNN cares about human-rights violations in Muslim countries? Incredible. Obama gave billions to Muslim countries with long records of human-rights violations—most notably the Islamic Republic of Iran—and CNN never said a word. Bloody hypocrites. Their only interest was in bringing President Trump down.

I told Ostrovsky that advertisers should not be supporting a news organization that promotes and incites violence, whitewashing, and obscuring the jihad ideology. He said, "I'm Jewish!" I responded, "That doesn't give you a blank check to destroy. You're a left-wing Jew. You guys are the worst. You're a Jew for jihad, you're a kapo. I can't believe that the little advertising I still get, you want to extinguish. You want to silence all voices that don't support your vicious agenda. You should be ashamed of yourself. How do you sleep at night? How do you look in the mirror? You brought me here to talk about the freedom of speech, and you are working to destroy it."

He said, "We'll talk about the freedom of speech." I said, "No, we won't. You have no intention of discussing how my freedom of speech is being abridged."

And I walked out.

CNN would not accept or allow my earning 30 bucks a day from AdSense. Even this pittance kills them, so they assigned this tool Ostrovsky to go after my advertisers, the handful that they were.

Did CNN advertisers know that this was where their ad dollars are going, to destroying Americans and their livelihoods?

The Sarsour Protest

CNN hated me, but they sure loved Linda Sarsour.

On May 25, 2017, several thousand patriots gathered in New York City to protest the City University of New York (CUNY)'s invitation to anti-Israel BDS (Boycott, Divestment, Sanctions) leader Linda Sarsour to keynote their commencement ceremony.

Sarsour was the hijab-wearing feminist icon who led the ridiculous

Women's March on Washington the day after Trump's inauguration. Nothing exposed how phony and leftist the feminist movement really was more than the fact that the absurd vagina hat protests against Trump were led by this vicious supporter of jihad and sharia.

Sarsour was invited by Ayman El-Mohandes, the dean of CUNY's Graduate School of Public Health and Health Policy. Even after being barraged with complaints, CUNY stood by its decision to honor this vicious Muslim activist. Such sanction was so malignant and so evil, it could not be ignored. There was a responsibility for the time we are living in.

We had to reschedule the protest from June 1 (the day of Sarsour's keynote speech) because it was the Jewish holiday of Shavuot, and so many proud Jews wanted to attend. It was wrong for CUNY to have scheduled the commencement ceremonies on Shavuot—the day that the Torah was given by G-d to the Jewish people. Over 25% of CUNY's student body was Jewish. The fact that the commencement address was on Shavuot was another reason CUNY should have canceled Sarsour and rescheduled the commencement. What were Jewish students supposed to do? They either had to violate their holiday or miss their graduation.

Speakers at our event included New York State Assemblyman Dov Hikind, who did yeoman work in exposing many of Sarsour's shady activities; John Guandolo, a former FBI agent, counter-terror expert, and founder of *UnderstandingTheThreat.com*; Lauri B. Regan of the Endowment for Middle East Truth and National Women's Committee of the Republican Jewish Coalition; David Wood of Acts 17 Apologetics; ex-Muslim human rights activist Nonie Darwish; and conservative gadfly pundit Milo Yiannopoulos.

Universities have disinvited Ayaan Hirsi Ali, Nonie Darwish, Ann Coulter, Yiannopoulos, and legions of conservative thinkers and voices in defense of freedom, but a pro-sharia and anti-Israel activist they will defend to the death.

An outspoken critic of Israel, Sarsour avidly supports the BDS movement, a Nazi-like initiative to pressure institutions into dropping all ties with Israel. In October 2012, she tweeted that "nothing is creepier than Zionism."

In 2004, Sarsour revealed that a close friend and her cousin were both serving time in Israeli jails for their efforts to recruit jihadists to murder Jews. She also disclosed that her brother-in-law was serving a 12-year prison term because of his affiliation with Hamas.[39]

In October 2011, Sarsour declared that "Muslim New Yorkers" stood in "solidarity and support" for the communist Occupy Wall Street movement.[40] That same year, Barack Obama honored her as a "champion of change."[41]

In May 2012, Sarsour claimed that the Detroit "underwear bomber" was a CIA agent.[42] When the Muslim who had plotted to kill me, Usaama Rahim, was killed by the police he attacked, Sarsour commented: "At the end of the day, a Black man was shot on a bus stop on his way to work and we should treat this like any other case of police violence."[43]

She also claimed that the killing of Shaima Alawadi was a racist-Islamophobic-anti-Muslim killing.[44] In reality, Alawadi was killed by her husband, but when that came to light, Sarsour never retracted.

The left's chokehold on the nation's most powerful institutions continues, despite a Trump presidency and a Republican congress, but this was a step too far.

There was enormous press coverage surrounding my demo against CUNY's obscene invitation to, as Yiannopoulos succinctly put it, "sharia-loving, terrorist-embracing, Jew-hating, ticking time-bomb of progressive horror," to keynote their commencement ceremonies.[45]

The event was a smashing success, a triumph. Thousands came out in the pouring rain and cold to protest the monstrous invite to a monster.

And that was the lede story. The make-up of the crowd was the lede story. Mostly young, mixed, everything—true Americana. For me, that represents a sea-change in our movement. Seeing that, the enemedia had to spring into action. Not one hour after the event was over, the deranged left-wing *New York Daily News* crafted a false story headlined "Wild brawl breaks out at rally against CUNY's commencement speaker civil-rights activist Linda Sarsour," but of course, there was no wild brawl.[46]

In a minor incident, two violent left-wing morons were arrested for attacking our people. That was news? That's standard operating procedure for those violent goons. But the *News* wrote it up that the violent hooligans were the ones attacked. They just make this stuff up. Did they talk to any of the speakers? No. Did they talk to any of the victims of those arrested? No. The *News* said there were no arrests. But there were. And of course, every other media outlet picking up on the story said that there were no arrests. Did any one of these "journalists" even make a call to the NYPD?

The *Daily Mail* also covered our protest against the invitation given to a pro-terror, pro-sharia, Jew-hater. What was so telling is every major news organization picked up the *News*'s fake news story about a wild brawl. There were two arrests—violent leftists, of course. It was our people who were attacked. We didn't clash. The violent left-wing thugs were agitating and menacing our peaceful protest for the whole of the event.

The news story here wasn't about violence at our event. The story was that we were pushing back against this leftist/Islamic goose-stepping army. Why the police put these violent morons right up against our stage is an interesting question.

It was a turning point.

The fact remained the only reason the cowards at CUNY didn't cancel Sarsour is that they were afraid her co-religionists and their leftist lapdogs would blow the place up if they did.

The theme of our protest was this: we were mad as hell and we weren't going to take it anymore.

Can We Recover?

The real question isn't whether free speech is under threat in the United States, but rather, whether it's irretrievably lost. Can we get it back? Not without war, I suspect, as is evidenced by the violence at colleges whenever there's the shamefully rare event of a conservative speaker on campus.

Free speech is the soul of our nation and the foundation of all our other freedoms. If we can't speak out against injustice and evil, those forces will prevail. Freedom of speech is the foundation of a free society. Without it, a tyrant can wreak havoc unopposed, while his opponents are silenced.

With that principle in mind, I organized the free-speech event in Garland, Texas in the wake of the world being rocked by the murder of the *Charlie Hebdo* cartoonists. My version of "Je Suis Charlie" was an event here in America to show that we can still speak freely and draw whatever we like in the Land of the Free. Yet even after jihadists attacked our event, I was blamed—by Donald Trump among others—for provoking Muslims. Two days after jihadis attacked my free speech event, Trump said to Megyn Kelly:

> I watched Pam earlier, and it really looks like she's just taunting everybody. What is she doing drawing Muhammad? I mean

it's disgusting. Isn't there something else they could be doing? Drawing Muhammad? . . . . They can't do something else? They have to be in the middle of Texas doing something on Muhammad and insulting everybody? What is she doing? Why is she doing it? It's probably very risky for her—I don't know, maybe she likes risk? But what the hell is she doing?[47]

And if I tried to hold a similar event now, no arena in the country would allow me to do so—not just because of the security risk, but because of the moral cowardice of all intellectual appeasers.

Under what law is it wrong to depict Muhammad? Under Islamic law. But I am not a Muslim, I don't live under sharia. America isn't under Islamic law, yet. For standing for free speech, I've been:

- Prevented from running our advertisements in every major city in this country. We have won free-speech lawsuits all over the country, which officials circumvent by prohibiting all political ads (while making exceptions for ads from Muslim advocacy groups);

- Shunned by the right, shut out of the Conservative Political Action Conference;

- Shunned by Jewish groups at the behest of terror-linked groups such as the Council on American-Islamic Relations;

- Blacklisted from speaking at universities;

- Prevented from publishing books, for security reasons and because publishers fear shaming from the left;

- Banned from Britain.

A Seattle court accused me of trying to shut down free speech after we merely tried to run an FBI poster on global terrorism, because authorities had banned all political ads in other cities to avoid running ours. Seattle blamed us for that, which was like blaming a woman for being raped because she was wearing a short skirt.

This kind of vilification and shunning is key to the left's plan to shut down all dissent from its agenda—they make legislation restricting speech unnecessary.

The foundation of my work is individual rights and equality for all before the law. These are the foundational principles of our constitutional republic. That is now considered controversial. Truth is the new hate speech. Truth is going to be criminalized.

The First Amendment doesn't only protect ideas that are sanctioned by the cultural and political elites. If "hate speech" laws are enacted, who would decide what's permissible and what's forbidden? The government? The gunmen in Garland?

There has been an inversion of the founding premise of this nation. No longer is it the subordination of might to right, but right to might. History is repeatedly deformed with the bloody consequences of this transition.

J'accuse the Left

The June 2017 shooting of Republican Congressman Steve Scalise at the Congressional baseball practice by an SPLC-supporting Bernie Sanders devotee was the obvious and logical consequence of the left's treasonous war on America.[48]

This was but another assassination attempt by a left-lauded Southern Poverty Law Center supporter. SPLC, a vicious hate and smear machine, continued to be held up as some kind of authority by the elite media and academic institutions. SPLC enthusiast Floyd Corkins shot up the Family Research Council with the hope of killing as many employees as possible in August 2012.

But this was just the tip of the iceberg.

For years, the left and its media lapdogs have created narratives out of whole cloth about the impending violence from the right. President Obama, inciter-in-chief, regularly used violent rhetoric to gin up the Democrats: "If they bring a knife to the fight, we bring a gun." He supported the most violent, seditious movements of 21st-century America (Black Lives Matter, Occupy Wall Street, Muslim Brotherhood groups, to name a few), while directing the Department of Homeland Security to track "right-wing extremists"—in other words, Americans like you and me.

For years, the street thugs have been agitating, and for years the elites in the Democrat Party have egged them on, giving the violence legitimacy, sanction, and their imprimatur. All the while, they blamed the right for unrelated violence. While there was no connection between what a Norway mass-murdering madman did when he killed 77 people on July 22, 2011, and what we said—our recommendations for countering jihad terrorism and brutal sharia—the left blew up and blood-libeled us almost to the point of extinction. When it came out in court that this Norwegian madman was inspired to violence by al-Qaeda and Hamas, that was not widely reported.[49]

The left always blames us for violence, no matter how nonexistent the ties. Even when I was the target of an assassination plot in Garland, the left blamed me because I would not adhere to the blasphemy laws under sharia.

Bernie Sanders fundraised by blaming Sarah Palin and conservatives in general for the 2011 shooting of Arizona Congresswoman Gabby Giffords. The *Daily Caller* reported that "there was never any actual evidence presented that Jared Loughner, a diagnosed schizophrenic who pleaded guilty to the shooting, was a Palin fan, a Tea Party supporter, or that he had ever seen Palin's 'crosshairs' map" that was widely blamed for the shooting. In fact, according to the *Caller*, "one friend tweeted that 'he was left wing, quite liberal.'"[50]

Another shooter in Portland, also in June 2017, was likewise a Bernie supporter; he ranted against Christians, Jews, and Muslims but the enemedia reported his shooting of two people as an "Islamophobic... hate crime."[51]

I have been covering leftist and Islamic protests for years, and they are rife with hate and violence that never get reported in the mainstream media. There is a systematic, organized movement to overthrow American freedoms and install an enemy regime. At every pro-America, pro-Trump, anti-sharia, counter-terrorism protest, leftists show up full of bloodlust and primed for battle. These primitives agitate, incite, and attack our people whenever we peacefully assemble. And their stooges in the media, like clockwork, then report what happened as follows: "Violence breaks out at far-right rally..." "Far-right" is the media's term for anyone who doesn't submit to these goose-stepping, jackbooted thugs.

At my rally against CUNY's invitation to terror-inciter Linda Sarsour to give its commencement address, New York City Mayor "Red Bill" de Blasio directed the NYPD to put the violent leftists not three feet from our people.[52] It was not pretty.

Conservative and pro-Israel speakers are attacked and silenced on the rare occasions they are even invited to speak. Trump supporters have been beaten at rallies and demos in support of the President.[53] From Berkeley to Brooklyn, college campuses have become nothing short of war zones.

As the *Daily Wire* noted: "In recent years, under the tender tutelage of the Obama Department of Justice, mass violent action by leftists has become commonplace across the country, from the Occupy Wall Street movement to Black Lives Matter-inspired mob violence in Ferguson and Baltimore, from campus chaos at California State University of Los Angeles to this sort of violence at Trump rallies."[54]

This is not static. This situation on the ground is fluid. Do the leftists think freedom-lovers will continue to stand down? Does the left want war? They are going to get it. Because we know where this road leads. We saw this same kind of violent thuggery in the 1930s in Germany. And we have seen what happens when good people do nothing.

As for the "good people" in the Democrat Party, where are they? Where are the mass protests where Democrats proclaim, "Not My Party!" Why aren't we seeing that the way we are seeing "Not My President!"

If you are a Democrat Party member, you are part of the problem.

The West Has Lost the Will to Live

The most basic, primitive honor a nation owes to its dead is to fight to defend itself—to defeat the enemy and win. And yet the West won't.

The West is hanging on by a thread and doesn't even know it. We are living off the fumes of the accomplishments of our forefathers and those who fought and died in the cause of freedom and individual rights. But the thread is wearing thin. Time is running out.

After every murderous jihad attack comes the predictable Western response: not resolute self-defense, but weepy candlelight vigils, protestations of unity, and hashtags. After the jihad attacks in Garland, Chattanooga, the University of California Merced, and so many others, and the scores of arrests of American Muslims working for ISIS (the FBI has 900 ISIS-related investigations currently ongoing), our top priority should be to crush the enemy.

Instead, we get pathos and pitiful memes. After the jihad attacks in Paris in November 2015, where 137 innocent people were murdered in a coordinated attack across the city, NBC reported, "Paris residents were using the hashtag #PorteOuverte—French for 'open door'—on Twitter to offer safe haven to strangers stranded after a string of deadly attacks Friday night."[55] Everyone was congratulating himself over this hashtag. "Twitter users in other countries," NBC added, "also began using the hashtag to share their delight that social media was being used for a good cause"—colossal stupidity.

Share their delight? This delight was misplaced. I would have expected nothing less than that Parisians should have offered safe haven: just because savages are at war with us doesn't mean we should be less human.

This hashtag was just another part in of the endless stream of sophomoric, embarrassing, preening self-indulgence that is endemic in our sick culture. It was reminiscent of "Boston Strong" after the Boston Marathon jihad bombings in 2013 that killed three and maimed dozens more. After the bombings, the media and Boston elites refused to call the attack jihad. The Boston city government refused repeatedly to run our AFDI counter-jihad ads, but ran vicious Jew-hatred ads regularly. What's strong about Boston? What stand did Boston take against jihad?

Equally revolting was the Eiffel Tower peace symbol that was circulating around. Did the leftists think the ISIS jihadis would see this and lay down their arms?[56] If the Christians and Yazidis in Syria made the peace sign, would all be well? If the nearly 200 kidnapped Nigerian schoolgirls—who disappeared in 2014 and are now sex slaves to jihadis—made the peace sign, would they be freed? Such idiocy was an affront to every freedom-loving human being.

The endless patting ourselves on the back that citizens of Western countries engage in after a mass slaughter by jihadists is disgusting. People crow about hashtags and blood donations as if this was somehow new. Of course we care. We always care. That is our value system, that is a Western value. The United States of America is the most charitable nation on earth. That is who we are.

What no one is talking about is taking on these savages. That is what is so morally depraved about our response. The idea that we're not allowed to take the appropriate measures to defeat the global Islamic jihad is obscene. The idea that the United States of America cannot defeat the Islamic State or al-Qaeda is absurd, and the whole world knows it. But we choose not to use our strength. We choose to be victims. It's shameful.

And clearly, since everybody knows that we are not physically weak, where is the basic dignity that any nation should have, to stand up for its own values? If nothing else, when we find ourselves involved in a war, we should fight it and finish it. You either win or you will be defeated.

Is it proper for us to defend ourselves and to take the appropriate action to defend this country? Of course. One of Obama's historic crimes during his presidency was that he allowed our superiority to deteriorate. But that doesn't mean our enemies have disappeared, or that we cannot or should not defend ourselves against them. Just hours after Obama insisted that he had contained the "Junior Varsity team" ISIS, they laid siege to Paris.[57] And this goes unchallenged.

When Muslims attack, the left attacks us. MSNBC, the *Guardian*, and *Salon* all ran pieces blaming the "right-wing" for those November 2015 Paris attacks.[58] Outrageous, but not surprising. The enemedia was and is aligned with the jihad force. As the jihad heats up in the West, the media is becoming more clumsy and desperate in its attempts to deflect attention away from the jihad and back to its favorite bogeyman, "right-wing extremists."

Even when the evidence of Islamic jihad responsibility is everywhere, "journalists" still find ways to put the blame on the "right-wing" that they hate far more than they do bloodthirsty jihadis, whom they don't dislike at all.

If you have an ounce of self-esteem, when someone comes at you with a gun, you answer with force. If he is out to destroy you, you owe it to yourself to defend yourself. We need to understand that the left is as dangerous, if not more so, than the suicide bomber, for obscuring this basic fact. Because leftists have the legitimacy of the mainstream, the imprimatur of respectability, they wield this spurious legitimacy like a club to destroy all opposition to their totalitarian agenda.

We need to go to war against the left. We have to get that into our heads. We have to accept that terrible reality. They want to destroy our freedom. They want to destroy our country. They want to steal our children. That's war. There is no one on the right who has the correct philosophy about this. The left demands the right to lie, and they are lying to the American people on a massive scale, even to the extent of making people think there is something wrong with loving and defending our nation.

The idea that the November 2015 attacks in Paris happened on the eve of a global conference to discuss not global jihad, the gravest threat to freedom, but climate change, speaks to how unreal and sick we are as rational beings. The fact is, global jihadists, whether they're ISIS or al-Qaeda or Hamas or Hezbollah, are monstrous aggressors. We don't have to wait for the first sign that they are attacking; they have declared war against us. They must be destroyed. We can't complain about what we should or shouldn't be doing, we have to correct it. The idea of containment is absurd—an intermediate state.

There is no intermediate state. It's either/or. This is war. We have to fight it.

The terrible consequence of the left's and the spineless, gutless right's attacks on the rational voices in the counter-jihad movement is the extinguishing of voices of those who are brave enough to tell the truth. This creates a vacuum filled by the worst of the fringe—racist demagogues such as white nationalist Richard Spencer to whom the left and the enemdia are more than thrilled to give a platform.

The Coming Civil War

The left has been at war against America for decades. The right represents those of us who favor individual freedom and capitalism—and the left are those who want government controls and socialism.

Political violence became an essential and successful means of leftist warfare in the 1960s, the decade of destruction. The success of the violent "student rebellion" in 1964 and the so-called Free Speech Movement has set the table for the left's warmongering and treason. It was clear from the outset that the "student revolution" violently ushered in at Berkeley in the mid-sixties would come to this. The left is evil, and they mean to destroy our way of life, our freedom, and us. It took decades to norm their anti-Americanism and their hatred of freedom and individual rights, but they have reached their tipping point. And the long beaten and battered among us have had it.

Ayn Rand explained why the left is seeking nothing less than the breakdown of American society:

> The attempt to solve social problems by means of physical force is what a civilized society is established to prevent. The advocates of mass civil disobedience admit that their purpose is intimidation. A society that tolerates intimidation as a means of settling disputes— the *physical* intimidation of some men or groups by others—loses its moral right to exist as a social system, and its collapse does not take long to follow.
>
> Politically, mass civil disobedience is appropriate only as a prelude to civil war—as the declaration of a total break with a country's political institutions.[59]

The left is targeting the most powerful office in the world—the Presidency. But, as the shooting of Congressman Scalise and others at the Congressional baseball practice shows, they're targeting everyone on the right. There will be more of this.

President Trump was elected by Americans who oppose the left-wing coup and are fed up with living under the left's oppressive boot. Trump is our proxy. We fought back the non-violent way—through the ballot box. From the moment he was elected, the left refused to accept the will of the people. Freedom lovers are beaten at rallies against jihad and sharia by left-wing fascists who mockingly call themselves antifa, short for "anti-fascists," or "anti-fascist action."

The deck is stacked against us. We must get off the defense.

AFDI 18-Point Platform in Defense of Freedom

I get this question all the time, "What can we do? How can the jihad be stopped?"

We developed the AFDI 18-point Platform in Defense of Freedom in strategy sessions after the International Freedom Defense Congress of the international group Stop Islamization of Nations (SION), which was held in New York City at the UN Millennium Plaza Hotel on September 11, 2012, directly across the street from the United Nations headquarters (as devout Muslims were attacking our embassies in Libya and Egypt).

At the Congress, which included representatives of European nations, as well as India, Israel, Malaysia, and Egypt's Coptic community, world-renowned authorities in legal strategy and political action addressed the attendees.

We formulated this Platform for Defending Freedom as a tool for counter-jihad activists and a set of principles to unite the counter-jihad movement in the wake of the Boston jihad bombings. We needed to press our politicians and parties to accept these goals and pursue political action to make them reality, and to rate politicians on the basis of these points. We plan now to form an international group of politicians and activists committed to these principles in countries across the globe.

Here is the plan to saving America... and the West. Join us.

— AFDI calls for the US and other non-Muslim governments to recognize officially that Islam is a political movement and therefore not solely religious in the strict sense of the US Constitution. AFDI recognizes that Islam in its mainstream theological formulations and its dominant form throughout its history, not "extremist Islam" or "hijacked Islam" or "Islamism," but Islam in the Koran and Sunnah, as understood by Islamic jurists and theologians, can and should be regarded as an authoritarian and supremacist political system as well as a religion. Thus, Muslim groups should be subject to all the scrutiny and legal requirements of political organizations, without being able to shield their political activities behind the protection of religious freedom.

— AFDI denounces the crippling rules of engagement under which our soldiers are forced to labor. They should be given the freedom to defend themselves and protect their comrades.

— AFDI calls for profiling of Muslims at airports and in hiring in professions in which national security and public safety could be compromised.

— AFDI calls for immediate investigation into foreign mosque funding in the West and for new legislation making foreign funding of mosques in non-Muslim nations illegal.

— AFDI calls for surveillance of mosques and regular inspections of mosques in the US and other non-Muslim nations to look for pro-violence materials. Any mosque advocating jihad or any aspects of sharia that conflict with Constitutional freedoms and protections should be closed.

— AFDI calls for curriculum and Islam-related materials in textbooks and museums to describe Islamic doctrine and history accurately, including its violent doctrines and 1,400-year war against unbelievers.

— AFDI calls for a halt of foreign aid to Islamic nations with sharia-based constitutions and/or governments.

– AFDI denounces the use of sharia law in any Western court or nation.

– AFDI advocates deportation hearings against non-citizens who promote jihad in our nations.

– AFDI calls for an immediate halt of immigration by Muslims into nations that do not currently have a Muslim majority population.

— AFDI calls for laws providing that anyone seeking citizenship in the United States should be asked if he or she supports sharia, and investigated for ties to pro-sharia groups. If so, citizenship should not be granted.

– AFDI calls for the cancellation of citizenship or permanent residency status for anyone who leaves the country of his residence to travel for the purpose of engaging in jihad activity, and for the refusal of reentry into his country of residence after that jihad activity.

— AFDI calls for careful investigation of Muslim residents in any non-Muslim country who have obtained naturalized citizenship or permanent residency status, to ensure that that status was not obtained under false pretenses.

— AFDI calls for the designation of the following as grounds for immediate deportation: fomenting, plotting, financing, attempting, or carrying out jihad attacks; encouraging or threatening or attempting to carry out the punishments Islamic law mandates for apostasy, adultery, blasphemy, fornication, or theft; threatening or attempting or carrying out honor murders, forced marriage, underage marriage, female genital mutilation, or polygamy.

— AFDI calls for the US and other free nations to have jihad, as it is traditionally understood in Islamic jurisprudence to involve warfare against and subjugation of non-Muslims, declared a crime against humanity at the U.N., or to withdraw from the U.N. and have its headquarters moved to a Muslim nation.

– AFDI calls for legislation to make the foreign funding of Islamic Studies departments and faculty positions in our universities illegal.

– AFDI demands the repeal of U.N. resolution 16/18 and any other resolutions that might limit the freedom of speech.

– AFDI calls for all Muslim chaplains in prisons and the military to be thoroughly vetted, and dismissed if they have ties to any Islamic supremacist group, or if they advocate jihad.

– AFDI calls for the development of energy policies that will free us from dependence upon oil from Muslim countries.

— Through SION, AFDI establishes a common American/European coalition of free people determined to stand for freedom and oppose the advance of Islamic law, sharia. Islamic law is not simply a religious system, but a political system that encompasses every aspect of life; is authoritarian, discriminatory, and repressive; and contradicts Western laws and principles in numerous particulars. SION respects Muslims as fellow human beings and rejects Islamization as a comprehensive political, religious, cultural and social system of behavior and ideology.

AFDI and SION stand for:

— The freedom of speech—as opposed to Islamic prohibitions of "blasphemy" and "slander," which are used effectively to quash honest discussion of jihad and Islamic supremacism;

— The freedom of conscience—as opposed to the Islamic death penalty for apostasy;

— The equality of rights of all people before the law—as opposed to sharia's institutionalized discrimination against women and non-Muslims.

These are the precepts we must follow. These are the policies we must pursue in culture and then in Congress. We can't change laws and policies without changing the *zeitgeist*. You can't change politicians. Politicians are mirrors of public opinion. So talking politics is like putting the cart before the horse. Before we can talk politics, we must first learn everything, and then teach everyone in our sphere of influence.

The left has always understood this. It's why they made that long march through the institutions. Steadily, step by step, beginning in the 1960s, they took over the academic institutions, the educational system, the mainstream media, the entertainment industry, and more. They got footholds and pried open the doors, hiring only their friends and allies, until they had total control. They never broke ranks, never gave in to infighting.

This is the lesson we must learn from the culture wars. The left has mastered it.

The left stands shoulder to shoulder with their soldiers, no matter what their crime. The right abandons their allies at the slightest whiff of trouble. The left circles the wagons. The right sets up a circular firing squad. Anyone who thought, *What difference does it make what happens to Pamela Geller? So what?* doesn't realize the situation. They thought it would end with me. But it boomeranged. When they allowed the blacklisting and smearing, and the destruction of my good name, and that of others like me, they opened the floodgates. No one is too big and no one is immune. They're taking down the President. They've eliminated everyone in his inner circle, with the exception of his daughter. This is the fault of the right. The left protects its own.

What we are experiencing now is very much like the run-up to World War II. The same thing is happening.

If this book is proof of anything, it's that one person can make a difference. That means YOU. You must be unafraid. You must embrace the smear, defamation, and libel. You must get on social media and shout. You must share the websites, articles, and activism on your pages, social media channels, and email contacts.

You must go to protests, events, conferences, and networks—meet people, network, start a group, invite us to speak. *Do something.*

So much depends upon one person deciding to act. That could be you. That must be you.

I am one person. So are you. Together we are an army.

Acknowledgments

This incredible journey has been one wild, raucous ride. I never imagined that those who stood for Americanism, freedom and individual rights would be deemed the enemy, our names dragged through the mud. I wish to thank all of my readers, supporters, and followers who refused the lies and stood with me despite the blowback and hate.

I am deeply grateful to my colleague Robert Spencer, who embarked on many a dangerous project with me and never faltered, never stood down. I want to thank my lawyers David Yerushalmi and Robert Muise for their indefatigable courtroom efforts to defend the freedom of speech on our behalf. And a special shout-out for colleagues such as Pamela Hall for their wonderful collaboration.

This book would not have been possible without the courage and backing of Milo, who embraced the idea of publishing my book and scoffed at the threats that accompany such an undertaking.

Lastly, I want to thank my parents Libbie and Reuben Geller, who set the moral example and showed me how to live an honorable life.

I will never stand down. I fight for them and all freedom-loving people

Notes

1 The End of the World as I Knew It

1 Tom Leonard, "The 9/11 victims America wants to forget: The 200 jumpers who flung themselves from the Twin Towers who have been 'airbrushed from history,'" *Daily Mail,* September 11, 2011.

2 The Workshop

1 "'Islam is Peace' Says President," Remarks by the President at Islamic Center of Washington, D.C., September 17, 2001.

2 "Clip: Defense Department Briefing," *C-Span,* May 9, 2006.

3 "PM Erdogan: The Term 'Moderate Islam' Is Ugly And Offensive; There Is No Moderate Islam; Islam Is Islam," *Middle East Media Research Institute,* August 21, 2007.

4 Ayn Rand, "Theory and Practice," *Capitalism: The Unknown Ideal,* 138. http://aynrandlexicon.com/ayn-rand-works/capitalism-the-unknown-ideal.html

5 James Wolcott, "A Touch of Class," *Vanity Fair,* November 16, 2005.

6 Tyler O'Neil, "Southern Poverty Law Center: 'Our Aim in Life Is to Destroy These Groups, Completely,'" *PJ Media,* September 1, 2017.

7 Karen Zraick, "Terror Suspects in New Jersey Plead Guilty," *New York Times,* March 3, 2011.

8 Jeff Baker, "'Truth' review: Dan Rather and CBS blew it, and so does this movie," *The Oregonian,* October 29, 2015.

9 Hassan M. Fattah, "At Mecca Meeting, Cartoon Outrage Crystallized," *New York Times,* February 9, 2006.

10 *Bat Ye'or, Europe, Globalization, and the Coming of the Universal Caliphate,* Rowman & Littlefield, 2011, p. 171.

11 "Islamophobia is as dangerous as racism: Turkish PM," *World Bulletin*, September 12, 2013.

12 Hassan M. Fattah, "At Mecca Meeting, Cartoon Outrage Crystalized," *New York Times*, February 9, 2006.

13 "Danish Cartoon Controversy," *New York Times*, n.d..

3 Muslim Girls

1 Bob Mitchell and Noor Javed, "'I killed my daughter. . . with my hands,'" *Toronto Star*, June 16, 2010.

2 Joe Warmington, "Aqsa Parvez rests in numbered gravesite," *Toronto Sun*, December 10, 2008.

3 Pamela Geller, "Going Forward on Aqsa," *PamelaGeller.com*, February 19, 2009.

4 "Pics reveal CAIR backstage coordination of media in Rifqa Bary case and how the media kept silent," *Jawa Report*, December 14, 2009; "CAIR Attorney Demands Ban and Seizure of all Christmas Cards sent to Rifqa Bary (Bumped) ***And Updated***," *Jawa Report*, December 10, 2009.

5 Pamela Geller, "CRUSHING CLAMPDOWN ON CHRISTIAN RIFQA: No 'Approved Visitation' List for Apostate," *Atlas Shrugs*, November 23, 2009.

6 Pamela Geller, "Fatima Abdallah Honor Killing Cover-up: Complaint Filed with Medical Examiners Commission," *Atlas Shrugs*, June 23, 2011.

7 David Caton, "Tampa Police CSI tech admits *'fear of Muslim reprisal'* in Palestinian woman's death," Florida Family Association, August 9, 2011.

8 Pamela Geller, "Media Jihad: Lying for the Barys, Lying About Rifqa, Lying About Apostasy, Lying about the Laptop—Rifqa bought it, not 'doting dad,'" *Atlas Shrugs*, August 30, 2009.

9 Rene Stutzman, "Problems with Rifqa Bary Began with a Laptop Gift," Orlando Sentinel, August 30, 2009.

10 Phyllis Chesler, "Worldwide Trends in Honor Killings," *Middle East Quarterly*, Spring 2010, pp. 3-11.

11 ibid

12 Ahmed ibn Naqib al-Misri, *Reliance of the Traveller: A Classic Manual of Islamic Sacred Law*, Nuh Ha Mim Keller, translator. Amana Publications, 1999, o1.1-2.

13 Robert Spencer, "Trump's new executive order on immigration requires a log of honor killings," *Jihad Watch*, March 6, 2017.

4 The Ground Zero Mosque

1   Ralph Blumenthal and Sharaf Mowjood, "Muslim Prayers and Renewal Near Ground Zero," *New York Times*, December 8, 2009.

2   ibid

3   Pamela Geller, "It's Official: Ground Zero Mosque Defeated!," *Breitbart*, September 26, 2015.

4   Arun Shourie, Harsh Narain, Jay Dubashi, Ram Swarup, and Sita Ram Goel, *Hindu Temples: What Happened to Them, Volume 1: A Preliminary Survey*, Voice of India, New Delhi, 1990.

5   Pamela Geller, "Giving Thanks," *Atlas Shrugs*, December 8, 2009.

6   "Community Board Meeting re: Mosque at Ground Zero," Flickr, May 25, 2010.

7   Chris Earle, "Good Muslims, Bad Muslims, and the Nation: The 'Ground Zero Mosque' and the Problem With Tolerance," *Communication and Critical/Cultural Studies*, February 4, 2015.

8   C. Lee Hanson and Eunice K. Hanson, "A Mosque That Stirs the Passions," *New York Times*, August 3, 2010.

9   Robert Spencer, "SIOA at Manhattan Community Board meeting on the 9/11 Mosque—the fix was in," *Jihad Watch*, May 25, 2010.

10 Community Board 7 Manhattan, Resolution, October 5, 2010.

11 Justin Elliott, "How the 'ground zero mosque' fear mongering began," *Salon*, August 16, 2010.

12 Pamela Geller, "Fox News: Geller vs. CAIR," *Atlas Shrugs*, May 30, 2010; Pamela Geller, "911 Mega Mosque: Pamela Geller vs Islamic Supremacist Liar on CNN Sunday Morning June 6, 2010," *Atlas Shrugs*, June 6, 2010.

13 Pamela Geller, "CNN Ground Zero Mosque Debate: Geller vs. Muslim American Society," *Atlas Shrugs*, July 15, 2010; Pamela Geller, "VIDEO Round 2: Geller Vs Ramey, Muslim American Society Debate the Ground Zero Mega Mosque," *Atlas Shrugs*, July 19, 2010.

14 Pamela Geller, "Fox and Friends: Pamela Geller vs Nicole Neroulias on Ground Zero Mosque and Bus Campaign," *Atlas Shrugs*, August 11, 2010.

15 Pamela Geller, "RLTV VIDEO: Pamela Geller vs 'Palestine Center' Rap Artist, Debate Staten Island Mosque Victory, 'Mosques in America,'" *Atlas Shrugs*, July 25, 2010; Pamela Geller, "RLTV Video: 911 Mega Mosque Debate: Pamela Geller vs Robert Salaam," *Atlas Shrugs*, June 8, 2010; Pamela Geller, "RTV VIDEO: Pamela Geller on Ground Zero Mega Mosque Landmark Decision," *Atlas Shrugs*, August 3, 2010; Pamela Geller, "Pamela Geller on Bill O'Reilly Rebuts CAIR's Fallacious Accusations," *Atlas Shrugs*, August 4, 2010; Pamela Geller,

"Unindicted Co-Conspirator Hamas-linked Muslim Brotherhood Front CAIR Smears Pamela Geller on O'Reilly," *Atlas Shrugs*, August 4, 2010.

16 Pamela Geller, "911 Mega Mosque: The Joy Behar Show with Pamela Geller and Daisy Khan," *Atlas Shrugs*, May 26, 2010.

17 Pamela Geller, "Hannity: Ground Zero Mosque Debate Pamela Geller vs David Lane, Liberal Lawyer," *Atlas Shrugs*, August 12, 2010; Pamela Geller, "HANNITY: Geller vs Gross on Ground Zero Mosque," *Atlas Shrugs*, August 23, 2010.

18 Pamela Geller, "Hamas-linked CAIR on FOX: Hate Sponsor Ibrahim Hooper Soils Himself with Geller Obsession," *Atlas Shrugs*, August 17, 2010.

19 Pamela Geller, "CNN on Ground Zero Mosque: It's All Geller's Fault!," *Atlas Shrugs*, August 18, 2010.

20 Pamela Geller, "FOX Business TV Appearance: Geller on the Dove Church Qur'an Burning," *Atlas Shrugs*, September 7, 2010.

21 "Sean Hannity Show: Pamela Geller Debates Michael Ghouse (Muslim American Congress) 911 Mega Mosque," *YouTube*, May 13, 2010.

22 "BBC Radio: Ground Zero Debate Geller vs Shahed Amanullah," *YouTube*, August 15, 2010.

23 Pamela Geller, "Here's the Geraldo Hit Job Video," *Atlas Shrugs*, September 12, 2010.

24 Pamela Geller, "Fox Business: Pamela Geller vs Black Panthers Leader Malik Shabazz on Money Rocks," *Atlas Shrugs*, September 12, 2010.

25 Pamela Geller, "FOX Business: Hate Sponsor CAIR on Steroids, Waterboy Bob Beckel Squeal and the Ground Zero Mosque," *Atlas Shrugs*, September 27, 2010.

26 "Rauf's Group Claims Credit for 'Training' NY Times Reporter," *IPT News*, September 20, 2010.

27 "Memo to media: Pamela Geller does not belong on national television," *Media Matters*, July 14, 2010.

28 Pamela Geller, "Atlas TV Alert: Hardball Tonight UPDATE: HARDBALL CANCELS," Atlas Shrugs, July 14, 2010.

29 Pamela Geller, "WPIX: 'what's more insulting and offensive -- that image of truth, or a 15 story mega-mosque looking down on the sacred ground of Ground Zero?,'" *Atlas Shrugs*, August 9, 2010.

5 Stealth Turkey Jihad

1   http://www.butterballcorp.com/corporate-information/facts/

2   Pamela Geller, "AFDI Victory! Butterball Backpedals on Bismillah Brouhaha: "Butterball products are not certified halal," *Atlas Shrugs,* November 20, 2012.

3   Pamela Geller, "Happy Halal Thanksgiving," *American Thinker*, November 21, 2011.

4   Pamela Geller, "Clean Up, Meat Aisle: Talking Heads Exploding over Halal Butterballs," *Atlas Shrugs*, November 24, 2011.

5   ibid

6   Pamela Geller, "Secret Selling of Halal Meat in the US," *Human Events*, October 16, 2010.

7   Email to Pamela Geller, October 17, 2011.

8   Hannah Arendt, "Eichmann in Jerusalem—I," *New Yorker,* February 16, 1963.

9   Richard J. Bernstein, Hannah Arendt and the Jewish Question, *MIT Press*, 1996, p.161.

10 Pamela Geller, "Documents reveal British banned Geller and Spencer because of their 'pro-Israeli views,'" *Daily Caller*, December 1, 2013.

11 ibid

12 Andrew Gilligan, "Muslim hate monitor to lose backing," *Telegraph*, June 9, 2013.

13 Andrew Gilligan, "The truth about the 'wave of attacks on Muslims' after Wool-wich murder," *Telegraph*, June 1, 2013.

14 Pamela Geller, "There Was a Muhammad Before Those Cwazy Cartoons!," *Atlas Shrugs*, February 22, 2006.

6 CPAC and What's Wrong with the Right

1   Mark Hosenball and Michael Isikoff, "The Flying Dutchman: Free-speech hero or an anti-Islamic publicity hound? Geert Wilders is coming to America," *Newsweek,* February 17, 2009.

2   "Coughlin Sacked," *Washington Times,* January 4, 2008.

3   Franklin Foer, "Grover Norquist's Strange Alliance With Radical Islam," *The New Republic*, November 11, 2001.

4   Franklin Foer, "Grover Norquist's Strange Alliance With Radical Islam," *New Republic,* November 11, 2001.

5 David Horowitz, "Why We Are Publishing This Article," in Frank J. Gaffney, Jr., "A Troubling Influence—An Islamic Fifth Column penetrates the White House," *FrontPageMagazine*, December 9, 2003.

6 See images of checks Alamoudi wrote to Norquist's Islamic Institute at http://www.sperryfiles.com/images/8-1a.jpg.

7 Steven Emerson, "Strange Bedfellows on the Campaign Trail," *IPT News*, January 14, 2008.

8 Franklin Foer, "Grover Norquist's Strange Alliance With Radical Islam," *The New Republic*, November 11, 2001.

9 Frank J. Gaffney, Jr., "A Troubling Influence—An Islamic Fifth Column penetrates the White House," *FrontPageMagazine*, December 9, 2003.

10 See images of checks Alamoudi wrote to Norquist's Islamic Institute at http://www.sperryfiles.com/images/8-1a.jpg.

11 Frank J. Gaffney, Jr., "A Troubling Influence—An Islamic Fifth Column penetrates the White House," *FrontPageMagazine,* December 9, 2003.

12 Robert Spencer, "Guilty as Charged," *FrontPageMagazine*, April 20, 2006.

13 Scott Johnson, "The lies of Grover Norquist," *PowerLine*, December 10, 2003.

14 "CAIR Executive Director Placed at HAMAS Meeting," Investigative Project on Terrorism, August 2, 2007.

15 "CAIR Identified by the FBI as part of the Muslim Brotherhood's Palestine Committee," Investigative Project on Terrorism, August 8, 2007.

16 Paul Sperry, "Norquist's Muslim Protégés," *FrontPageMagazine*, June 3, 2008.

17 "Suhail Khan," Discover the Networks, http://www.discoverthenetworks.org/individualProfile.asp?indid=2348.

18 Justin Elliott, "Pamela Geller versus CPAC," *Salon*, February 12, 2011.

19 ibid

20 Byron Tau, "Right fractures over Islam," *Politico*, February 12, 2011.

21 J. P. Freire, "DOJ Voting Rights attorney resigns over Black Panthers stonewalling," *Washington Examiner*, May 17, 2010.

22 Brian Sidler, "Geller Continues Fight Against Creeping Sharia At CPAC 2012," *Critical Post*, February 13, 2012.

23 Pamela Geller, "CPAC 2012: Pamela Geller Wins Anti-Jihad Blogger of the Year," *Atlas Shrugs*, February 11, 2012.

24 Jennifer Rubin, "CPAC missteps again [UPDATED]," *Washington Post,* March 5, 2013.

25 ibid

26 Nick Hallett, "Geert Wilders Wins 'Politician Of The Year' Award For Third Time," *Breitbart*, December 15, 2015.

27 "Churchill on Islam," *The Churchill Project*, March 4, 2016.

28 "Muslim groups nervous about King hearings," *Politico*, January 11, 2011.

29 Pamela Geller, "Zuhdi Jasser's Own Private Islam," *Atlas Shrugs*, May 19, 2009.

30 Pamela Geller, "Jasser's Jihad," *Atlas Shrugs*, May 13, 2009.

31 M. Zuhdi Jasser, " American Islamists Find Common Cause with Pamela Geller," *American Thinker*, February 13, 2011.

32 M. Zuhdi Jasser, "American Islamists Find Common Cause with Pamela Geller," *American Thinker*, February 13, 2011.

33 Zuhdi Jasser, "'Alt-Jihadists': Useful Idiots of the Global Islamist Establishment," *Reform This!*, March 12, 2017.

34 Pamela Geller, "The Grand Mufti of the Stealth Jihad: Zuhdi Jasser Says 'There's No Greater Threat' Than Pamela Geller and Her Colleagues," *Geller Report*, March 14, 2017.

35 "Our Team," American Islamic Forum for Democracy, https://aifdemocracy. org/our-work/our-team/

36 Jeffrey Weiss and Kevin Krauss, "2 Garland shooters' lives twined to tragic end," *Dallas News*, May 2015.

37 Sean Holstege and Matthew Casey, "Elton Simpson's slow, isolated descent into ISIS, jihad," *Arizona Republic*, May 9, 2015.

7 The Ad Wars

1 Pamela Geller, "Islamic Law Comes to Dearborn," *Human Events*, June 23, 2010.

2 http://www.smartbus.org/Smart/mktg/advertise.aspx

3 Pamela Geller, "Rifqa Bary Death Threat: Exhibit A, The Document: FATWA (Death Penalty) for Apostasy," *AtlasShrugs.com*, September 21, 2009.

4 Jennifer Fermino, email to Pamela Geller, September 20, 2011.

5 Matthew Popowsky, "Judge Engelmayer Preliminarily Enjoins MTA's Advertising Policy on First Amendment Grounds," *SDNY Blog*, July 20, 2012.

6 "NYC's Islamophobic and anti-Arab 'savages' bus ads to go ahead," *Al-Bawaba*, July 21, 2012.

7 Mona Eltahawy, "Why Do They Hate Us? The real war on women is in the Middle East," *Foreign Policy*, April 23, 2012.

8   "Palestinians in Gaza celebrate terror attack at Jerusalem synagogue," *Reuters*, November 18, 2014.

9   Jessica Schulberg, "The 'World's Number One Self-Hating Jew' Goes to Jail," *New Republic*, January 6, 2015.

10 Andrew Rice, "Kunstler Protege Stanley Cohen Brings American Rights to Hamas," *Observer*, October 1, 2001.

11 Peter Noel, "Homeland Terrorism," *Village Voice*, September 25, 2001.

12 Pamela Geller, "Free Speech Victory: 'Proud Savage' Mona Eltahawy Has to Pay Restitution In AFDI Ad Vandalism Case," *Breitbart*, December 26, 2014.

13 Mona Eltahawy, "If anti-Muslim ads are protected, so must be my free speech right to protest," *The Guardian*, October 12, 2012.

14 "Ridley v. Massachusetts Bay Transportation Authority," http://caselaw.findlaw.com/us-1st-circuit/1059632.html.

15 U.S. District Court, District of Massachusetts, "American Freedom Defense Initiative, Pamela Geller and Robert Spencer, Plaintiffs, v. Massachusetts Bay Transportation Authority and Beverly Scott," December 20, 2013.

16 Mohamed Akram, "An Explanatory Memorandum on the General Strategic Goal for the Group in North America," May 22, 1991, Government Exhibit 003-0085, US vs. HLF, et al. P. 7 (21).

17 Omar Sacirbey, "Muslims launch campaign to 'understand' sharia," *Religion News Service*, March 2, 2012.

18 ibid

19 Bob Christie, email to Pamela Geller, March 13, 2012.

20 Pamela Geller, "NY Times Allows Another Full-Page Anti-Catholic Ad; Rejected AFDI's 'Anti-Islam' Ad in 2012," *PamelaGeller.com*, July 4, 2014.

21 Ann Bayefsky, "Apartheid Palestine?," *Jerusalem Post*, March 17, 2013.

22 "SF Supervisors Unanimously Pass Resolution Condemning Islamophobic Bus Ads," Council on American-Islamic Relations, March 21, 2013.

23 Jaxon Van Derbeken, "3 held in alleged anti-gay BB shooting in S.F.," *SFGate.com*, March 4, 2010.

24 "Shafiq Hashemi, Muhammad Habibzada and Sayed Bassam: Three men pleaded guilty Monday to the BB-gun shooting of a San Francisco man they believed to be gay," *Fugitive Watch*, April 20, 2010.

25 Pamela Geller, "BOMBSHELL COVER-UP in San Francisco Muslim Shooting of Gay Man," *Atlas Shrugs*, March 4, 2010; Pamela Geller, "Video of San Francisco Muslims Shooting Gay Man Shows 11 Other Attacks in a Single Night Laughing as they fired the gun," *Atlas Shrugs*, March 13, 2010.

26 Daniel Greenfield, "Head of San Francisco Human Rights Commission Claims Iran is More LGBT Friendly than America," *FrontPageMagazine*, March 20, 2013.

27 Chris Stedman, "Stop trying to split gays and Muslims," *Salon*, April 2, 2013.

28 Isabel Vincent, "No community programs at 'Ground Zero' mosque a year after the controversy," *New York Post*, December 9, 2012.

29 Mark Koenig, email to Pamela Geller, April 3, 2013.

30 Arnold Ahlert, "Erasing the 'Faces of Global Terrorism,'" *FrontPageMagazine*, June 27, 2013.

31 Gabe Finger, "FBI: It's too racist to show pictures of terrorists," *Daily Caller*, June 26, 2013.

32 Gabe Finger, "'Offensive to Muslims': Dem congressman calls on FBI to take down photos of terrorists," *Daily Caller*, June 20, 2013.

33 "Hate Crime Statistics 2010," Federal Bureau of Investigation, https://ucr.fbi.gov/hate-crime/2010/narratives/hate-crime-2010-victims.

34 Jeff Cummings, "Dishonorable ads pulled," *Edmonton Sun*, October 30, 2013; Pamela Geller, "CTV: 'City removing "controversial" [freedom] ads from Edmonton buses,'" *PamelaGeller.com*, October 29, 2013; Paula Simons, "Hate groups have no charter rights to hijack ads on ETS buses," *Edmonton Journal*, October 5, 2016.

35 Phyllis Chesler, "Worldwide Trends in Honor Killings," *Middle East Quarterly*, Spring 2010, pp. 3-11.

36 "Ads on RTD buses mislead on ethnic cleansing in Mideast," *The Denver Post*, November 4, 2013.

37 "Former British Rapper Reportedly Under Investigation for James Foley Beheading," *Billboard*, August 23, 2014.

38 Jennifer Fermino, "Shocking anti-Islam ad campaign coming to MTA buses, subway stations," New York *Daily News*, September 19, 2014.

39 Jennifer Fermino, "Shocking anti-Islam ad campaign coming to MTA buses, subway stations," *New York Daily News*, September 19, 2014. The phrase was later removed from the online version of the article.

40 New Israel Fund 2012 Annual Report, https://issuu.com/newisraelfund/docs/nif_2012_ar; Hank Sheinkopf, "Former Clinton PR Advisor, Conservative PR Leader Condemn New Israel Fund," *FrontPageMagazine*, February 26, 2015; Helene Fragman Abramson, "New Israel Fund Tries to Explain its Way Around BDS Ban," *Jewish Press*, June 19, 2014.

41 Ron Kampeas, "For Murray Koppelman, a distasteful Tehran scene inspires a gift to New Israel Fund," *Jewish Telegraph Agency*, April 23, 2012.

42   Ronn Torossian, "The Extremist, Radical New Israel Fund," *Truth Revolt*, November 26, 2014.

43   "Profile: Alisa Robbins Doctoroff," *Encounter*, http://www.encounterprograms. org/who-we-are/participants/profile-alisa-robbins-doctoroff

44   Dina Kraft, "US Jews boosting Arab employment in Israel," *Jewish Telegraph Agency*, May 18, 2009.

45   Kevin McCauley, "Sarid Moves Forward," *O'Dwyer's*, January 6, 2015.

46   https://www.facebook.com/newisraelfund/posts/140339495989359? comment_id=1112596&comment_tracking=%7B%22tn%22%3A%22R3%22 %7D

47   Sam Sokol, "Birthright Israel cuts ties with New Israel Fund," *Jerusalem Post*, November 28, 2014.

48   Ronn Torossian, "UJA-President, Alisa Doctoroff, and Her Radical Support of Palestinian Non-Violent Activism, And New Israel Fund," *Jewish Press*, February 22, 2015.

49   Ronn Torossian, "Revealed: UJA President A Donor to Radical Left-Wing Anti-Israel Organization," *Truth Revolt*, February 19, 2015.

50   "Edith and Henry Everett Foundation Partners With Anti-Israel Organizations," *Jewocity.com*, December 4, 2014.

51   Anne Herzberg, "NGO silence on PLO terror verdict," *Jerusalem Post*, February 24, 2015.

52   Lauren Evans, "MTA Votes To Ban All Political Ads From Subways And Buses," *Gothamist*, April 29, 2015.

53   Pamela Geller, "SION/AFDI Counters Muslim Brotherhood's ICNA Ad Campaign to Mainstream Sharia," *Atlas Shrugs*, February 7, 2012.

54   Adam Carlson, "Billboard campaign on Prophet Muhammad comes to Atlanta," *Atlanta Journal-Constitution*, June 1, 2015.

55   "About ICNA," Islamic Circle of North America, http://www.icna.org/ about-icna

56   Mohamed Akram, "An Explanatory Memorandum on the General Strategic Goal for the Group in North America," May 22, 1991, Government Exhibit 003-0085, US vs. HLF, et al. P. 7 (21).

57   ibid

58   Bukhari, *Sahih al-Bukhari: The Translation of the Meanings*, translated by Muhammad M. Khan, Darussalam, 1997, book 56, number 186; book 9, number 304; and book 56, number 236.

59   Abu Muhammad al-'Adnani ash-Shami, "Indeed Your Lord Is Ever Watchful," September 21, 2014.

60 Paul Miller, "Lamar Outdoor Advertising Under Fire for Anti-Israel Billboard," *Observer*, February 19, 2016.

61 ibid

62 Paul Miller, "Lamar Outdoor Advertising Under Fire for Anti-Israel Billboard," Observer, February 19, 2016.

63 Pippa Crerar, "Sadiq Khan: There will be no more 'body shaming' adverts on the Tube," *London Evening Standard*, June 13, 2016.

64 Caleb Pershan, "Muni Bans All Political, Offensive, And Violent Advertising On Buses And Trains," *SFist*, April 5, 2017.

65 Dan Rivoli and Stephen Rex Brown, "Muslim parody posters banned by MTA are not political ads, judge says," *New York Daily News,* October 7, 2015.

66 Jonathan Stempel, "New York's MTA must run 'Muslim' movie posters in subways: judge," *Reuters*, October 7, 2015.

8 CAIR vs. The Truth

1 Ibn Warraq, *Why I Am Not A Muslim*, Prometheus Books, 2003, p. 115.

2 Art Moore, "Did CAIR founder say Islam to rule America?," *WorldNetDaily*, December 11, 2006.

3 ibid

4 Mohamed Akram, "An Explanatory Memorandum on the General Strategic Goal for the Group in North America," May 22, 1991, Government Exhibit 003-0085, U.S. vs. HLF, et al. P. 7 (21).

5 U.S. District Court for the District of Columbia, Iftikhar Saiyed vs. Council on American-Islamic Relations Action Network, Rene Arturo Lopez, et al, vs. Council on American-Islamic Relations Action Network, November 23, 2012.

6 ibid

7 "CAIR OK'd to meet in Capitol," *Washington Times*, March 11, 2007.

8 Steven Pomerantz, *The Journal of Counterterrorism & Security International*, Spring 1998.

9 S. A. Miller, "Muslim group: 'Who cares' if US terrorists in Kenya mall siege," *New York Post*, September 24, 2013.

10 Art Moore, "Did CAIR founder say Islam to rule America?," *WorldNetDaily*, December 11, 2006.

11 Charles C. Johnson, "Somali-American leader: 'I tried to warn America' about homegrown radicalization," *Daily Caller*, September 23, 2013.

12 Kris Van Cleave, "New Hitler ads on Metrobuses stir up controversy," *WJLA*, May 17, 2014.

13   Pamela Geller, "Hate Group Hamas-CAIR Responds to AFDI with Deception About Converts on DC Buses," *PamelaGeller.com*, June 11, 2014.

14   Cathy Grossman, "Muslim and anti-Muslim bus ads battle heads to Round 3," Cathy Grossman, *Religion News Service*, June 11, 2014.

15   Paul Nussbaum, "SEPTA to accept anti-Muslim ads, but changes will bar future ads," *Philadelphia Inquirer*, March 27, 2015.

16   Bob Stewart, email to Pamela Geller, March 26, 2015.

17   Pamela Geller, email to Bob Stewart, March 26, 2015.

9 Jewicidals

1   Bruce Finley, "Colorado Jewish, Muslim and Christian leaders launch love campaign," *Denver Post*, December 24, 2012.

2   Bukhari, *Sahih al-Bukhari: The Translation of the Meanings*, translated by Muhammad M. Khan, Darussalam, 1997, book 8, number 670.

3   "Algerian Army Marching Drill: Kill, Slaughter, and Skin the Jews," Middle East Media Research Institute (MEMRI), November 1, 2015.

4   "Rafah Cleric Brandishes Knife in Friday Sermon, Calls upon Palestinians to Stab Jews," Middle East Media Research Institute (MEMRI), October 9, 2015.

5   "Gaza Preacher Raises Explosives Belt in Friday Sermon: We Will Turn You into Scattered Body Parts," Middle East Media Research Institute (MEMRI), October 23, 2015.

6   "Palestinian people do not exist," *JTF News*, November 11, 2014.

7   Ayn Rand, *For the New Intellectual*, Signet, 1963, p. 165.

8   Andrew Gilligan, "Muslim hate monitor to lose backing," *Telegraph*, June 9, 2013.

9   Fiyaz Mughal, "Pamela Geller—Deemed 'Not Conducive to the Public Good,'" *Times of Israel*, December 18, 2016.

10   ibid

11   ibid

12   Julia Gorin, "Ending the Balkan Quagmire at *American Thinker*," *American Thinker*, July 4, 2007.

13   Fiyaz Mughal, "Pamela Geller—Deemed 'Not Conducive to the Public Good,'" *Times of Israel*, December 18, 2016.

14   ibid

15   ibid

10 Garland, Texas: ISIS Attacks the Homeland

1   Oliver Duggan, "Hunt for gunman in Charlie Hebdo attack: What we know," Telegraph, January 7, 2015.

2   Jenny Doren, "Muslim group gathers for peace, faces threats, protest," WFAA, January 17, 2015.

3   "Book of Mormon Musical: Church's Official Statement," The Church of Jesus Christ of Latter-Day Saints, February 7, 2011.

4   "Megyn Kelly On Trump And The Media: 'We're In A Dangerous Phase Right Now,'" NPR, December 7, 2016.

5   Justin Wm. Moyer, "Megyn Kelly, Michael Moore have televised love-in after Trump debate debacle," Washington Post, January 27, 2016.

6   "North Carolina Man Charged with Conspiring to Provide Material Support to ISIL," United States Department of Justice, August 4, 2016.

7   Katie Zavadski, "FBI Agent Apparently Egged on 'Draw Muhammad' Shooter," Daily Beast, August 4, 2016.

8   "The New Era," JustPasteIt, May 5, 2015.

9   Pamela Geller, "Email of the Day: 'You Deserve to Be Raped by Hordes of Muslims….," PamelaGeller.com, November 23, 2015.

10 Pamela Geller, "Muslim Issues DEATH THREAT on my Facebook Page," PamelaGeller.com, February 20, 2016.

11 Pamela Geller, "'WORTH RAPING AND CHOPPING': Mark Zuckerberg ALLOWS SAVAGE DEATH THREATS by Muslims but CENSORS Posts Critical of Muslim Migrants," PamelaGeller.com, March 6, 2016.

12 "Hannity and Pamela Geller Battle Anjem Choudary Who Says Geller Should Be Put to Death," YouTube, May 6, 2015.

13 Andrew Bostom, "Hey Hannity, Koran 5:60 Refers to Jews as 'Apes and Pigs,'" American Thinker, January 25, 2013.

14 Kevin Johnson and John Bacon, "Dozens of FBI surveillance teams tracking suspects," USA Today, June 4, 2015.

15 ibid

16 Ray Sanchez, Evan Perez and Shimon Prokupecz, "Boston shooting: Suspect plotted to behead Pamela Geller, sources say," CNN, June 3, 2015.

17 "Activist says Boston beheading plot targeted her; police express doubt," Reuters, June 4, 2015.

18 Daniel Greenfield, "Boston Beheader Plotted Murder of Pamela Geller Who Had Been Condemned by His Imam," FrontPageMagazine, June 3, 2015.

19 Patrick Poole, "Phoenix Mosque Attended by Garland Jihadists Previously Spawned Two Other Terrorists," *PJ Media*, May 8, 2015.

20 Milton J. Valencia, "ISIS supporter to plead guilty in US court," *Boston Globe*, September 20, 2016.

21 "Warwick man to be sentenced in terror plot," *ABC6.com*, March 23, 2017.

22 "Man Pleads Guilty to Conspiring to Commit Acts of Terrorism to Support ISIL," U.S. Department of Justice, September 22, 2016.

23 "Affidavit of FBI Special Agent Joseph Galietta," June 12, 2015.

24 Adam Goldman, "Man charged with supporting ISIS allegedly had links to attack in Texas," *Washington Post*, August 4, 2016.

11 Freedom of Speech in the Age of Jihad

1   "Guidelines for Countering Racial, Ethnic and Religious Profiling," Society of Professional Journalists, October 6, 2001.

2   ibid

3   ibid

4   ibid

5   ibid

6   ibid

7   ibid

8   "Jihad Against Jews and Crusaders," World Islamic Front Statement, February 23, 1998

9   "Pamela Geller," Southern Poverty Law Center, n.d.

10 "A Journalist's Manual: Field Guide to Anti-Muslim Extremists," Southern Poverty Law Center, October 25, 2016.

11 ibid

12 ibid

13 "Pamela Geller," Southern Poverty Law Center, n.d.

14 "A Journalist's Manual: Field Guide to Anti-Muslim Extremists," Southern Poverty Law Center, October 25, 2016.

15 ibid

16 ibid

17 ibid

18 "Federal Government Authorizes Facebook, Twitter, and YouTube to Censor 'Anti-Islam' Speech; Lawsuit Filed," *American Freedom Law Center*, July 13, 2016.

19 ibid

20 Michael Nunez, "Former Facebook Workers: We Routinely Suppressed Conservative News," *Gizmodo*, May 9, 2016.

21 Javier E. David, "Angela Merkel caught on hot mic griping to Facebook CEO over anti-immigrant posts," CNBC, September 27, 2015.

22 ibid

23 Dexter Van Zile, "Why is Facebook Enabling Anti-Semites?," *Algemeiner,* February 4, 2014.

24 Sharona Schwartz, "An Israeli Group Created Fake Anti-Israel and Anti-Palestinian Facebook Pages. Guess Which One Got Taken Down?," *The Blaze*, January 5, 2016.

25 "Shurat Hadin Proves Facebook Likes Palestinian Incitement [video]," *Jewish Press,* January 5, 2016.

26 Pamela Geller, "Left Press Lashes Out Against Our Free Speech Lawsuit," *Breitbart*, October 13, 2016.

27 Nick Wingfield, Mike Isaac and Katie Benner, "Google and Facebook Take Aim at Fake News Sites," *New York Times*, November 14, 2016.

28 ibid

29 ibid

30 Jessica Roy, "Want to keep fake news out of your newsfeed? College professor creates list of sites to avoid," *Los Angeles Times*, November 15, 2016; Paul Thornton, "Fake news writers: 'Hillary Clinton, here are your deplorables,'" *Los Angeles Times*, December 3, 2016; "Fake news writers abuse the 1st Amendment and endanger democracy for personal profit," *Los Angeles Times*, December 1, 2016.

31 "The Demonetization of YouTube is Fast Underway; Dissidents Will Be Silenced," *ZeroHedge*, April 5, 2017.

32 Michael Hernandez, "US Muslim groups welcome changes to Google results," Anadolu Agency, July 26, 2017.

33 Liel Leibovitz, "Google's New Hate Speech Algorithm Has a Problem With Jews," *Tablet,* July 28, 2017.

34 ibid

35 Thomas Lifson, "Facebook cowers and complies with sharia," *American Thinker*, July 12, 2017.

36 "MGM Resorts will match employees' donations to civil rights groups, including ADL," *JTA*, August 20, 2017.

37 William A. Jacobson, "Charlottesville is being exploited to attack freedom of speech and internet freedom," *Legal Insurrection*, August 20, 2017.

38 Pamela Geller, email to Lauren Kirchner, August 18, 2017.

39 Sarmad S. Ali, "Kerry Drew Disenchanted Arabs in Bay Ridge," *Columbia Journalism*, November 15, 2004.

40 Trevor Loudon, "Who's Behind Occupy Wall Street?," *New Zeal*, October 25, 2011.

41 "Linda Sarsour," Champions of Change, *WhiteHouse.gov*, n.d.

42 Linda Sarsour, "Underwear bomber was the #CIA all along," Twitter, May 8, 2012.

43 "Islamists Use Boston Shooting to Sow Hatred of Law Enforcement," IPT News, June 2, 2015.

44 Linda Sarsour, "My Take: My hijab is my hoodie," CNN, April 5, 2012.

45 Valerie Richardson, "Ralliers decry CUNY's selection of Muslim activist Linda Sarsour as graduation speaker," *Washington Times*, May 25, 2017.

46 Sarah Gabrielli and Rich Schapiro, "Wild brawl breaks out at rally against CUNY's commencement speaker civil-rights activist Linda Sarsour," *New York Daily News*, May 25, 2017.

47 Jenn Selby, "Donald Trump Lambasts 'Disgusting' Pam Geller for Baiting Muslims with 'Draw the Prophet' Contest in Texas," *Independent*, May 5, 2015.

48 Jessica Lussenhop, "James T Hodgkinson: What we know about Virginia suspect," *BBC News*, June 14, 2017.

49 "Anders Breivik details Norway massacre plans, cites Al-Qaeda inspiration," *Associated Press*, April 20, 2012.

50 Alex Griswold, "Sanders Fundraised in 2011 by Falsely Blaming Sarah Palin for Tucson Shooting," *Daily Caller*, June 14, 2017.

51 Patrick Lion and Caroline Mortimer, "'White supremacist's' chilling rant hours before he 'murdered Good Samaritans defending Muslim girls from racist abuse on Portland train," *Mirror*, May 29, 2017; Guy Benson, "Surprise: Portland Killings Blamed on Trump Rhetoric Actually Perpetrated by Bernie Supporter," *Townhall*, May 31, 2017.

52 Pamela Geller, "Aligned with Sarsour, NYC Mayor De Blasio's SABOTAGES AFDI CUNY Protest," *Geller Report*, May 29, 2017.

53 Ben Shapiro, "How The American Left Made Political Violence The New Normal," *Daily Wire*, n.d.

54 ibid

55 Jillian Sederholm, "#PorteOuverte: Paris Residents Open Doors to Those Stranded By Attacks," *NBC News*, November 14, 2015.

56 Pamela Geller, "Eiffel Tower Peace Symbol: The Least Appropriate Thing Ever," *PamelaGeller.com*, November 15, 2015.

57 Jim Sciutto, Evan Perez, Kevin Liptak and Z. Byron Wolf, "Why did Obama declare ISIS 'contained' the day before Paris attack?," CNN, November 16, 2015.

58 Brad Wilmouth, "MSNBC Frets 'Tsunami of Hatred' Will Meet French Muslims, Right Wing Will 'Take Advantage,'" *MRCNewsBusters*, November 14, 2015; Natalie Nougayrède, "Paris attacks leave France in trauma, fearing for the future," *Guardian*, November 13, 2015; Chauncey DeVega, "And so the hate speech begins: Let Paris be the end of the right's violent language toward activists," *Salon*, November 14, 2015.

59 Ayn Rand, *Capitalism: The Unknown Ideal*, Signet, 1986, p. 256.